Socioeconomic Injustices: Pakistan in Whirlpool

Socioeconomic Injustices: Pakistan in Whirlpool

Mr Waqas Ahmad Saad

KALPAZ

ISBN: 978-93-5128-146-7

Price: ₹ 900

First Published, 2016

Published by

Kalpaz Publications
C-30, Satyawati Nagar,
Delhi – 110052
E-mail: kalpaz@hotmail.com
Ph.: 9212142040

Printed at: G. Print Process, Delhi

Cataloging in Publication Data—DK
Courtesy: D.K. Agencies (P) Ltd. <docinfo@dkagencies.com>

Saad, Waqas Ahmad, author.
Socioeconomic injustices : Pakistan in whirlpool / Mr Waqas Ahmad Saad.
pages cm
Includes bibliographical references.
ISBN 9789351281467

1. Pakistan—Social conditions. 2. Pakistan—Economic conditions. 3. Pakistan—Politics and government. 4. Justice. I. Title.

HN690.5.Z9I55 2016 DDC 306.095491 23

Dedicated to Nelson Mandela –African revolutionary leader considered among the greatest proponents of socioeconomic justice in modern history

Contents

Preface

Production of any research oriented work is not possible without extensive hard work and consultation which I also undertook with a passion and energy. Though I have been writing articles extensively since 2007, yet as per my experience writing a book is a much more laborious and difficult job in comparison to writing articles. During the last few years, I have studied extensively about ongoing socioeconomic and political atmosphere in the context of regional and international affairs and its repercussion on my country and reproduced my thoughts in the form of articles in leading newspapers of the country. In my articles I have not been able to produce all systemic failures and their impacts as the focus of articles were mainly on the reporting of the rapidly occurring changes and their repercussions on Pakistani society during a particular span of time. I decided to write this book in order to discuss and critically analyse all the core issues responsible for the massive ongoing socioeconomic and political injustices in Pakistan, which is not possible in the scope of articles.

Acknowledgments

First of all I would like to thank "The Almighty" who has given me such a thinking brain and curious nature. This blessing makes me a celebrant of creativity, innovation and inquisitiveness. The Five W's- Where, When, What, Who and Whom is an integral part of my thought process and I utilise this for the solution of many mysteries by the grace of the Almighty.

Frankly speaking, I am not generous enough to bestow admiration and rarely show appreciation even for my dear and near ones. In trying to be honest with my readers, perhaps I am being brazen also in admitting my fault that being a proud fellow it has always been difficult for me to easily acknowledge the intellect of others in my surroundings, yet there are some special people whom I cannot refrain from acknowledging as without their kind disposition and cooperation the provision of this book might have been unthinkable.

I am very thankful to my parents particularly my mother who has always been very caring and loving towards me and her affectionate attitude and trust on me has always enhanced my confidence in life. I am also thankful to my brothers, Dr Mohsin Hassan and Dr Mubashir Hassan, who though being younger to me have always shown a mature, kind and cooperative attitude towards me which has helped me a lot in building concentration and focus in my work. My Sister Saadia Gul though youngest of all siblings, through her loving, caring and cooperative attitude has always produced good repercussions in my life and I am grateful to her from the core of my heart for her selfless behaviour and encouragement.

I would also like to mention some personalities from the field of Journalism who have positively impacted my career as a writer and journalist. Mujeeb-U-Rehman Shami (Editor-in-chief of *Daily Pakistan*) introduced me to mainstream journalism and provided me enough opportunities of working with liberty and ease which enhanced my confidence. Here I will not forget Mr.Abdul Jabbar Mufti (Resident editor of a national daily in *Multan*) who initially introduced me as a column writer in "*Daily Naway-Waqt*"- one of the leading newspapers of the country. I am also very thankful to Mr Qudrat-Ullah Ch a veteran journalist and renowned editor who was kind enough in sharing his journalistic experiences with me and I learned a lot from him as well. I am really very grateful to Mr Sohail Warrich (Editor Editorial of *Daily Jang* Lahore) who has encouraged me a lot, during my brief meetings with him, he has always been very kind hearted and loving towards me and I respect him from the core of my heart.

Among my friends in Lahore, Professor Abdullah Bhatti (A renowned scholar and author) is of key importance, he has always extended his integral support and encouragement which enhanced my self-belief. I am really thankful to my friend Syed Irfan Shah (Editor of Media world line and a renowned spiritual personality) whom I consider as an elder brother, his affectionate attitude has provided me much courage in life. I am really very thankful to Professor Nasir Bashir who is not only a very good poet and an intellectual but also a very nice human being, his company has always been an opportunity of learning for me. Here I can't forget Mr Usman Mujeeb Shami a young and energetic editor who also gave me good company and bundle of new ideas during my meetings with him.

I would like to thank my maternal uncle Advocate Mian Abdul Waheed who has always been a great source of encouragement for me, I would also like to include here the name of renowned lawyer and seasoned politician Senator S.M. Zafar with whom I discussed the contents and title of my book, his kind attitude inspired me a lot. Here I will also pay tribute to the memories of the kindness and cooperation of a very dear friend - Muhammad Iqbal Afaqi (Editor of Monthly *Aawaz Digest*) whose support played an integral part in the publishing of this book and lastly I am thankful to my publisher for showing faith in my abilities and definitely the provision of this book would not have been possible without his trust and investment in me.

**Special acknowledgments for my mother
Mrs Amna Arain whose untiring support has always
been a great source of courage for me throughout life.**

Part I

1

Little Glimpse of Modern Day Pakistan

- **Today's Pakistan**

With more than 192 million pale faces Pakistan Seems to be the land of hunger, terror, injustices, discriminations, diseases and misery in the year 2015. With a very minute per capita income (1265 US dollars) its more than 40 per cent population is living below the poverty line on less than 1.25 dollars income per day. Pakistan ranked 147th out of 175 for its severe economic circumstances in 2013, statistics of 2013 showed total volume of its GDP (Gross domestic product) 236.518 billon US dollars, which looks too minute in comparison with its massive population and excessive inflation of 11.2 per cent (Dec 2013). Value of its currency is going down in comparison to United States dollar. In the year 2008, one United States dollar was equivalent to 58.25 Pakistani rupees (PKR) but in 2013 dollar reached its highest position in the country's history in comparison to PKR. In September 2013 one US dollar was equivalent to 109 PKR, now in 2014 it is around 100 PKR.

Unemployment is a great matter of concern for the massive fraction of population in the country. Frustration and conflicts among the youth (64 per cent of total population) is touching the skies due to its miserable economic circumstances. According to human development index (2012) 61.3 per cent of total population is living on less than two US dollars per day in the country. With a very uneven distribution of wealth, super elite and elite classes possess the major portion (78.20 per cent) of the wealth of the country. Jobs (including both public and private sectors) are very limited; bribes and political influence are two main and familiar sources for getting a public office in Pakistan. Corruption is widespread and deep-rooted in the country, according to statistics of 2013 published by *Transparency International* Pakistan stands 129th out of 175 countries as per corruption precipitation index. Political elite and Civil-military bureaucracy is considered as most corrupt fraction of society. In 2012 Transparency International calculated that Pakistan has lost more than 8.5 trillion PKR in corruption, tax evasion and bad governance during the Pakistan People's Party (PPP) led collation government between 2008-2013. Above mentioned PPP government is alleged as most corrupt by its political opponents.

Corruption has produced severe repercussions on the very fabric of the country-shaken badly due to this, office holders of public and semi-government institutions in Pakistan are notorious for looting public money through abuse of power. Admiral (retired) Faseeh Bukhari former chairmen of National Accountability Bureau (NAB) once admitted (during his regime as NAB chairman 2010-12) that more than 8 billon PKR is looted every day in the country. Media has exposed many scams of corruption in the country during recent past, Hajj corruption, Pakistan steel mills, National Insurance Corporation Limited (NICL). scam are some of the famous cases among these. Activism of superior judiciary (Lower judiciary has been still not able to make an impact) and media has made a little progressin exposing and countering corrupt mafias in the country during recent past but their efforts are not sufficient enough to bring a major change.

Repercussions of hunger, unemployment and disease are severe enough on massive fraction of population. Growing Talibanisation and extremist attitude particularly in youth is a result of widespread poverty in the country. Thousands of religious schools (Madarsas) widespread in the country are recruiting hundreds of thousands of students from lower income groups every year. However, population belonging to middle, upper middle and more than middle (an income group between upper middle and elite class) class are familiar with western style of education. Currently one hundred and twenty six universities and colleges that award degrees (both in public and private sectors) are under operation. But most graduates are not fortunate enough to find good jobs after the completion of their degrees from these institutes. Most among the white collar jobs are under possession of upper income groups. Key positions in civil, military, bureaucracy, top semi-government organisations and multinational corporations are in the possession of upper middle and more than middle classes. Super elite and elite classes (Comprising of feudal lords and industrial tycoons) are fully involved in politics.

As more than half of population in the country is not able to fetch basic human necessities for their families so the provision of modern education to their children is almost impossible. Lower income groups are easy victims of orthodox groups in the country who utilise this massive fraction of population for their heinous purposes such as suicide attacks etc. At the time of independence (1947) there were only 189 Madarsas (religious schools) in Pakistan but in 2013 total number of Madarsas in Pakistan (registered and non-registered) were more than 50,000. These widespread religious schools

An image of Corporal Punishment by TTP Milltants in FATA

Children Gathered to Collect Food from a Slum in Peshawar

Faction of Deprived ones getting Chairty Food in Lahore

Images of TTP Miltants in Nortren Part of the Country

located from Karachi to Gilgit currently have more than two million students. Regime of military dictator Zia-ul-Haq proved most favourable for the expansion of religious schools in Pakistan. Due to foreign funding and involvement (Arab Countries like Saudi Arabia are familiar to support Madarsas of Sunni sect in Pakistan) some Pakistani Madarsas are involved in sectarian violence which has escalated during last two decades. After the September 11 attacks on United States some Western journalists and television commentators widely associated Pakistani Madarsas with the provision of fundamentalism and terror in the world. At a very critical juncture of its history Pakistan Muslim League Nawaz (PML N) led government is trying to negotiate with Taliban –indicating its weak position against extremist factions of the society. Tehrek-e-Taliban Pakistan commonly called as TTP started its operations after 2006 for the enforcement of Shariah (Orthodox Islamic laws) in the northern part of the country and now in 2014 it has influence over two thirds of the country. TTP with more than 50,000 militants is trying to further enhance its in settled areas of the country as well. Currently, Federally administrated tribal areas (FATA) are almost under the control of Taliban militant groups. Some other religious militant groups possessing close ties with Taliban such as Lashkar-e-Jhangvi (LeJ), TehrekNizam-e-Shariah Muhmmadi and some other minute groups have also gained influence in different parts of the country.

Global war against terror is going on Since October 2001 and it has produced severe repercussions on Pakistan as well. According to a senior military official, "Pakistan has paid the cost of war against terrorism more than any other country in the world. Human loss in war on terror is more than 50,000 including armed force personnel and civilians during the last twelve years, but even then the world is not recognising our sacrifices". *Daily Times* among one of the reputed English newspapers in the country, recently published a report about the economic loss of Pakistan since 9/11, the report stated that country has faced an economic loss of 82.64 billons PKR during the last 13 years out of which loss of 24.68 billons PKR has occurred within just last two years (2011-13). It was month of November in the year 2001when United States troops just started operations in Afghanistan and when Al Qaeda lunched its first attack on Pakistani soil. It came as result of United States led NATO invasion of Afghanistan. Pakistani orthodox political and non-political groups ran a massive protest in September-October 2001 in various cities against Pakistan's involvement in the attack and in support of United States polices but military dictator Pervaiz Mushraf took a firm stand which led Pakistan towards difficult circumstances in future.

- **Is this the Land of Pure?**

Major factions of population in the country feels proud to declare themselves as "Sons of land of pure" but due to too many impurities present in Pakistani atmosphere, food and even in culture this does not seems to be a suitable title for them. Blood is thicker than water anywhere else in the world but not in so called land of pure as blood too possesses impurities here. It can be said that the dual attitude of majority among the masses and impurities in food and life style has made blood thinner as compared to water both in the moral and physical sense respectively. Impure food, milk and water might be available in other less developed parts of the world but blood mixed with water is only available in the so called land of pure. It's a matter of fact that blood is life, without it no human being is able to survive. Hundreds and thousands of people lost their lives in ancient times when man was not able to transfer blood from one person to another. With the passage of time man has been improvising the techniques and equipment for transforming human life on earth. Education, timely justice alongside with basic health facilities are considered among the basic human rights in any civilised part of the world. Health insurance is available to commoners in Europe, United States and many other countries in the world.

Formation of first blood bank during early 1915 in United States is considered among major achievements in medical sciences, storage facilities of human blood led towards reduction in death rate in later periods. It was the Mount Sinai hospital in New York which acted as the first blood bank in the world, doctors of this hospital used sodium citrate for the preservation of human blood first time in human history. By the late 1920s blood banks became an essentiality in all the civilised societies in the world.

But what is happening with blood in the land of pure? Young and energetic investigative journalist Iqrar-ul-Hassan has exposed mafias of blood banks in the country in his show *Sare-e-Aam* (*Without fear*). This mafia is involved in different cities in trading in saline mixed impure blood so as to increase the quantity. Blood is combination of Red Blood Cells (RBC), White Blood Cells (WBC) and platelets. After collection, blood is preserved at a specific temperature to ensure its quality until usage. But in the land of the pure quantity matters a lot as compared to quality so blood banks here are involved in increasing quantity. Majority among the blood banks in Pakistan receives blood through donations. Pakistanis are familiar for charity and donations in the world so donation of blood is also considered a great charity here but the receivers (blood banks) sell this blood at very high prices, not only they sell it but majority among these blood houses make it impure.

It seems that the land of pure has become a hub of impurities as nothing pure is available in modern day Pakistan. Masses are not able to attain pure food, water, basic health and education facilities and justice too is not available in pure form to the ordinary citizens of the country. It's a matter of great concern for commoners in Pakistan that provision of basic health facilities to its citizens is not a priority of any government in the country. Condition of public hospitals in the country are so miserable that sometimes it seems that citizens of Somalia, Rwanda and Afghanistan are more fortunate than Pakistanis as they too are atleast able to get better and pure healthcare. Doctors in public sector are reasonably paid but a massive fraction of doctors working in public sector organisations are in the habit of shirking their duties. Doctors being an integral part of educated elite in the country are involved in physical exploitation of masses through their corrupt norms and values. A massive fraction of doctors (almost 99.99 per cent) working in public hospitals also run their private business like clinics, maternity homes, medical complexes, medical colleges and universities etc. So they (doctors) are familiar for not entertaining patients in Public hospitals and suggest them to visit their private clinics after the so called duty hours. "Earning of a private surgeon in Pakistan is more than their counterparts in Turkey, Malaysia, Singapore, South Korea or any other country of the developing world", said Dr Shahid, a young FCPS fellow. "I am familiar with an eye surgeon earning more than five million PKR per month but he is such a greedy one that he possesses no human values for the patients of lower income groups, he is also doing a government job with very rare performing duties and has a notorious reputation for inhuman treatment of poor patients even in the public hospital where he serves.—— I did MBBS from Cuba, worked as a trainee for one year in United States and am now doing specialisation in Pakistan but such inhumane and merciless attitudes of doctors towards poor patients, I have only seen in Pakistan", Shahid added more.

It's a great dilemma in modern day Pakistan that not only is the major fraction of doctors in public hospitals not performing their duties in a regular manner but they are also the part of loot and corruption through various means. Amir Karim a human right activist from Islamabad while discussing on the same issue said that "Doctors are working like a mafia in Pakistan". According to him the entire health department of the country is involved in the exploitation of the poor population of the country and doctors are playing a vital role in this chain. He claimed that doctors in public hospitals are involved in receiving heavy bribes from pharmaceutical companies for the recommendation of their medicines. Nabi Bukhsh a PHD in pharmacology working with a renowned multinational medicine cooperation based in Thailand said that pharmaceutical companies in Pakistan are bearing lot of extra expenditures as they have to keep a lot of people happy for the sake of their business such as the bureaucracy of federal and provincial health departments and doctors as well. "That's why standard of medicine in Pakistan is too low, medicine with same nomenclature in Middle East, Singapore, China and even India would be more pure and effective in comparison to Pakistan", Bukhsh added more.

Tharparkera desert based area in rural Sind faced severe draught in recent days that caused severe repercussions. More than 200 people including women and children lost their lives and more than 5000 succumbed to severe diseases due to absence of food and safe drinking water. Qaaim Ali Shah the Chief Minister of ruling PPP claimed that the bureaucracy of the Province was involved to a great extent for making circumstances so miserable. According to Chief Minister, political leadership of Province was very much aware about the upcoming situation so 6000 bags of wheat and other food items were arranged but in a hurry but bureaucracy was involved in mishandling the situation. Later CM sacked the Provincial Director General of Health and also dismissed the Sind government's Minister for relief and rehabilitation. Media reports stated that one major cause for the too much casualties was Irresponsible and cruel attitude of majority of doctors–remained absent from their duties in that much backward part of the country during these severe circumstances. It looks great human dilemma of modern day Pakistan that country's doctor community is losing human values and norms in a rapid manner, More rapidly than any other fraction of society. Moral values and norms once were an integral part of human attitude in country now replaced with materialism and cooperate culture. But Pakistani society especially the massive poor fraction of the society is suffering a lot from this change.

Qaaim Ali Shah the 82 year old veteran politician serving as the chief minister of Sindh for the 3rd term, took oath of the office of chief ministership for the very first time in the year 1988 during the term of Benazir Bhutto as the prime minister. Ms Bhutto selected a loyal feudal lord for the important office of chief minister and since then Mr Shah has held an important position in PPP. Mr Shah commonly called as Saain (A typical word used in Sind for an aged man) is considered as the most weak and incompetent among all chief ministers of the country but he has the trust of party chairperson Bilwal Bhutto Zardari and PPP co-chairperson Asif Ali Zardari, former President of the country due to his loyal services for the Bhutto family. According to Ayaz Lateef Paleejo President of Awami Tehreka Sindhi Nationalist leader from

Hyderabad, PPP has failed to deliver anything for the masses in the country during its four regimes after Zulifiqar Ali Bhutto, the founding chairman of PPP, who ruled the country between 1971-77. While talking to media persons in recent days Paleejo claimed that leaders of PPP are just involved in loot and corruption and have no sympathies for the poor people of Sind. Incident of Thar is just the glimpse of the cruel picture of rural Pakistan where incidents of this type are a matter of routine for the massive poor population of the country.

- **A little about Education and Justice**

We have had enough discussions about the miserable circumstances of health facilities for the commoners in the country, now let's have a look at education and justice as well. According to the latest report of UNESCO (United Nations education programme) Pakistan stands at 180th position among 221 countries list for the provision of basic education facilities to its citizens. Literacy rate has always been a great matter of confusion in Pakistan as there is massive difference between the statistics of government and non- government organisations working for the betterment of education in the country. According to census of 1998 literacy rate in the country was 43.92 per cent, currently government claims that it has reached near 56 per cent. In a male dominating conservative society of the country female fraction of the society is less educated so the literacy rate in men and women specifically was 54.81 per cent and 33.02 per cent respectively according to census of 1998. Literacy rate in the urban areas of the country is about 63.08 per cent and 36.64 per cent in the rural areas. In the year 2014 Pakistan Muslim league led government had claimed that over all percentage of literacy has reached the figure of 62 per cent but apparently this figure is not acceptable as hundreds of thousands of children are still out of schools. Even if the government figure of 62 per cent is accepted it would be lowest in SAARC region (With the exception of Afghanistan which is not actually a part of SAARC). If we have a comparison between India and Pakistan in education sector we conclude that India has gone miles forward from its neighbour. Currently, literacy rate in India is more than 90 per cent, second highest after Sri Lanka (96 per cent) in the South Asian region. In recent days, India has shown its significance and competency to the whole world in various fields of knowledge such as medicine, engineering, commerce, business administration etc.

While studying in Faculty of Agriculture Engineering and Technology in University of Agriculture Faisalabad I became familiar with the names of J. K. Gupta, S. V. Kulkarni and R. S. Khurmi who are famous Indian authors having significant contributions in the fields of civil, mechanical and agriculture engineering. Book of S. V. Kulkarni *Surveying and Leveling* and RS Khurmi's book *Thermal Engineering* is familiar all over the world. I do not have the name of any Pakistani author possessing calibre and fame like Gupta, Khurmi and Kulkarni. Contrary to this, Pakistani professors and research scholars are familiar for corruption, loot and fake publications. According to Anne Sofi Olson a PhD scholar from Sweden studying in Himachal Pradesh, a north Indian state, "there is a massive difference in quality of education between India and Pakistan" "I am doing PhD from an Indian University but I came to research on herbal medicines in Pakistan but it was very shocking to me that Pakistani students are very unfamiliar with actual research, plagiarism is very common among the students and most of the publications are based upon plagiarism, professors are involved in loot and corruption, funds for research are looted mercilessly" She added more. A PhD scholar from a very renowned public sector university of the country also stated in these words, "Sir we are not able to do any research here as our supervisors (Professors) are involved in massive corruptions, funds for research projects are going in their kitty and students are in miserable circumstances but we have to bear this for the sake of our future".

Now let us shift our focus back to the miserable circumstances of basic education in the country. It's a great matter of concern for the government that more than one quarter (26 per cent) of school going age children were out of schools in 2014. This massive fraction of children in the country is involved in child labour in every corner. Hundreds of public schools in rural and urban areas of the country including rural Sind, Baluchistan and South Punjab are under the possession of feudal and urban lords. Concerned governments have failed to take charge of these public buildings from these mafias. A report was published about ghost schools (a terminology for non-functional schools in the country) in *Daily News,* one of the leading English newspaper of the country on September 13,2013. The report stated that currently 4,450 ghost schools are present in Pakistan. Majority of these ghost schools are present in Sind province, currently 2,181 schools in the province of Sind can be considered as non-functional. Teaching and non-teaching staffs of these ghost schools are drawing salary without doing any work, so tax

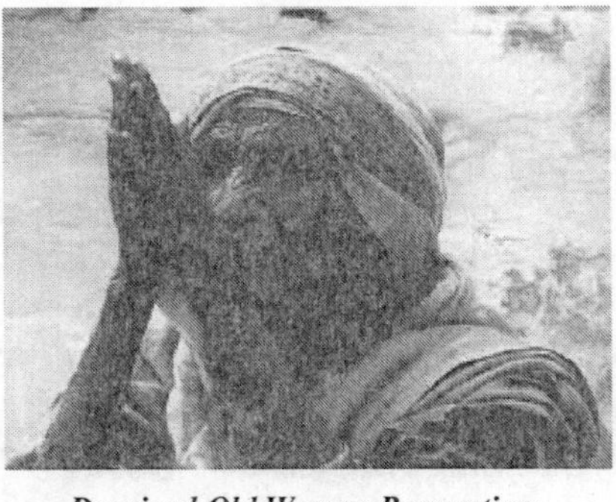

Deprived Old Women Requesting Officals for Help

Image of a Slum in Karachi

payers of the country are bearing a great loss but are still not able to bring any change in the system. One can easily imagine the level of education of the country which is not able to provide basic education to its massive fraction of the population.

Non-functional or ghost school is only one side of the picture, the other side which reflects the miserable circumstances in public schools and colleges is more heinous and dark. If we have a look at the conditions of public schools in the country it will be clear that massive fraction of these schools is no more able to provide quality education to the children of the nation due to various reasons. First and foremost reason for the decline of public schools in the country is the allocation of a very low budget for education. Currently 1.9 per cent of GDP on education is not sufficient for the provision of quality education in the country. Due to its very minute expenditure on education in comparison to its neighbours, Pakistan is not able to enhance both the rate and quality of education in a scenario of rapid growth in education systems in its surroundings. Low allocation of budget and corruption also has produced severe repercussions on public schools in the country during the last two decades. Massive factions of public schools in the country possess very less furniture and other basic human facilities such as toilets, play grounds, computer labs, etc. Due to very uncomfortable circumstances in the public schools, upper income groups of the society do not send their children to public schools, only children of few factions of lower income groups study in the public schools of the country.

Public school teachers are rated as third grade citizens and treated in an inhuman manner by the bureaucracy and administrators. Due to very low wages and facilities bulk of teaching staff belongs to lower income group of the country. As massive fraction of population in the country is heavily influenced by wealth and material possessions so the teachers being part of lower income groups possess a shaky confidence and ungroomed personalities. This low confidence is playing a vital role in less interaction between student and teacher in the public schools of the country. Majority among the public school teachers and students are not familiar with the importance of student-teacher interaction. Massive fraction of students studying in public schools of the country is shy and do not like to ask questions during class, similarly teachers too are rude and do not like being questioned by students during lectures. Contrary to this massive fraction of private schools in the country is spending relatively more on infrastructure and laboratories and some private (not all as there is a mafia in private sector educational institutes as will be discussed later) educational institutes are paying handsome salaries to their teaching staff as well. Private sector has played its part in a significant manner in the recent past in education field that's why a massive fraction of upper income group including elite, more than middle (An income group between elite and upper middle class) and upper middle classes of the country has become an integral part of private sector educational system during the last two decades. Children belonging to super elite fraction of the country like to study abroad, in this way public schools in the country are the hub of students belonging to lower income groups.

Like too many other basic necessities of life pure, economical and timely justice is also like a dream for majority population of the country which never comes true. According to Willem Penn, "justice delayed is justice denied" but here in Pakistan with the exception of some very fortunate people who can get justice or even injustice in time, justice is otherwise always being delayed. It's almost impossible to fetch justice within the time frames of international standards in Pakistan as procedure of getting justice is always lengthy, expensive and journey to justice is fraught of hinders and fears.

Judiciary is well known as the 3rd pillar of the state in the modern world, used for strengthening the very fabric of state in all civilised countries, but Pakistan is unfortunate enough that its judicial system is not yet able to deliver accordingly. In the early period of the country's history judiciary favoured the military dictators who used it as a tool to impose military rule for a long span of time, this action of judiciary produced severe repercussions on it derailing it from its original objectives. General Ayub Khan was involved in first coup d'état against a civilian government of the country in October 1958, the judiciary fully supported the military action and provided a firm constitutional support to the military dictator. This role of judiciary was also followed in later periods. Nowaday's too much judicial activism of a superior judiciary in the country is another factor behind delayed justice in the country. Judicial activism has become an integral part of judicial system during the long regime of popular chief justice Iftkhar Muhammad Chaudhry (retired from the office on 13-12-2013). Mr Chaudhry the former CJP was consider as Suo Moto king among the superior judges of the country, his over interference in state affairs produced severe repercussions on the functioning of the higher judiciary machinery of the country.

Lower judiciary is consider more responsible for delayed or denied justice in comparison to its superior fraction as more than 95 per cent of delayed or pending cases in the judiciary belongs to its lower fraction. Superior judiciary of the country is restricted for the interpretation of constitutional affairs, and limited to hear only high profile cases so massive portion of the population depends on the lower judiciary for justice. Police also have a vital role in any judicial system of the world as the collection of evidence for the provision of justice has always been a responsibility of the police. But the police in Pakistan have failed to deliver role efficiently, reputation of the police among the masses is not good enough and disliking towards the police in masses is widespread. Police is considered among most corrupt public sector organisations in the country, its substandard investigation and cruel attitude towards masses is producing many hurdles for the provision of timely justice. We will discuss the role of judiciary and police in later chapters here we recapitulate all in these words, "So called land of pure is not a land of pure in any sense as among all basic rights of human beings namely, Education, Health and Justice, nothing is available in purified form here".

2

Collapse of Economy and its Repercussions

- **Economic Failures of the State**

Pakistan with its massive population of 192 million (2014) is the sixth most populated nation of the world. The economic volume of the country is not in proportion to its immense population or in other words expansion of economy is not in accordance with the expansion rate of population. Majority of the population is living in hunger, diseases and unemployment. As compared to his predecessors Syed Naveed Qamar and Abdul Hafeez Sheikh (2008-13, during the regime of PPP) Mr Ishaq Dar, our present federal minister for finance seems more composed, competent and determined and this is perhaps reflected in his attainment of some success during last six months in the form of improvement signs in the nation's economy such as appreciation of the Pak Rupee against the US dollar and increase in foreign exchange reserves of the country. Yet even then much needs to be done as the country is very much still in the shackles of miserable circumstances. If we even take a fleeting economic comparison between Pakistan and its neighbours like India, China and Iran it will be clear that our country stands far behind.

The dear and near friend of Pakistan, China has an economic volume of 9.75 trillion (US dollars) and is the second largest economy in the world after the United States. The per capita income of China is not in accordance or in proportion to the speed of its economic growth –countries of Europe, North America, Oceania (massive fraction with the exception of few) and Middle East rank higher with respect to per capita income in comparison to China. With per capita income of only 6711 US dollars, the living standard of the citizens' of China is considered below par than the least developed countries of Europe such as the Baltic States. Never the less the economic growth rate of 7.74 per cent (December 2013) and a very minute inflation rate of 2.25 per cent (Feb 2014) makes China one of the most rapidly growing nations of the world. Similarly, another neighbour of Pakistan and its traditional rival,

India also possesses better circumstances in the economic field. According to experts Pakistan looks no near to India in various fields now due to the economic boom that India witnesssed during the last decade under the leadership of its economist Prime Minister (Dr Manmohan Singh). India has a massive population of 1250 million and is the second most populated country in the world after China. Meeting the challenge of such a massive population is not an easy task, provision of food, shelter, education and justice to the second largest population in the world is really a difficult job but due to expansion its economy it has been able to face this challenge. Though the speed of development is not too rapid –India is growing in gradual manner but even then its progress is more than its neighbour Pakistan. India is included among the most rapidly growing nations of the developing world after China and Turkey. India's GDP nominal is 1.87 trillion dollars (10th in the world) while its GDP per capita is 5.05 trillion (third in the world, after USA and China). Its economic growth rate was almost five per cent (For the fiscal year 2013-14). In 2013, its exports were 312.35 billon dollars making it one of the top exporters of the world.

Comparing it with its two giant neighbours, Pakistan posseses miserable economic circumstances, Pakistani economy is facing difficulties since the mid of 2005 and the years during 2008-13 remained among the worst period of its history. Pakistan's GDP nominal is only 245 billon dollars and the volume of economy is not sufficient for its massive population. Currently, Pakistan stands 45th in the world in economic volume while bearing the weight of the sixth most populated nation of the world, with more than half of its population living below the poverty line. Federal finance minister admitted in his recent press briefing that the massive fraction of the population of the country is living below the poverty line with earnings less than two US dollars per day. Finance Minister also described new parameters to define population below the poverty line. In 2008, the international criteria to define poverty line was revised by the World Bank to an earning of 1.25 US dollars per day from one US dollar per day due to the increased rate of inflation. In Pakistan, with due to the massive decline of the rupee in comparison to the US dollar the international parameters were adjusted by our Finance Minister and the poverty line was set at two US dollars per day so as to make it comparable with the international parameters. Following this standard of poverty, more than 50 per cent of our population is living below the poverty line, but even an earning between 2-5 US dollars per day looks minute in contrast with the massive inflation of 10.82 per cent (2013)–and can hardly meet the basic requirements of a person.

Report of the International Monetary Fund (2013) stated that with per income (GDP) of 3149 US dollars, Pakistan stands at 140th position in the list of 180 countries. Due to very low per capita income, living standard of a massive fraction of its population has dipped to immensely low levels of misery and disaster. Average per capita income annually in most of the developed countries of the world is between 4500-5000 US dollars. Qatar, a small country in the Middle East with its highest level of individual income generation (10434.2 US dollars in 2013) stands first in the latest IMF list of per capita income. Central African Republic with the lowest per capita income (542 US dollars in 2013) stood 180th among the list of the 180 countries. 2013 reports of IMF and World Bank mention that Pakistan's worst economic circumstances as reflected by its GDP (PPP) makes it stand last among the bigger and recognised economies who are also facing adverse circumstances, like Iraq (war affected), Egypt, Bhutan, Iran (facing international sanctions) and even Sri Lanka.

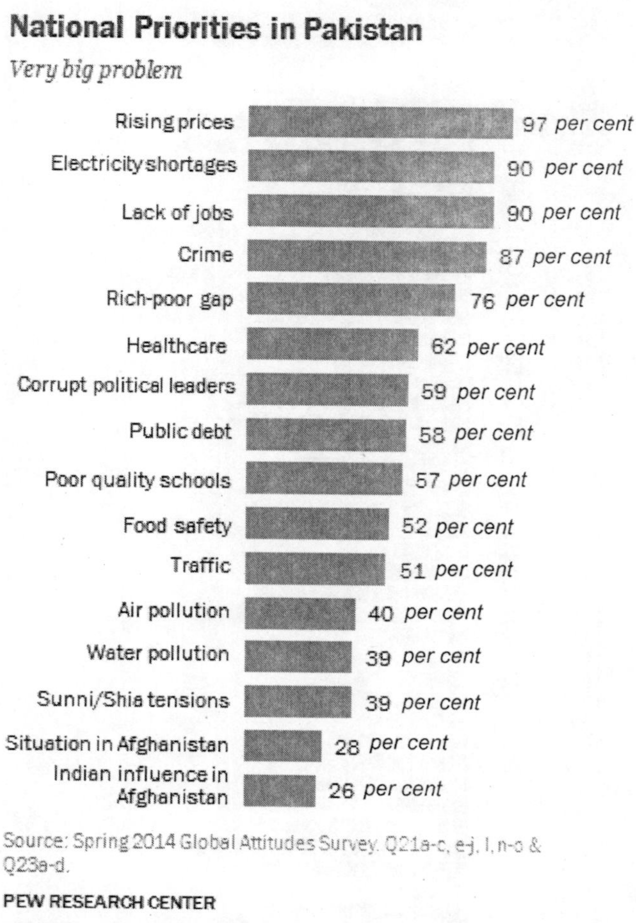

A demo of Public Problems in Pakistan Relesed by Pew Reserach Centre Wasingtion.

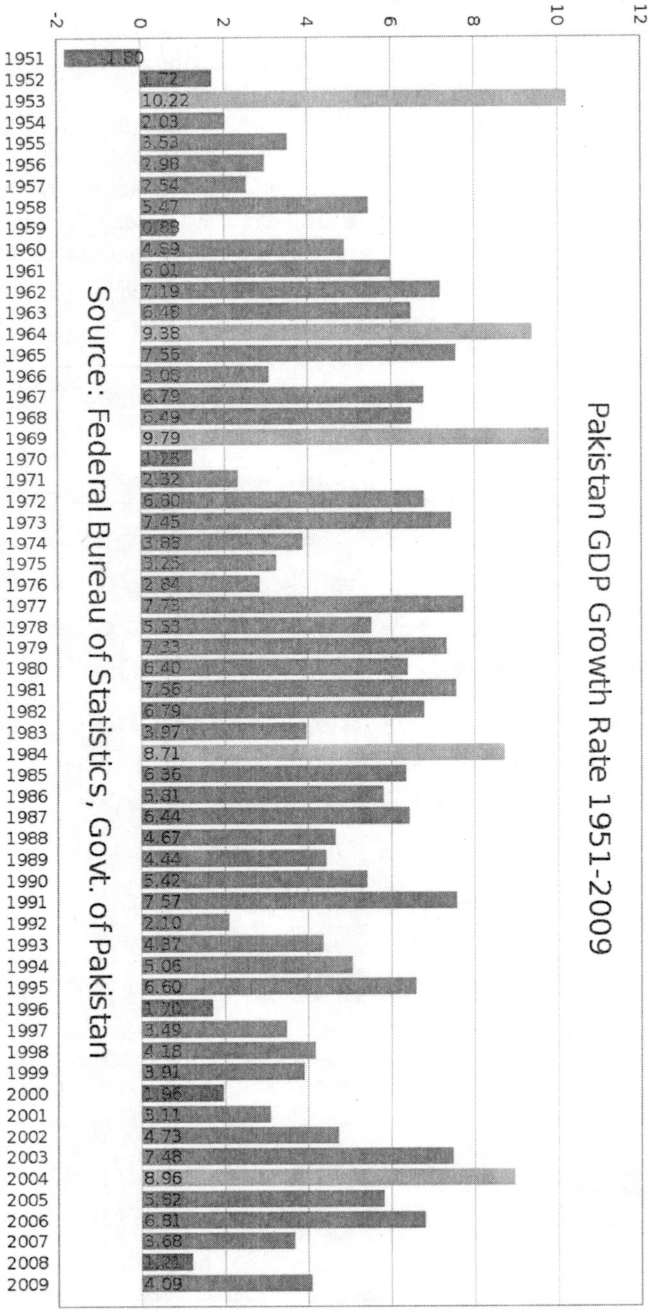

An Image of GDP Growth Rate in Pakistan

With massive inflation of 10 per cent (2013) Pakistani rupee has lost its value leading to immense price hike during last five years. Media reports state that there has been more than 500 per cent price hike in the country during the last decade. Population belonging to the lower income group has suffered a lot and its massive fraction is still suffering as its purchasing power to buy general goods like food, clothes etc., has gone down to great extent during the last decade. The living standards of relatively stronger economic groups of the country that is the middle and upper middle classes have also gone down during this span of time.

According to Salman Hussein a forty seven years mid - career IT (Information Technology) professional from Rawalpindi, "life for the middle class is not easy in Pakistan now, inflation has created too much price hike and now our buying power has gone down in comparison to the past" he added "I was used to shopping for my colleagues every three months only a few years back but now I am hardly able to manage clothes and other basic necessities of life even for my family———, astonishingly my income has also increased several times in comparison to the past but the speed of inflation is more than the enhancement in my income", Salman added more.

According to some economic experts the middle class has almost vanished from the country during the last decade, but some other experts have partially denied this theory, as per them the middle class has not vanished yet but very severe economic circumstances in the country has pushed the country's middle class towards the lower middle class segment and the lower middle class of the recent past has now become the part of the lower class. So what happened to the lower class of the recent past? Experts say that it has gone down below the poverty line. At US $ 2 per day as standard for poverty line the massive fraction of the population is living below the poverty line, so where is the middle class? Let's have a close look on all the income fractions of the society. Population below the poverty line is more than 50 per cent of total population, Remaining 50 per cent or less include all income groups other than the lower class, and includes lower middle, middle, more than middle, elite and super elite classes. Super elite, elite, more than middle (a newly emerged wealthy class between the middle and elite classes mainly comprise of corrupt civil-military bureaucrats and urban mafias) and middle classes are hardly 15 per cent of the total population of the country. So a massive fraction of population (35 per cent) belongs to lower income group including lower middle class and lower class. So in reality there is very minute middle class remaining in the country.

According to some very renowned economic experts of the world foreign investment in any country is closely associated with the existence of middle class. Stronger middle class better implies better foreign investment and vice versa, as investors invest on "Buying Power" of the consumers of the country, more buying power attracts more foreign investment. We can prove this theory by presenting here the example of India -the next door neighbour of Pakistan which possesses the largest middle class population in the world (members of Indian middle class were between 500-600 million in 2013), is a great hub of foreign investment in the modern day. India attracts foreign investments from countries like USA, Canada, Australia, Europe and China due to mutual interests of trade, man power, etc. created between India and these countries.

According to report published in "*Daily Dawn*" one of the leading English language newspapers of the country, on September 12, 2013, IMF warned Pakistan about its poor economic growth in the recent past. Report further stated that during the last five years GDP growth remained less than three per cent and the there serves of the Central bank (State Bank of Pakistan) had dipped to a very low volume of 6 billion US dollars from 14.7 billon US dollar during the fiscal year 2011-12. The International Monetary Fund extended Pakistan's three year 6.7 billon dollar loan in September 2013 on very tight conditions. IMF also warned Pakistan that future contracts between it and loaning countries would be done only by following its terms and conditions in a true sense. According to a senior official of IMF, the organisation has faced criticism from various countries for the provision of more privilege to Pakistan; the senior official also stated that those countries had failed to fulfil their commitments with the organisation (IMF) during the recent past years.

Pakistan with a massive burden of foreign debts is going through miserable economic circumstances. Major portion of its collected revenue is used up for the payment of instalments of foreign loans. Currently (2013), Pakistan

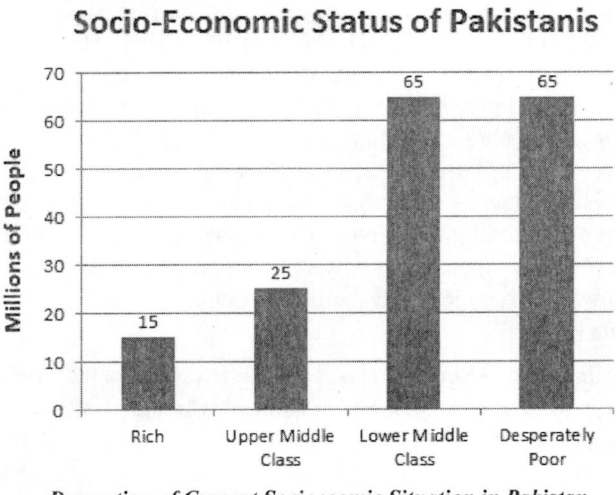

Descrption of Current Socioecomic Situation in Pakistan

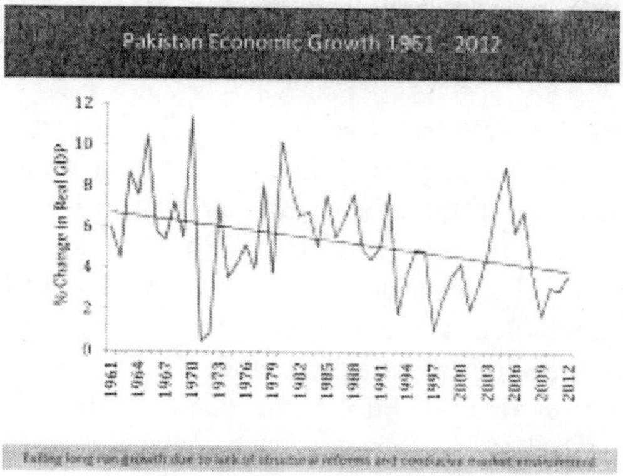

Fluctuating Econmoy of Pakistan

has a debt of 62 billion dollars borrowed from International finance organisations and different countries of the world. Pakistani's are unfortunate enough that they have to bear not only the load of foreign debts but also the load of debts of national banks as well due to massive loans taken from them by the different governments during their regimes. A report published in Daily Dawn on February 28, 2012 about the internal debts of the country, stated that domestic borrowing had accelerated to a great extent during past years. According to the report up till 2012 different governments have borrowed more than 130 billons producing severe repercussions on the country's economy. Poor economic circumstances are considered one of the top ranked reasons for causing anarchy, conflicts and frustration among the masses. There has been a heinous rise in suicides among a vast fraction of the population during the last five years, every year thousands amongst the ordinary Pakistanis commit suicide due to miserable economic conditions. Basic human necessities of proper food, shelter and basic healthcare looks too far away from the range of a massive fraction of population and suicide remains the only option for them to get rid of such difficult circumstances.

Massive fraction of men and women living below the poverty line have been seen collecting food (particularly in smaller and backward areas) form garbages and slums in modern day Pakistan. More than two million people in the larger cities of the country got their daily food from charity organisations. Some generous individuals are also running food centres to provide food items twice a day to this miserable fraction of the population. Some religious institutions like shrines of the Sufi's and Saints also provide free food to pilgrims and the poor population in their vicinity. Famous shrines like 'Data Gunj Bux' in Lahore, 'Golrah Shareef' in Rawalpindi , 'Shabaz Qulandar' in Sehwan, are providing food to massive fractions of the poor classes. Many people also donate to the Shrines of the country as they believe that these institutes provide great social and religious services for the needy. "Lungar" is the common name of that food which is distributed among the pilgrims and poors with the combined collection of donations.

"Suicide the only way to escape poverty" was the title of a report published in "Daily Dawn" on 15th February 2012; the report indicated the great percentage of suicides in the country in comparison to its neighbouring countries. According to the report, 1600 people had committed suicide due to miserable economic circumstances during January 2011 to October 2011. Pakistani economy has collapsed to a great extent during the last ten years and now its widespread repercussions are evident in each and every corner of the country. Interest rates of public and commercial utilities has risen alarmingly during the last five years negatively impacting smaller and medium sized enterprises. Federal and provincial governments due to very limited resources are involved in continuous borrowings. Many times recently, the opposition has blamed the Federal government for borrowing excessively from International financial organisations and for the excessive printing of currency notes. Excessive printing of currency is increasing inflation and devaluing the rupee vis-a-vis the US dollar and is also enhancing foreign debts. Devalued currency is producing severe repercussions on internal economic situation and affecting the buying power of the people of the country. Budget deficit is rapidly increasing every year and to overcome it governments are imposing more taxes on the commoners, the elite and super elite classes of the country are very rarely concerned about taxes as most of them are involved in tax evasions to a great extent.

Commoners in the country are paying various types of taxes like general sales tax, petroleum levy etc., but these taxes are not enough for the relief of the massive fraction of population. An ordinary citizen using a cellular phone in the country has to pay a tax of 40 rupees (directly and indirectly) on the recharge of 100 rupees, contrary to this the super elite and elite classes of the country who possess more than ninety per cent of the country's total income rarely pay taxes, most of this affluent class owns industrial estates, agricultural and urban lands, businesses in the country and abroad as well. All the political elite of the country including the mainstream leaders of PPP, PML (N) and PTI have businesses abroad and are known to be involved in tax evasions to a great extent. According to Imran Khan, chairman of PTI and a leader of opposition, there are more than 1000 billon tax evasions every year in the country. Super elite and elite classes of the country are involved in loot, corruption, and tax evasions with full ease and liberty and face no accountability for their heinous crimes.

- **Energy Crises and Economic Disaster**

Energy (electricity and natural gas) crises in Pakistan is going on from 2005 and has produced severe repercussions. It has produced severe impacts on smaller and medium sized industry and businesses during the last decade, due to high cost of energy, cost of manufacturing and production has increased several times and this has led to the sabotage of the process of industrialisation in the country. Similarly the energy crises has increased unemployment and poverty in the country. Workers of smaller and medium size industrial units and even sometimes of large industries too have to face a certain period of unemployment every year due to shortage of electricity and natural gas. Industry in the country is utilising both natural gas and electric power to generate production; smaller and medium size industrial units like flour mills, cotton factories, poultry shades, textile power looms depend on electricity while heavy industries such as fertilizers factories and Sugar mills depend on natural gas, for their operations. Mega shortfall of electricity has produced severe repercussions on smaller and medium size enterprises in the country, due to unavailability of power supply through government organisations these industrial units are utilising generators for the provision of electricity. This action of self-provision of electricity has enhanced the manufacturing cost to a great extent. Due to high manufacturing rate open market prices have also greatly increased. Now have a look on another aspect of the situation, due to provision of limited electricity and natural gas industrial units are not able to yield full working hours in a year and its repercussions are also severe. Factories were not able to fulfil their international consignments on time in the initial years of energy crises leading to loss of their regular international customers.

As we discussed earlier that self-provision of electric power through generators is an expensive action. A minute fraction of heavy industrial units possess their own generators (power stations) so they are able to produce electricity of their own use, but smaller industrial units are totally dependent on state owned power distribution companies. When these smaller units use little generators for the purpose of power generation cost of production almost doubles as smaller power generators use large quantities of petrol and diesel which are very precious in modern day Pakistan. Hence energy crises is playing a very vital role behind the excessive price hikes in the country. Similarly massive fraction of heavy industries is using natural gas as fuel but shortfall of natural gas in the winters create too much difficulties for the running of these types of industrial units. Large scale utilisation of compressed natural gas in motor vehicles has produced a great shortage of natural gas for the industrial units during the last five years. Up till 2005, Pakistan possessed enough resources of natural gas, sufficient enough for both domestic and industrial usage; but then a flood of CNG (compressed natural gas) stations in the country after 2005 (though it started in early 2000 but got boom after 2005) absorbed a major portion of natural gas reserves of the country. Massive fraction of public and goods transporters converted their vehicles from petrol or diesel to CNG–a cheap option in comparison to the other two fuels. Due to instalment of CNG kits in busses and other heavy vehicles margin of profit enhanced several times in transport business but it did great damage to industry, as burning of precious natural gas in vehicles was heavily paid for by the industrial sector of the country. Pakistan lost its massive reserves of natural gas during the last seven to eight years due to its merciless utilisation in vehicles, this action though benefited a specific mafia (both CNG owners and transporters were integral part of this mafia). Mafia controlling the CNG licenses earned billons of rupees with the provision of licenses to specific individuals and later these CNG owners earned trillions of rupees with this business with in a very short span of time. CNG stations got natural gas on a very low and subsidised price but these gas stations got massive profit (more than five hundred times) which resulted in a flood of CNG stations in a very short span of time. Similarly, when transporters witnessed a very cheap fuel they utilised it too in a merciless manner, initially concept of CNG was designed for smaller vehicles of lower middle and middle classes of the country but this fraction was not able to fetch its fruits fully. Transporters initially experimented with smaller vans on CNG which enhanced their profits more

Energy crisis in Pakistan and effect of energy crisis on the economy of Pakistan

People protesting against the ongoing elctrcity crises

than double, later induction of big busses on natural gas suck a massive of the standing reserves.

Pakistan possesses the sixth largest population in the world so more than 192 million people are facing extremely severe energy crisis in the world. This crises of energy has produced a very harsh impact on the lives of this massive fraction of population of the world. Businesses are going down, unemployment is increasing, living standard of massive portion of population is hugely distributed, conflicts and frustration among the masses is touching the sky and over all the entire life cycle of the common people has been rendered miserable.

Electricity (power supply) is considered as life energy for the people in the modern day, all fields of life including agriculture, industry and business are heavily dependent on the provision of electricity. Massive short fall of electricity is capable of causing large scale disturbance and destruction in each and every sector, industry, firm and households in today's Pakistan. Demand for electricity for both domestic and commercial purposes in Pakistan is not more than 2,000 MW (twenty five times lesser than its neighbour India-currently producing more than 3,00,000 MW of electricity). Our country has been hardly able to produce 10,000-13,000 MW (Maximum) during last five years. There always remained a massive difference between demand and supply of electricity (up to 10,000 MW in summers) during the last decade. Result of this immense difference between demand and supply of power is the massive load shedding (black out) of 10-14 hours in urban areas (larger cities) and 14-18 hours per day in rural areas of the country. The hot and humid summers in specially in the plains and deserts are very harsh and miserable for the majority of people. As majority among the population belong to lower income groups so this miserable fraction of population is not able to afford generators or other systems of power supply when electricity is not available through public connection. Shortfall of power in summers goes up particularly in rural areas (More than 64 per cent of total population is living in rural areas of the country) and misery for massive fraction of population living in villages and towns and adjacent cities starts. When women and children in high temperatures of 50°C cry for relief it seems that this part of world is living in the era of 1500s. During massive unavailability of electricity major portion of population living in rural areas face severe repercussions like scarcity of even drinking water and poor crop yield.

Shortfall of 6,000-10,000 MW electricity during most of the year causes severe repercussions on industry, business and urban life of the country. Smaller and medium sized industrial units, business of lower middle class and domestic lives are also disturbed during the darkened hours. Most of these urban small business and self-employed people are also not able to generate electricity during the power cuts of the state-owned electric supply cooperations. One major dilemma of electric power sector in the country is 100 per cent dependency on state-owned power generation and distribution companies for provision and distribution of electricity in the whole country. As provision of electricity is only dependent on state-owned organisations so population is forced to rely on these poor performing institutes. Most among the modern and civilised countries in the world has allowed private sector to invest in power sector. Contrary to Pakistan its next door neighbour India has allowed the private sector to invest in power sector as a result of which there is excessive production of electricity in many parts of the country. India in recent times has been able to supply electricity at very reasonable rates. Massive involvement of private sector in power generation projects in India made rate of electricity economical and has also reduced the pressure on public power generation companies, but Pakistani's are not that fortunate as due to non-involvement of private sector in power sector they have to rely on poorly functioning state owned power generation and distribution companies who have failed to a great extent to reduce shortfall and line losses during the last decade in the country.

Group of Very Dpeived ones from Faisalabad who Sold thier Kideneys for only 3 Lakhs Rupess

Image of Food Distribution by a Generous Man in Peshwar

Repercussions of this massive shortfall of electricity are widespread and deep routed on urban business. As we discussed earlier that smaller and medium sized industrial units like power textile looms, flour mills, poultry shades operating in cities are not able to function properly due to unavailability of electricity for most of the year. So the workers working on daily wages in these organisations too face unemployment for particular period of time every year. Larger industrial groups in the country are now focusing on self - provision of electricity. Tapal industries and few sugar mills are also generating electricity as well, but these private power generators are not allowed to sell this electricity to the masses.

- Importance of agriculture is not negligible in any economy of the world but agriculture is of key importance for the economy of Pakistan as more than 62 per cent of the total population is directly or indirectly associated with agriculture. Agriculture of the country is also facing severe repercussions due to energy crises in the country. Pakistan possesses a relatively fertile land among the other agricultural countries of the world, most part of its cultivated land is able to produce good crop yield, but availability of ground water (canal water) is always been a great matter of concern for the farmers of the country. Though the country has the largest irrigation system in the world even then this system is not able to sufficiently meet the irrigation needs of the farmers. So most of the farmers in the country use turbines and tube wells to irrigate their lands but due to massive shortfall of electricity tube wells cannot run for most of the time and ground water is either not available or too expensive to access. Agro, based industry in the country like tillage industrial units, cotton factories etc are also facing severe repercussions due to massive load shedding in the country. Unlike their counterparts in neighbouring countries, farmers in Pakistan are utilising very expensive electricity, India is providing free and subsidised electricity (free electricity is provided for a specific limit i.e. 500 units then a very nominal price is charged) to its farmers and this has produced good results for the agriculture of the country in terms of increase in crop yield.

- **Terrorism and Economy**

Terrorism has played a vital role for the collapse of the economy in Pakistan during last decade. Repercussions of terrorism on economy are widespread and deep-rooted like energy crises. Different local and international terror groups have produced widespread and deep-rooted networks in a large part of the country during the last few years. Religious, ethnic and different nationalist militant groups possesses widespread networks in the country and activities of these militant groups has produced huge impacts on the economy of the country. Foreign investments in the country have gone down to lowest levels during 2007-13 due to multidimensional militancy in the country. According to the latest report of IMF (March, 2014) 'there is a very minute improvement in the economy of Pakistan but militancy will remain as a constant threat for the economic conditions in the country in future as well. Country has faced terrorism as a tool for its economic destruction in recent past and still it looks like a hanging sword for its prosperity. Industry and businesses in the country has faced severe repercussions of this militancy and terror and ultimate result of insurgency provided by terrorist organisations in the country has gone against the poor and miserable masses of the country'.

Different local and international militant organisations set up their networks in various parts of federally administered tribal areas (FATA) in mid 2000's in a reaction to United States invasion of Afghanistan after September 11, 2001. These organisations expanded their networks in settled areas of Khyber Pukhtunkhawa i.e. Dera Ismile Khan, Baunu etc., Punjab, (southern part of Punjab is much under the influence of different religious militant organisations) and Karachi. Baluchistan the largest Province in the country (3,47,190 sq.km.) is already facing great anarchy and disharmony since 2004. Death of Akbar Buggtti, the former chief minister, governor and a nationalist leader in a military operation in 2006 has opened the doors of militancy and conflicts in the province. Militancy in Baluchistan extended during the PPP led coalition government from 2008-13 and the province went under constant conflict and disorder.

It's a matter of fact that terrorism and militancy are directly associated with poor economic conditions, miserable circumstances of economy for the massive fraction of population in Pakistan is also playing a vital role for enhanced militancy in the country. For example, Baluchistan is considered as the most backward part of the country, it possesses very less infrastructure and public machinery in comparison to the other provinces of the country. Immense reaction was shown by State actors against nationalist leaders like late Nawab Akbar Buggti who raised their voices against socioeconomic injustices and discriminations with the people of Baluchistan. Death of Akbar Buggti enhanced insurgency in major part of the province. Movement for its liberation that started in early 1960's got momentum just after the military operation. This militant movement against the state of Pakistan destroyed the remaining economy of the largest province of the country. The minute industry that Baluchistan possessed got destroyed and its already shaky business went under permanent decline.

Tariek-e-Taliban Pakistan commonly called as TTP initially started its operations in north-western parts of the country in December 2007. Islamic clerics of TTP set a network in federally administrated tribal areas of the country for the enforcement of Islamic laws (Shariah) in the country. They destructed the writ of state in most parts of the tribal agencies and Northern Province (KPK) in a very short span of time and introduced orthodox Islamic laws as a replacement of state laws. State machinery almost vanished from major part of tribal areas after the invasion of Islamic clerics. Just after attaining control of the particular territory these clerics destroyed dozens of girl's schools and ordered women not to go out of their homes. Citizens of these areas were warned against modern education, clerics ordered the population to register their children in religious schools. The clash between the State and Islamic militant groups consisting of hundreds and thousands of militants has produced severe repercussions on the economy of the country and particularly on the economic circumstances of FATA and its adjacent province KPK. FATA a nowadays has become a 'no entry' area for law enforcement agencies of the country and Taliban has strengthened its writ in the territory during last three years.

Islamic militants in Pakistan are involved in kidnapping for ransom, smuggling, and smuggling of weapons for the generation of funds. To enhance their revenues few fractions of these militant groups are also involved in drug business and robberies in big cities. Islamic militants in the country have set a widespread and deep-rooted network for the collection of their imposed taxes, collection of so called taxes is going on at a large scale in FATA and major portion of "KPK". Settled areas (not part of tribal territory) of KPK like Peshawar, Dera Ismile Khan, Charsadah, Bannu and Mardan are under constant threat from these militant groups. Numerous operations launched by Islamic militants during the recent past in these above mentioned areas has caused loss in faith of their ordinary citizens on the State's law enforcement agencies and writ. According to a recent report of Geo news the business community in Peshawar (the capital and largest city of KPK) has shown great concerns about the declining business in the city due to militancy. The report stated that traders in the city are very much frightened with rapidly growing incidents of kidnapping for ransom and robberies. Hundreds of traders were kidnapped for ransom during the last five years in the city of Peshawar and many were looted through robberies. Islamic militants and other criminal gangs in the country are also involved in the collection of Bhatta, a certain amount on monthly or weekly basis, from the business community in various parts of the country. According to a senior journalist from Peshawar business community, "in major part of the province of KPK business men are forced to pay monthly Bhatta to these militant organisations". "Law enforcement agencies have failed to provide security to the business community in this part of country", he stated more.

It's a great dilemma of KPK that majority among the leading industrialists and businessmen in the province are in the process of transferring their business abroad in countries like Malaysia, Singapore, Thailand, Sri Lanka, Bangladesh, Kenya etc. Some are also shifting their attentions towards relatively peaceful cities within the country like Lahore and Islamabad.

"Militancy and terrorism has destroyed business in Pakistan particularly in KPK", said Amir Hayat a businessman from Peshawar. "We are paying heavy amounts to these militants for the survival of our businesses and families; no one is willing to lose his life or any among his family members by refusing these wild beasts. Someone who refuses to pay will either lose his life and business or any among his family members. Ultimate repercussion would be the explosion in your shop or business centre or the kidnapping of your son", Hayat continued. "We are paying ransoms and monthlies to these militant organisations and law enforcement agencies in the country are very well aware of it but the officials of these agencies are not able to help us as they too feel afraid of these militants. People voted for change in the province in the general elections of 2013, that's why Pakistan Teherk Insaf (PTI) came into power but we are still very disappointed. PTI has proved itself not more than a traditional political party who is also involved in loot, corruption and bad governance like other political parties of the country" Hayat added more. "According to a senior journalist from Peshawar political change in the province has proved to be more heinous for the miserable people of the province as now massive fraction of the population believes that the circumstances are going towards a point of no return." "A civil war is very imminent in the country if these circumstances continue", he added more.

Ongoing terrorism in the country has not only destroyed the economy of northern part of the country but also produced severe repercussions on other populated provinces of the country like Punjab and Sind. With a massive population of 21.5 million (Statistics of 2013) Karachi , the commercial capital of the country, is the 3rd largest city in the world after Shanghai and Beijing. Karachi is playing a vital role in the economy of the country as it is a hub of all types of industries and businesses and a generator of a massive portion of taxes for the country. Sind industrial estate in Karachi, among the oldest industrial zones in the country, possesses more than 2500 factories of various types. Karachi Chamber of Commerce and Industry, the representative body of industrial and trader community has more members than any other indigenous body of this type. Karachi, the largest city in the country, has been the centre of foreign and local investments during the era of 1960 to mid - 1980's,but as of now its economic grandeur has gone down to a great extent due to massive violence, target killing and disorder, going on since at least the last thirty years. After mid 1980's an ethnic war has started in the city which has destroyed its peace and writ of the state, governments after mid 80's have failed to control this widespread anarchy and gang war is still going on in various parts of the city.

Currently different ethnic and religious groups are involved in target killing and kidnapping for ransoms. Target killing is taking place since almost three decades in the city and different ethnic and religious militant groups are involved in it, this massive gang war in most parts of the city has caused immense human and economic losses during last eight years.

It's a true saying that peace and economy are directly associated with each other. Progress and prosperity of cities, provinces and countries are not possible without peace. Terror, militancy and destruction of law and order always causes economic collapse, a situation Karachi has been facing during the last three decades. Initially in the 80's and 90's the different ethnic groups were only involved in financial crimes but now orthodox militant groups are also involved in collecting monthlies and kidnapping for ransoms. Different banned Islamic groups (Military ruler Pervaiz Mushraf banned many religious militant organisations in 2002 due to their alleged involvement in violence and target killing) and religious organisations also started moving towards Karachi in mid - 2000's sensing it favourable for their future.

Talibanisation is a term widely used by western media since September 11, 2001 for the widespread network of militant Islamic groups associated with Al Qaeda and Taliban all over the world particularly in Pakistan, Afghanistan and Iraq. Talibanisation has spread to a great extent now but was not so widespread up till the mid 2000's. TTP started its activities in north western part of the country in December 2007 but soon it started to flourish its network in all the corners of the country. With the exception of federal capital, upper and central Punjab, (This exception is even not fully correct as Islamabad and Rawalpindi possesss many hubs of Islamic clerics in guise of religious institutes). The Taliban have now spread their network in every part of the country and majority among this widespread system was established after December 2007.

Nowaday's different groups of Islamic clerics are involved in heinous activities and are trying to establish a state within a state (They possess a state in FATA as well) by challenging the writ of state in a furious manner. They are also involved in the extraction of so called taxes (monthlies) from the traders and industrial class in the name of Islamic Shariah. Monthly (a forced amount received by these militant groups from different fractions of the society at the start of every month) has been a great matter of concern for the business and industrial community of the city since mid 1980's.

Whether an ordinary vendor or an industrial giant, no wall are familiar with the monthly collecting mafia in Karachi. Monthly is a great source of fund generation for most of these ethnic and religious militant groups operating in the commercial capital of the country. The business community of Karachi lives under constant threat from these militant groups and are forced to pay monthlies as a tribute to these criminals as per their volume of business, that is if a small shop keeper has to pay an amount of 2000 PKR per month then an industrialist has to pay more than a million rupee per month to save his life, family and business. Business community is too much fed up with this situation but have no other option.

Parchi or ticket is also a much used means of collecting funds by these militant organisations. Militant groups utilise the method of Parchi when they possess lesser funds in specific circumstances. Many among these militant groups in Karachi also have political affiliations (some have seats in parliament as well), these groups need funds for their political assignments and most among them use Parchi or ticket method for gathering funds for such special occasions. Parchi or ticket of a specific amount is thrown in the office or house of a businessmen or other professionals like doctors and engineers with a certain deadline. If receiver fails to fulfil the order with in the stipulated time frame he is victimized through various brutal means like killing of a family member or destruction of business through bomb blast. Different industrial groups, businesses outlets and even some commercial banks of the private sector have been forced to pay specific amounts as Parachi in the recent past. According to a very senior commerce reporter from Karachi a market oriented commercial bank transferred its headquarter from Karachi to Lahore as administration of bank was very much fed up by the huge payments of Parchis, some other sources said that in the recent past the bank had had to pay at least 250 million PKR every year to a militant group for the security of its business.

- **Tax Evasions in Pakistan**

Tax evasion has played a vital role in the collapse of the economy of Pakistan. Tax of every type, of hundreds of billions, is going in the kitty of corrupt mafia. The Federal Board of Revenue (FBR) is considered as the most prime organisation of the country for the implementation of tax laws. FBR also runs various promotional campaigns for increasing the awareness of the masses and motivating them for the payment of their due taxes. Yet FBR being a premier tax collector has failed to deliver in the real sense, as tax evasion has become a matter of great concern for governments in modern day Pakistan. Sources say that the country is losing tax reckoned at 1000 billons every year and this great loss is responsible for producing severe repercussions on the economy. Former chairmen of NAB Admiral Faseeh Bukhari (retired) admitted during his tenure of chair (in 2013) that there is a massive tax evasion of seven to eight billions every day in Pakistan. Tax evasion is one of the major types of the ongoing corruption in Pakistan. Super elite and elite classes of the country are committing this crime with absolute ease and liberty. Feudal and industrial classes alongside with business tycoons of all types such as real estate developers, owners of media outlets etc. are involved in this loot to a great extent. Above mentioned organisations of corporate sector have earnings of billons every year but majority among these private sector organisations files very minute tax returns, and the repercussion of this loot and corruption is widespread hunger and disease for the commoners of the country.

Political elite being an integral part of economic cream is involved in tax evasion to a great extent. Most among the political elite in the country also belong to the feudal and industrial classes. Mainstream leadership of all political parties including PML (N), PPP and PTI are facing severe allegations of tax evasions and hiding their assets. As we discussed earlier that corruption and politics are directly proportional to each other in Pakistan and politicians have been facing the allegations of corruption and tax evasion from a very long span of time. According to a February 12, 2012 report of *Express Tribune,* one of the leading English newspaper of the country, more than sixty per cent of the cabinet miniters and two-thirds among the federal law, makers paid no taxes during the fiscal year 2011-12. Report mentioned the statistics was provided by investigative journalist Umar Cheema who stated that a members of parliament of Pakistan possesses an average wealth of 8,82,000 US dollars (Record of 2012) and this fraction of society is not paying taxes accordingly. Report also mentioned the names of parliamentarians and details of paid taxes during the fiscal year 2011-12. Figures given in this report are so astonishing that it seems hard to believe them. The report stated that Senator Mushaid Hussain (Secretary General of PML - Q) then the third largest party in the country, and ruling party during 2002-07, possessing national tax number 2955343-1 paid only 82 rupees tax during the fiscal year 2011-12. Above mentioned example is just a glimpse of the larger picture which suggests that there are thousands of such politicians in Pakistan who possess the assets of billions of rupees but cringe from paying even a single penny to the government of Pakistan.

Prime Minister of Pakistan Nawaz Sharif has been facing severe criticism during the recent past from his political opponents, Imran Khan, chairman of PTI, the third largest political power in the country after PML(N) and PPP, has claimed many times in public meetings that Premier Sharif paid only 5000 PKR tax during the fiscal year 2010-11. Imran Khan too faced criticism by his political opponent PML (N) for hiding his wealth and assets, some senior leaders of ruling PML (N) have raised questions about the lavish life style of Imran Khan. Similarly former President of Pakistan and Co-chairman of PPP, (Five times ruling party of the country during 1971-2013)

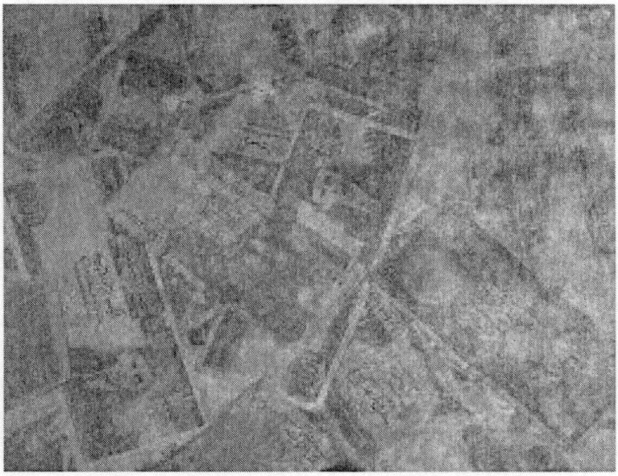

Inflation a Great Curse for Country Since Early 1990's

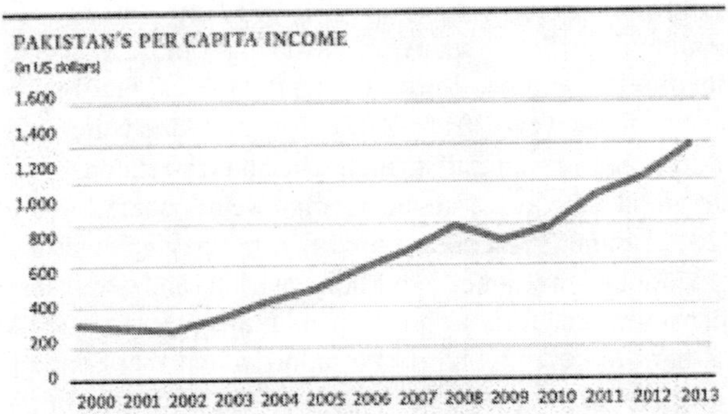

View of per capita income in Pakistan

Asif Ali Zardari has been severely criticised by his political opponents and some fractions of media for his alleged involvement in corruption, tax evasion and hiding assets.

Health and educational institutes in the country belonging to private sector are also involved in tax evasion to a great extent, many medical complexes of corporate sector in the country are registered as welfare trusts and seek tax exemptions on this behalf do not paying a single penny as tax but in reality these private sector organisations are not working as welfare trusts. These corporate sector medical complexes have earnings of billions of rupees every year. Several Mafias are also involved in this business of running healthcare complexes and medical colleges as welfare units but their actual motive is to evade taxes by utilising such tactics. As tax collection per capita in Pakistan is very low as compared to other countries in the region so the government is thinking of broadening the tax net by including some other sectors (currently not in tax net) within in the purview of the taxation system. This will not at all be easy for the concerned authorities as major fraction among the tax exempted belong to the influential classes of the country.

It's a matter of great concern for the government that private educational institutes are also among the non-taxpaying organisations or are paying very minutely. Universities, medical and general colleges of this non-tax paying category serve the upper income groups of the country and the commoners derive no benefits from them. Majority among the private sector educational institutes seek tax exemptions and relaxations in the name of education. But education in more than ninety per cent of these institutes is out of range for even the middle class of the country due to the massive tuition fees charged by them which only the elite can pay. Like private sector hospitals these educational institutes also earn in billions of rupees every year but do not pay tax in a proper manner. Majority among these types of organisations registered as social welfare units generate heavy funds in the name of social services but do nothing in this regard.

Government should take necessary steps to enhance its tax net and improve tax collection system by reducing corruption in concerned departments. For this it should impose taxes on health and education institutes belonging to private sector as these organisations are involved in massive revenue generation through their commercial tactics.

Media has become a great source of power through its influence on various fractions of society, especialy after 2000. Industry and business tycoons who invested in media to enhance their influence and image among the masses, widely utilised tax evasion as a tool for financing their investments. This attitude not only badly damaged the image of media among the masses but also produced severe repercussions on the economy. Many media outlets are utilising their influence as a weapon and are involved in tax evasion of billons of rupees every year. An industrialist-cum-politician turned media tycoon was arrested by NAB in 2002 for his involvement in massive tax evasions, later he was released against a plea bargain with the authorities. Same year his media group invested in media, initially a nationwide newspaper was started but in 2008 it started a news channel as well. Now the particular media / industrial group is considered among the largest pressure groups in the country. Apart from the three media houses- Jang/Geo group (the largest independent media corporation in the country), Naway-Waqat group and Dawn –a massive fraction of other media outlets are owned by industry and business tycoons who utilise the media as a tool for their own protection or shelter.

Another businessman-cum-politician later turned media tycoon has also come under severe allegations of corruption during his tenure as a Mayor in a metropolitan city. Above mentioned media tycoon started his career in 1985 as an educationist and established a group of educational institutes within a very short span of time. His business expanded during his eight years tenure of Mayorship to a great extent and he invested in other sectors as well. He launched a news channel as well and entered in the arena of media. After completion of his second term as a Mayor apparently he quit politics but he was a strong candidate for the office of chief minister (care taker) in Punjab before general elections of 2013. Noway's his media group has also grown in popularity and influence amongst the masses making him a media tycoon with a back channel role in politics as well. Some other business tycoons from the fields of gold, real estate etc. have also invested money in media during the last few years and they too are utilising their new business (Media) as a tool to protect their original business and to save taxes to a great extent.

Journalists are facing severe repercussions due to above mentioned business people of the country: Businessmen and industrialists are investing in media to protect themselves from NAB and other concerned authorities against corruption and tax evasion charges, so they have no sympathies for the journalists. This categoryof business people initially invests in media to enrich their influence in the society and when they get the desired results they leave their workers in miserable circumstances. Many among newly opened media houses whose owners are industrialists and businessmen are going through severe circumstances as the workers of these media houses are facing immense economic pressure, but the owners are happy as they were able to use media as a tool to hide their corrupt practices and tax evasions.

Too much tax evasion has produced severe repercussions on the economy of the country; it has shaken badly the very fabric of economic infrastructure of the country. It has promoted the culture of corruption among lower income groups of the country as well. Corruption in government services is widespread in Pakistan and officials of all ranks are involved in this business. Loot and corruption by upper income groups including the political elite, feudal and industrial class and top ranked government officials has encouraged same attitude in lower income groups as well. Business community of middle class is also involved in tax evasions, electricity theft similarly. Low ranked officials are also practising massive corruption by following their seniors. Upper middle and middle class business community of the country are also involved in artificial price hikes with an ease and liberty as they feel no fear of accountability. Owners of grocery stores, medical outlets, cloth shops and stores of general items in both larger and smaller cities are involved in loot and corruption for enhancing their profits.

"Most among the merchant community in Pakistan are involved in over charging" said Sami Ch an Engineer from a South Punjab's district working in Lahore. "Though I am working in Lahore but I was a frequent shopper in my town in South Punjab", he said. "Once I entered a famous cloth outlet of the city and asked the price of a popular fabric, the merchant told me that it would cost me five thousand, but the same buy from a market in Lahore had cost my friend only three thousand five hundred PKR. I said to shopkeeper your margin of profit is too much why? He at once got furious and said that they are bearing more expenditure on servants and electricity bills that's why they charge more. When I explained that electricity charges are same in every part of the country he started abusing me and asked that why do people just blame small shopkeepers like him instead of the big crocodiles who are looting this country with both hands? I had no answer to this question of the shop keeper", Ch added more.

Pakistan has the lowest tax to GDP ratio according to a latest report of media point. Major cause of tax evasion in the country is due to massive mafias present in the business community of the country. As we discussed earlier that big giants of industry and business in the country are involved in tax evasion with the help of state machinery which has weakened the very fabric of the state. Adan Thoman, British high commissioner to Pakistan has written an article about tax evasion in Pakistan which was published in Express

Tribune on December 14, 2013. In this, Thoman stated that less than 0.5 per cent of total population is paying taxes in Pakistan. Tax revenue in Pakistan is only 0 9 per cent of its GDP. If we compare this with the other countries having similar per capita income, volume of economy and economic circumstances we can easily see that Pakistan lags far behind them in the matter of tax collection. Other countries with similar expansion of economy and per capita income have at least 14 per cent of tax to GDP ratio.

Huge tax evasion has produced great negativity about the country among the aid providing countries and International finance organisations. IMF and World Bank the two leading finance organisations in the world are very much familiar with the ongoing tax evasion in Pakistan, so these organisations have shown too much reluctance to renew the country's contracts with them. Tax evasion in the country has forced it to beg for foreign debts. Pakistan is under more than 64 billion dollars of foreign loans currently and over sixty per cent of the collected revenue is used up in paying the instalments of foreign loans every year. When tax net of the country is so poor and not able to collect enough revenue then government will face difficulties in the payments of foreign loans as well. That's why Pakistan is failing to pay its loan instalments in a proper manner and its repercussions are severe, interests on loans are increasing every year which multiplies the total debts.

- **Repercussions of Economic Failures**

Economic failures have produced very widespread and deep-rooted repercussions on the society in Pakistan. With such a low per capita income (1365 US dollars according to GDP nominal) life has become too much difficult for the ordinary citizens of the country and worst still the governments are involved in non-issues rather than focusing on the economy of the country. Ruling political party PML (N) is facing severe criticism by opposition parties especially PTI and media for not showing keen interest in fulfilling its promises regarding economic revival, made at the time of election in May 2013. PTI is involved in severe criticism against federal government as it thinks that government has failed to deliver in favour of the poor masses of the country. Opposition political party heavily criticised the project of metro bus system in Lahore of 45-50 billion rupees (Completed in Feb 2013). This system possesses new terminals, bridges and roads for special buses for the citizens of Lahore. Project got wide admiration in Lahore as ordinary citizens in the city got benefit through it but faced heavy criticism in other cities as opponents are of the view that in such times of severe economic circumstances the metro project was a waste of public money. Government has launched similar projects in Rawalpindi, Multan and in some other metropolitan cities of Punjab. Government of Punjab also uncovered a metro train project of cost 160 billons, for Lahore. Political opponents of PML (N) have put up a severe criticism on these projects with a viewpoint that government should think about the massive population (50 per cent of total population) of the country living below the poverty line rather than invest on roads and rails.

Ruling party PML (N) is said to be fond of construction projects in the country, Lahore to Islamabad motorway was completed during second tenure of Mr Sharif (1997-99, started in his first tenure 1990-93) as the Prime Minister of the country. Opponents of PML (N) and Sharif claim that these type of projects are designed for mega corruption. According to leaders of PTI metro bus projects in metropolitan cities of Punjab and Lahore metro train project will open the flood gates of corruption for the leaders of PML (N). Some leaders of opposition also said that Premier Sharif's family is directly involved in these mega projects.

PTI and other opposition political parties in the country are crying for economic reforms for the betterment of the poor masses of the country, currently living in miserable circumstances, but government seems involved in construction projects and is paying no heed to the cry of opposition. A fraction of economic experts is insisting for the formation of new industrial zones in the country. According to a senior Professor of economics from Lahore,'government should focus on new economic zones and foreign investments. Sharif's are borrowing money from abroad and wasting it on roads and rail road projects which is not a good sign for the overall economy of country, people are hungry and unemployed they want bread and employment not luxury motorways', he added more, 'If we discuss repercussions of economic failures on the society we will find a long list'. Poverty, unemployment, militancy, crime, and illiteracy are some major outcomes of economic collapse in the country; lets have a look on some among above mentioned ones:

- **Militancy and Crime**

Militancy and crime is a definite outcome of economic failure of the state. When state is not able to provide bread to its citizens what will they do? Heinous increment in militancy and crime rate is a great repercussion of state failures in economic matters. According to Gilani and Gill, two renowned economic scholars, "there has been a rapid increase in crimes during last five years in the country due to economic imbalance as compared to other countries in the region." Some other research scholars believe that over 90 per cent crime in the country is directly associated with economic problems of the criminals. There has been a rapid increment in organised crime in the country during the last decade, majority participants of this type of crime are educated young professionals of the country who are involved in these criminal activities due to massive and widespread unemployment in the country, ratio of unemployment among the educated class of the country has increased to 400 per cent during last five years and majority of these young educated guys are now part of different criminal gangs.

"When a graduate in the age group of twenty to twentyfive is not able to find a respectable position in society it produces severe psychological impacts on him", said Mrs Shahida Ali a psychologist from Lahore. "Economic disasters are great sources of frustration, conflicts and anarchies in societies, the youth in Pakistan is facing conflicts and frustration due to economic pressures", she added further. "Younger generation of lower income groups in Pakistan is deprived enough and is harbouring an extremely furious attitude towards the upper income groups .They have decided to deal with the economic cream of the country with weapons. Many young educated guys of lower income groups are involved in murder, rape and robberies of the upper income fraction of the society", she added more.

If the educated brain of the country is involved in organised crime then we can well imagine what the uneducated class of criminals would be doing. In fact they are committing crimes by means of severe and merciless methods. Majority among the dacoits in rural areas of the country including South Punjab and Interior Sind are familiar for their cruel and heinous attitude towards masses. These gangs of criminals kill people for even an ordinary wrist watch or for a cell phone.

"Criminal gangs in interior Sind utilise the jungle of Kucha as a safe haven", said Dhani Buksh a local Journalist working with a Sindhi newspaper in Hyderabad. These dacoits being an integral part of the economically deprived class in their early ages are mostly the victims of injustices by the feudal elite of Interior Sind. These dacoits operating in the interior part of Sind are considered crueller than their counterparts in urban areas of the country. Once they looted a marriage bus near a town adjacent to the city of Sukhar, they took each and every thing including cash and jewellery from men and women passengers. A little girl of nine or ten wearing gold tops in her ears was not willing to give those to the dacoits. The dacoits had enough loot in that particular robbery and could afford to neglect the little jewellery, but one among them shot that girl who died at the spot. "Such heinous attitude towards little children you can't find anywhere else in the world", he added more.

Religious militancy is also touching the sky in modern day Pakistan, and has gathered momentum during the last seven to eight years. Majority among the religious militant groups are spreading terror in the country with full ease and liberty, these orthodox militant groups have enhanced their networks to a great extent during the last few years. Manpower to these orthodox groups is provided thorough religious schools (Madarsas) of different sects. There is a widespread network of religious schools of different sects like Dev Bandi, Berlavi, Ahal Hadit Shiites, etc. but Dev Bandi run the majority of religious schools in the country. As majority of the population of the country is living under miserable economic circumstances so for the poor there remains no other option other than inducting their children in religious schools. Above mentioned fraction of population feel happy that atleast their children will get free bread twice daily in these religious schools alongside with religious education. As we discussed earlier that scientific education in the country is too expensive for major fraction of population in the country, so massive fraction of population relies on free religious schools to a great extent in modern day Pakistan.

Most of the Madarsas or religious schools in the country are operating with the help of charity, donations and foreign aids. Religious schools of different schools of thought receive substantial foreign aids every year from different donor countries. Countries like Saudi Arabia, United Arab Emirates and Iran possess sectarian interests in Pakistan and they are utilising manpower of religious schools in Pakistan for their sectarian benefits. Religious schools of Sunni sect are providing manpower to the militant groups of their sect. Sunni militant groups in the country have ties with some fractions in Saudi Arabia which provide financial resources to these religious schools. Similarly some Shiites militant organisations have links in Iran. Both these Sunni and Shiite militant groups are involved in massive sectarian violence in the country on behalf of their foreign masters. Banned religious organisations in the country are involved in heinous crimes like target killing, robberies and such other offenses. In 2002, military ruler Pervaiz Mushraf put a ban on several religious organisations which proved to be a good decision later. But soon within months of this ban these organisations changed their names, rebuild their infrastructure and started operations. According to a senior journalist, (covering crime since more than two decades) most among the banned organisations like Sipah –e-Shaba Pakistan (SSP), Lashkar Jhangivi (L J) and many more possess more sound and widespread network in the country with the changed names as compared to 2002.

- **Extremism**

Extremism is a great dilemma of modern day Pakistan, extremism of all types (not only religious) is widespread and deep-rooted in Pakistan. There are many factors behind these extensive extremist values in the society but again economic destruction is playing a vital role in the enhancement of extremist attitudes in the society. Socioeconomic injustices have led to conflicts and frustration among the masses which is leading towards extremist attitudes. According to a senior journalist from Karachi honour killing of women in most areas of Interior Sind, South Punjab, Baluchistan and KPK can be linked to deprived economic conditions. A family is subjected to immense social pressure when due to poor economic circumstances they are not able to get their girl(s) married or pay dowry.With too much complicated social norms and values massive fraction of population in the country like to interfere in the domestic affairs of friends and relatives which puts these poor families under increased social pressure. As a result, above mentioned families utilise violence to kill their daughters and sisters to get rid of their marriage reponsibilities and social pressure. Brother, father, cousin or any other relative of a girl can put false charges of illicit relationship on her and kill her.

Similarly domestic violence against women in lower income groups of the country is also increasing due to poor economic circumstances. People belonging to lower income groups in the country are familiar for possessing a cruel attitude towards women and women of this class has now grown habitual to this cruel attitude. Some women face immense cruelty in the form of domestic violence. Women fetching less dowry is treated very inhumanly among most fractions of lower income groups and in lower middle class as well. Disputes of properties in lower income groups of the country are also major cause of violence among them. With too much inflation, unemployment and poverty, family assets of lower middle and middle classes of the country has become a prime source of their livelihoods. With too much price hike, livelihood expenditures of lower middle and middle class families has gone up immensely during the last decade.

Massive fraction of population belonging to lower middle and middle classes are not able in current circumstances to purchase any new asset in the country so they have to depend on their ancestral assets. When population is growing at massive rate every family has seven to eight members on an average in the country. Population growth in lower and lower middle classes of the country is too high as compared to the upper middle and elite classes of the country. Members of lower income groups in the country attain very minute share in case of division in their ancestral properties. This causes extremist attitude in massive fraction of particular groups and they get involved in violence against each other.

'Brother killed younger sibling on property dispute', 'Son killed father on economic affairs' and many such types of news are very familiar in Pakistani newspapers nowadays. Massive fraction of population is tending towards massive extremism due to economic failures of state and this situation is turning towards point of no return day by day. Ultimate result of this heinous situation would be more conflicts, anarchy and maybe even a civil war very soon.

3

Influence of Heredity in Pakistan

- **Influence of Heredity as a Curse**

Influence of heredity or ancestral genetics possess key importance in one's success or failure in life in modern day Pakistan. Unlike the developed and civilised world calibre, abilities, esteem and merit possess no value for achievements in the so called land of pure. Massive fraction of population belonging to lower income groups is not able to even think of achieving glory in life in contrast to his counterpart in the civilised world. One can't find any William Jefferson, Bill Clinton, William Gates II (commonly called as Bill Gates the founding chairman of Microsoft) and Barrack Husain Obama here. None among the Pakistani youngster is able to think like Mark Zucker Burg (youngest billionaire in the world possessing a net worth of 17.28 billion dollars, founder of social media network face book) as they are unfortunate enough for being born in a culture that rewards heredity instead of calibre. Above mentioned examples of achievers belong to the United States of America the largest economy in the world the only Superpower which achieved its absolute power and glory by promoting merit and calibre. William Jefferson, Bill Clinton the former President of United States (held office during 1993-2001) was part of a lower middle class family, his father was an ordinary salesman and he spent his early life in severe economic circumstances. Bill Clinton spent a very hard time up till his late thirtees but his ambitiousness and passionate attitude and the system of United States provided him opportunity to achieve highest level in the society just at the age of forty six. Similarly, Barrack Husain Obama the current and 44th President of USA was also a part of lower income group and an ethnic minority (African American) but he is also among the youngest Presidents in United States just because of his level of intelligence and hard work. Contrary to this Pakistan provided opportunities to low calibre but influential fraction of society to run its system and result is in front of us. Our country is familiar to the world for its massive corruption, terrorism, conflicts and anarchy which may result in a civil war.

Massive fraction of population in the country is unfortunate enough that heredity is a great hindrance in their success as it's playing a vital role for success in any sort of career here. Influence of heredity is widespread and deep-rooted in every field of life including agriculture, industry, politics, religion, education, showbiz and even media (both print and electronic). In other words there is no place in Pakistan for a person who possesses intelligence, calibre and abilities but without an influential heredity and family back-ground.

Agriculture in the country belongs to renowned land owning families who possess massive portion of total cultivated land in the country. Few hundred families of traditional feudal lords own more than 90 per cent of fertile agricultural land of the country. Massive fraction of unutilised or relatively barren land is distributed among military, bureaucratic and political elite of the country for their so called services for the country every year. Hundreds of thousands of State-owned agriculture land has been handed over to retired armed forces officials alongside with few political families of the country during last decade. So no one is able to adopt profession of agriculture (by owning his land) in Pakistan with the exceptions of feudal lords, civil-military bureaucracy and political elite of the country.

Similarly process of industrialisation belongs to industrial dynasties only. No one other than industrial giants of the country is capable of participating in the process of industrialisation, in other words no one can grow as industrialists other than few royal families of the country. Industrial groups like Sharif's (family of Prime Minister of Pakistan, industrial tycoons and fourth richest family of the country which owns the industry of steel, sugar, poultry ....etc.), Zardari-Bhutto family (listed many former presidents and prime ministers of the country, including Asif Ali Zardari - former president of Pakistan 2008-13 and co-chairman of PPP who now leads the family), Nishat group (largest industrial group in the country, head of group Mian Mansha is the richest person in the country) and few more....possess their monopolies in the industrial field. Above mentioned industrial tycoons alongside few more have grown rapidly during the last three decades due to their political influences. Contrary to this, massive fraction of non-political or non-influential industrialists and businessmen of the country have gone towards massive decline due to ongoing immense energy crises, terrorism and business unfriendly atmosphere of the country.

Business community other than groups having political influence has faced miserable circumstances during the last two decades. Many among non-influential businessmen shifted their businesses abroad during last few years. Bangladesh, Sri Lanka, South Korea, Singapore, and Malaysia are the new destinations of the above mentioned class of the country. The country is no more under the industrialisation process due to barriers in investment and development in industrial field for commoners. System is proving no ease for smaller and medium size industrialists to grow and expand their business as the mafia holding the larger industrial units of sugar, fertilizers, cement, steel and poultry resent it. Majority among above mentioned industries belongs to political and bureaucratic elite of the country and this fraction of population is not willing to provide any space for new comers in the field, in other words like agriculture top businesses and industries too are restricted within few dozen families of the country and they have put up high entry barriers for others. According to a senior commerce reporter of the country from Lahore, "Hamza Shabaz Sharif (son of chief minister of Punjab, nephew of prime minister and member of parliament) is known as the *Don* of the poultry industry in Pakistan. His monopoly is controlling the poultry rates in Pakistan, in fact they (Sharif's) want to capture every business in the country". "If family of Prime Minister is involved in every type of business in this manner then nothing will remain for commoners", he added more.

The influence of some industrial groups on political parties of the country has produced severe repercussions on the economy of the country. Particular industrial and business groups feel lot of ease in their business as compared to their rivals possessing no political influences. This class is involved in writing off their debts from state owned and semi-government commercial banks. More than 100 billion loans were written off in the regime of military dictator Pervaiz Musharraff, massive portion of these loans belonged to industrial class of the country with political influences.

As we discussed earlier that heredity is the key to success in each and every field of life in Pakistan, we discussed impacts of heredity in Agriculture and Industry now we are moving forward towards politics. Though more than half of the country's history (almost thirty four years) is revolving around direct military rule (Martial Laws) but even then politics (in remaining half and with the coordination of military rulers as well) in the country is moving towards principal of heredity in Pakistan. Role of the ordinary masses in the country in politics is only restricted to discussing politics in streets and drawing rooms as their access to politics is not more than above mentioned places, they can't even think of becoming a Member of Parliament.

Political talk shows are very familiar among the masses in Pakistan as more than hundred news channels across the country are providing their services for the enhancement of political maturity in the country. Members of the parliament and mainstream politicians are now celebrities as they are fully utilising electronic media for their publicity and projection. But masses still are unfortunate enough that their favourite politicians are not able to deliver in their favour yet. Massive fraction among political elite claims that Martial Laws have played a key role in sabotaging the services owed to the masses. According to a senior politician from South Punjab, whenever elected governments in the country found a path towards socioeconomic empowerment of masses the process was sabotaged by military dictators. Contrary to this one massive fraction of population and some media icons believes that failure of political class is always been a cause of Martial law in the country. This fraction believes that massive corruption, favouritism, nepotism and bad governance of the political elite has always invited the military rule in the country and one can't blame military for it.

No doubt arena of politics is restricted for upper income groups of the country as game of politics is played with the tools of wealth and heredity in so called land of pure. Elite of the country is investing in politics for their corrupt motives and since they get many times more returns on their investments politics is a very profitable business for them. Feudal and industrial tycoons of the country are familiar for using their wealth and human resource to protect their political dynasties. More than ninety per cent among the renowned feudal and industrial families in the country have their own political dynasties. No space is available for educated lower middle and middle classes of the country in mainstream politics as all important offices in notable political fractions in the country are in the possession of the elite of the country.

All political parties in the country are mostly non-democratic (autocratic) in their approach towards distribution of important party offices and party offices in all notable political groups of the country are distributed on the bases of kinship. Such an undemocratic tradition has been producing severe repercussions on the whole political system of the country. Heredity has played a very vital role in derailing democracy in Pakistan; this undemocratic attitude of the political dynasties of the country is worse than dictators and has been the cause of strain between governments and different institutions such as the judiciary. Strain between civilian and military leaderships has ended up several times on imposition of martial laws.

No doubt South Asia is a great hub of political dynasties in the world. Gandhi family in India (Leading Indian National Congress), Sheikh's in Bangladesh and Nikeays in Sri Lanka have been into politics since a few generations. But Pakistan is facing worst impacts of influence of heredity on politics in the country. India with more than 810 million voters is considered as the largest democracy in the world. Unlike its neighbour (Pakistan) democracy is very deep-rooted in India and possesses no danger of military invasion, this has strengthened its democratic norms and values. Though corruption and favouritism is a part of political system in India as well but a proper system of accountability within political parties (and in system as well) has increased the chances of lower middle and middle classes of the country to become an integral part of the political elite.

Success of Bharatiya Janata Party (BJP) led National Democratic Alliance against Indian National Congress (INC) led United Progressive Alliance in the general elections of India in 2014 has shown the distrust of Indian voters against the politics of heredity. INC, ruling party of India during 2004-2014 (INC remained in power among the most period of Indian history with the exceptions of 1977-79, 1998-2004 and now 2014 onwards) seems as a dynasty of Gandhi's. Sonia Gandhi the Italian wife of former prime minister Rajiv Gandhi (who held office during 1984-89) leading Indian National Congress since 1998 was ready to hand over INC to her next generation. Rahul Gandhi the 42 years old son of Sonia (was party's candidate for the prime ministership in general elections 2014) and current Secretary General is more likely to fully command INC in near future. Even though a party based on kinship, INC has followed democratic norms and values in a much better way as compared to any political party in Pakistan. INC has also shown a different trait unlike any political dynasty in the world by having a separate party office and a separate government office. Mrs Sonia Gandhi led the party since 1998 but has never vied for prime ministership. After her assuming office as INC chairperson, party came in to power twice (2004-09, 2009-14) but both the times an economist belonging to lower middle class (Dr Manmohan Singh) took the office of prime minister. Dr Singh a veteran economist and member of upper house of Parliament possesses no political background but he is only prime minister of the country after Jawaharlal Nehru to hold the office for two successive terms.

Contrary to this, former (late) Prime Minister of Pakistan Benazir Bhutto appointed her son (at the age of 17) as chairperson of Pakistan People's Party and husband as co-chairman through a will. Pakistan people's party is among the largest political forces in the country and its history is revolving around heredity. We will discuss all political parties of the country in the later phase of the chapter but now let's once again focus on Indian democratic system which is presently providing massive opportunities to its lower fraction of population.

Narendra Modi current Prime Minister of India is a prime example of inducting lower income group at highest level due to merit and calibre. Modi being a part of lowest economic group faced severe circumstances to achieve highest level of glory but at last he is now the custodian of the largest democracy in the world. Modi now sixty three, started his career as a child labourer some fifty years ago and achieved the destiny of chief minstership within thirty years of his political career, he served as chief minister of Gujarat during 2001-14 for three consecutive terms and got BJP's prime ministerial candidateship in 2012. BJP possesses more democratic norms than any other political party in India. The current president of the party Raj Nath Singh is working as federal interior minister under the prime ministership of Modi, one of the relatively junior leaders. Two other former presidents and senior leaders of the party Nitin Gadkari and Venkaih Naidu are working as federal ministers under the Prime Minster Modi who was never party president but has proven his calibre more than any other leader of modern day BJP. Even Lal Krishna Advani, the senior most leader of BJP and twice a candidate for prime ministership, has accepted Modi's supremacy with an open heart which shows the deep-rooted norms of democracy in India's largest political party. Due to these widespread and deep-rooted democratic norms and values among massive fraction of its political groups, India truly deserves the title of the largest democracy in the world.

- **Political Dynasties**

As we discussed earlier that all political parties in Pakistan are working on the principal of heredity, almost all political fractions in the country have obtained leadership through ancestral means. It is an interesting fact that norms of heredity are widespread in all types of political groups namely, the Conservative, Moderate and Liberals. Liberal Pakistan People's Party (PPP), Moderate PML (N), the ruling party and PML (Q) and orthodox JUI (F) are all working under the principal of heredity. Let's have a discussion about the major political groups in the country.

- **Pakistan Muslim League (Nawaz)**

Pakistan Muslim League Nawaz or commonly called as N league (N stands for Nawaz Sharif the prime minister of Pakistan) is the largest political party in the country. After May 13, 2013 general elections it possess 187 members in the house of 342 in national assembly of Pakistan, moreover it formed government in Punjab the largest province of the country after the general elections. It is also a major coalition partner of National party in the government of Baluchistan. PML (N) has also got reasonable seats in the Provincial assembly of KPK and showed its representation in Sind assembly by winning more than half dozen seats after a long span of time. PML (N) currently possesses 15 members in upper house of the parliament (senate of Pakistan) and its rival PPP (ruling party during 2008-13) have majority with 39 members in the upper house. Demography is going to turn in favour of PML (N) in upper house of parliament as well next year with commencement of elections in March 2015.

As the name suggests it is a family party which is revolving around the family members of Sharif's. Punjab the largest populated province in the country is the centre of Sharif's political dynasty. With more than 100 million population Punjab possesses a great share among (more than 54 per cent of country's population belongs to Punjab) the total population of the country, Punjab remained a hub of PML (N)'s power since 1988. In Raiwind, a town adjacent to Lahore, is situated the magnificent palaces of the Sharif family. Most among the key government offices in current government belongs to Sharif family. Nawaz Sharif a sixty three years old veteran politician and the current prime minister is the head of Sharif dynasty since 2004 after the death of his father Senior Sharif. Chief Minister of Punjab Shahbaz Sharif, the brother of Prime minister, is another important member of Sharif family and key leader of PML (N). Both the Sharif's (Prime minister and chief minister of Punjab) are enjoying their third terms of their respective positions.

Founding father of Sharif family (Late) Muhammad Sharif was a poor man in 1935 and started his business with a borrowed amount of two hundred rupees in Amritsar (Now part of India) northern district of united Punjab. The family later shifted to Pakistan in 1947 after partition of the subcontinent into India and Pakistan. His elder son Nawaz Sharif entered in the arena of politics with the help of military dictator Zia-Ul-Haq a close aide of Sharif. Now Sharif family possesses industrial and political dynasties and is considered among the richest families in South Asia.

All India Muslim League (AIML) was founded in 1906 by some feudal Muslims of that time, Sir Sultan Muhammad Shah (44th spiritual leader of Ismailia) commonly known as Agha Khan III took the office of its first president in December 1906. Muslim elite of that time utilised AIML for the protection of its benefits for a long span of time. In 1934, Muhammad Ali Jinnah (Founder of Pakistan) was elected as President of AIML and it started to get popularity among the masses. AIML participated in three elections in the leadership of Jinnah before the partition of India in 1947. 1937 elections of provincial assemblies proved to be a bitter experience for AIML and it got only 106 seats out of 1585 while Indian National Congress got 707. Jinnah put his immense effort for making AIML as a true representative of Indian Muslims in early 1940's which resulted in 1945's Indian general elections when AIML won 30 out of 102 seats in legislative assembly. Similarly, in 1946 provincial assembly's elections it won 425 seats and got 26.81 per cent of total votes. This mandate was a clear indication for the creation of a new country.

After the creation of the country on August 14, 1947 Jinnah resigned from the office of Party president and took the office of Governor General of the newly created state. After his resignation Liquate Ali Khan (First Prime Minister of the country) who was very good administrator and right hand of Jinnah, (assumed the office of the President of Pakistan Muslim League. After Liaquate's assassination in October 1951 (within three years of Jinnah's death, Jinnah died on September 11, 1948) leadership of PML went into the hands of second class leaders who destroyed it within a very short span of time. Muslim League though was the founder party of the country but it lost its grandeur in early 1950's within few years of the creation of the country. It lost 1954 provincial election in East Pakistan (Now Bangladesh) which produced severe repercussions on its future. Emergence of military dictators in 1950's, 60's and 70's destroyed it completely later.

Fida Muhammad Khan an economist and lawyer gave a rebirth to Pakistan Muslim League on November 16, 1988 and held the office of PML's president till October 6, 1993. Nawaz Sharif current president of PML (N) (Prime Minister of Pakistan) assumed the office on October 7, 1993 and since then it has been a family party of Sharif's. Sharif remained as president of PML (N) till the coup d'état of Pervaiz Mushraf on October 12, 1999. After Sharif's arrest as a result of coup d'état wife of Sharif (Begum Kalsoom Nawaz) led the party during 1999-2000. Javeed Hashmi (Current president of Pakistan Tehrek –e-Insaaf) was the President of PML (N) during 2001-5 (during the exile of Sharif family). Sharif's was sent to exile (during which he lived in Saudi Arabia and London from 2000-07) through an agreement with military ruler Pervaiz Mushraf. Javeed Hashmi then senior vice president (2000) of PML (N) assumed office of party president and led the party through a very difficult span of time. Military ruler Musharraf formed Pakistan Muslim League (Quaid-e-Azam) from PML (N) and majority among the former parliamentarians of PML (N) (during 1997-99) left PML (N) and joined PML (Q). But Hashmi remained loyal with the Sharifs and faced too much severe repercussions during military regime. He was put behind the bars and faced severe violence. Sharif family heaved a sigh of relief when they settled down in London after leaving Saudi Arabia in 2005. They started political activities in London despite an agreement with military ruler Mushraf of not participating in politics for ten years. Just after feeling an improvement in political strength, the Sharifs removed Hashmi from the office of president and younger Sharif (Current chief minister of Punjab) took the office of president of PML (N) in 2005.

Current prime minister of the country Nawaz Sharif took the office of the president of PML (N) in 2011 again. Some other leaders who had provided loyal services to the Sharif family during their exile later faced same sort of situation like Javeed Hashmi. Zulifqar Khan Khosa a tribal chieftain and a veteran politician from south Punjab who also played a vital role for the survival of the party during military regime,was the president of party's Punjab chapter for a long span of time but in 2011 when junior Sharif handed over party's Presidentship to his elder brother, Khosa lost his office as junior Sharif was appointed as President of party's Punjab chapter again.

Nawaz Sharif was not a candidate for the office of Prime minister before the general elections in 1990, Ghulam Mustafa Jatoi was considered as favourite for the office as being a veteran politician of Islamic Jamorhiltehad (Islamic democratic alliance) he possessed widespread support in different factions of orthodox alliance. But after the general elections of 1990 Establishment and fraction of industrial politicians put their weight in favour of Sharif who took the office of prime minister in November 1990. Since then PML (N) is all about Sharif family who is running it like a family party. After winning general elections of 1990, 1997 and 2013 NawazSharif (who also remained as chief minister of Punjab during 1985-1990) took the oath of prime minister every time under the nomination of the party. Similarly his younger brother Shabaz took the oath of office of chief minister of Punjab in 1997, 2008 and 2013.

After 1997 general elections PML (N) got two-thirds majority in the national assembly and formed federal government and governments in Punjab and North western frontier province (Currently KPK) as well, it also was a part of a coalition government in Sind. Pervaiz Elahi a veteran politician from Gujarat and leader of PML (Q) was a part of PML (N) in 1997. Being a senior leader of the party at that time Elahi was a strong candidate for the office of chief minister of Punjab but after getting an overwhelming majority, Senior Sharif denied to appoint him as chief minister and appointed his younger brother Shabaz as chief minister of Punjab. According to a senior journalist from Lahore Nawaz Sharif promised Elahi and his cousin brother Ch Shujat Husain (another important political leader of the country and current President of PML (Q)) of giving them an important office in Punjab (Chief Ministership) but after getting an absolute majority the Sharifs turned down their promise. Very similar situation occurred in 2013 when PML (N) was not hoping for a single majority. Some senior leaders of PML (N) left the party during 2012-13 and joined an emerging political force PTI. Surveys and analysis were predicting a coalition government after the general elections of 2013. At this juncture of time senior Sharif had a fear that many among his aides will leave him and join PTI. So he promised some senior leaders of the party important offices including office of chief minister in Punjab. The Sharif once again came into an astonishing majority in general elections of 2013 and many among larger political forces including PTI refused to accept election results and accused PML (N) of rigging. After confirming single majority in national assembly and absolute majority in Punjab assembly Sharif once again turned down their promise and were not ready to appoint for the office of chief minister in Punjab a person other than Sharif family, this produced severe repercussions for the party. Just after one year of its tenure as governments in Centre and Punjab province, PML (N) is going through massive internal crises and party is divided among three major factions which are involved in leg pulling of their opponent for their own benefits.

Majority among the PML (N) members of parliament after general elections 2013 belong to former King's party PML (Q) who joined the party just before the elections. PML (Q) was carved by military establishment in 2001 and its massive fraction was part of PML (N) before the coup d'état of Pervaiz Mushraf. PML (Q) got 118 seats in the general elections of 2002 and formed a coalition government, many among the opposition parties including PPP and PML (N) of that time blamed Inter Services Intelligence (ISI) the prime secret agency of the country for supporting PML (Q) in the elections of 2002. PML (N) later (before the general elections of 2008) appreciated the members who had remained loyal with the party and had refused to join the

Prime Minester Sharif in his Palace in Raiwind an Image of Late 90's

dictator's party. But in the general elections of 2008 and even in 2013 top leadership of PML (N) once again ignored loyalty issues with the party and assigned positions to the aides of former military ruler Pervaiz Mushraf. Dr Shaifiq-ur-Rehman a middle class politician from a small district of south Punjab and also a writer, while in conversation to me said that "they (Sharif's) possess no sympathies for the loyal workers of the party who have foregone enough for the party and democracy". "I had a long standing with the PML (N) and faced severe repercussions during the regime of dictator Musharaf", said Dr Shafiq. "Being an integral part of educated middle class I realised the social problems of the society and did my best for the provision of relief to

Shabaz Shareef Enjoying the 3rd Term as Chief Minester in Punjab

the masses during my grass root level politics. I was hopeful for the party nominee for provincial assembly but party ticket of PML (N) was awarded to an integral person of Kings Party (PML (Q)) during the dictator's regime just because of his influential industrial background", the Dr added more.

Pakistan Tehek-e-Insaf commonly called as PTI emerged as a major political force after two conventional political parties PML (N) and PPP as a result of general elections 2013. PTI got thirty four seats in national assembly out of 342 and was also able to form a coalition government in north western province of KPK. PTI got immense mass following during 2011-12 and it seemed during this span of time that PTI would be in a position to sweep general elections of 2013 but at the end of day PML (N) won single majority. But PTI got the most votes after PML (N) in general elections of 2003. Analysts and political pundits were not hoping for the single majority for PML (N) before May 11, 2013- the Election Day, and this was a major reason for Sharif's flexible and moderate attitude towards second class leadership of the party. A massive fraction of journalists in the country has a strong opinion that both the Sharifs possess autocratic attitude towards second and third class leadership of the party. Shabaz Sharif chief minister of Punjab announced publicly that he is no more willing to hold office of chief minister after the general elections of 2013. He also said that if PML (N) got majority after general elections he would like to serve as a federal minister of water and power. Nisar Ali Khan federal minister for interior affairs and Khawaja Asif federal minister of water and power both were strong candidates for the office of chief minister in Punjab after the general elections of 2013. According to a senior political commentator top leadership of PML (N) was very much frightened with the growing influence of PTI amongst the masses during this span of time. This commentator also said that Khawaja Asif was very much hopeful of holding the office of chief minister as he was assured by Senior Sharif for this portfolio but once again after getting majority in Centre and Punjab, Sharifs decided not to break their status quo. Currently political dynasty of the Sharifs is occupying all the key government offices of the country.

Hamza Shabaz Sharif son of chief minister of Punjab, nephew of prime minister and member of national assembly from Lahore is the next generation representative of the Sharif. Hamza, 38, is often called de facto chief minister of Punjab, the bureaucracy and political elite of the province feel immense pressure from the crown prince of the Sharif family. According to a senior journalist from Lahore Hamza is like a *God Father* for the bureaucracy of the province. Shabaz Sharif, chief minister of Punjab, seemed more involved in federal government affairs as compared to those of Punjab, according to some senior journalists of the country. A senior political commentator from Lahore said that chief minister of Punjab likes to go on foreign visits with his elder brother the prime minister, and the largest province of the (Punjab) country he has handed over to his son. Bureaucracy waits for the orders of crown prince on important issues, similarly second class leadership of the party also looks up to Hamza for the resolution of party affairs and issues at district level. Grooming of Hamza Shabazis of key importance to the Sharif family. Two sons of Prime minister Nawaz Sharif, Hassan and Hussein, are fully involved in family businesses (which is spread all around the world from Pakistan to Middle East and Europe). Both Hassan and Hussein showed reluctance towards politics, that's why premier Sharif introduced his daughter Maryam and son-in-law Safdar in the arena of politics. Maryam Nawaz Sharif now 40 is currently heading loan based prime minister youth programmes, which is a project of more than 100 billon.

Maryam Nawaz started to emerge on the political scene of the country during 2011. Marvi Memon an industrialist lady from Sind former operational director of Inter Services Public Relation (ISPR) and coordinator of Prime Minister Youth programme is a political trainer of Maryam. On April 12, 2012 an article in Newsweek Pakistan declared Maryam as the new face and future of Pakistani politics. According to some senior journalists of the country premier Sharif gives much importance to the opinion of her daughter and she too is utilising her father's influence to gain political grounds. Premier Sharif has to face a lot of pressure from the youth due to widespread unemployment in the country. Pakistan Tehrek-e-Insaf (PTI) the political opponent of Sharif was much popular among the youth during general elections of 2013. Premier Sharif is feeling danger from PTI and to counter it he announced a youth loan programme within six months of his stay in prime minister office. This project is providing business loans to employed youth of the country at an interest rate of eight per cent, but a noted senior economist in the country has said that project is a flop scheme due to massive inflation in the country.

Influence of heredity in Pakistan is now so much widespread and deep rooted that not only actual family members of political dynasties are enjoying the key positions but extended family members are also involved in the state business. Cousins, second and third cousins, son-in-laws and daughter-in-laws and many more…are also playing their parts in loot and corruption with their relatives. Let's have a look on some more relatives of premier Sharif and chief minister Shabaz who are involved both in party and state affairs. Abid Sher Ali, a member of parliament from Faisalabad and state minister for water and power, is a nephew of premier Sharif. Sher Ali proved as most incompetent minister in Sharif's cabinet due to his massive failure in controlling energy crises in the country. He is also criticised for possessing hostile attitude and victimising some fractions of the society through his powers. But premier Sharif is not willing to sack him due to his kinship with the Sharif family.

Abid Sher Ali took charge as a state minister of water and power (considered as most corrupt ministry in Pakistan) under very difficult

Iamge of Sharif's Property in London

circumstances. There was massive energy crises in the country during June 2013 (still continuing), PML(N) appointed a veteran politician and a senior member of party Khawaja Asif as a minister of water and power alongside with young Sher Ali as his deputy (Minister of State) but both of them have still not been able to provide any break through. Former minister of water and power Raja Pervaiz Ashraf (later remained as prime minister of Pakistan for six months as well) commonly called as Raja Rental due to his alleged involvement in rental power corruption scandal has left a lot of garbage for his successors. As ministry of water and power became a great hub of corruption scandals and mismanagement during regime of Raja. PML (N) claimed that it would be able to deal with energy crises within six months of its government, during its election campaigns in April-May 2013. But its claims have gone with the wind and masses are severely criticising PML (N) for its false claims. Sher Ali came under heavy criticism when Peshawar electric supply corporation (PESCO) a power distribution company working under ministry of water and power made an agreement with electricity thieves. According to this agreement those thieves who are utilising direct electricity without meters in KPK will be allowed to continue their malpractice with the payment of only 700 PKR per month. In other words ministry of water and power failed to disconnect the power supply of influential thieves and was forced for shameful agreement. This type of incidents clearly depict the writ of government in the country. This seems highly unjust in the country where electricity is highly expensive and major portion of income of income groups upto middle class is used up for the payment of electricity, gas and water bills.

Images of Raiwind Palace Resddiency of Sharif Family

Captain (retired) Muhammad Safdar member of national assembly from KPK is the son-in-law of Prime Minister Sharif and another key member of Sharif dynasty. He was elected as member of national assembly on the ticket of PML (N) from NA-21 KPK. Mr Safdar is representing the party for the second time (elected in 2008 as well). Sources says that Safdar was a part of lower income group and fell in love with the Sharif's daughter during his duties in prime minister house as a civil servant in early 90's. Sharif family was reluctant to accept him as their son-in-law due to his ordinary family back-ground but now Safdar is playing an important role in the politics of KPK.

Senator Ishaq Dar, federal minister for finance, is also a close relative of premier Sharif and key member of Sharif dynasty. Prime minister Sharif's younger daughter is married with Dar's son and due to this close relationship Dar always remained as key person during all regimes of Sharif. Ishaq Dar now sixty three, assumed office of federal minister for finance on June 7, 2013 for the third term. He took the same office in March 2008 (In coalition government of PPP and PML (N) and in November 1998 as well). Now have a look on some other members of Sharif dynasty possessing key positions in the current regime of PML (N). Bilal Yaseen another member of Sharif dynasty holds a vital position in Punjab government, Yaseen who got the provincial assembly seat from Lahore is holding the office of minister for food in Punjab government. It is matter of fact that all important members of

Sharif family with the exception of Safdar got their seats from Lahore the safe haven of PML (N). One thing about the political dynasties in Pakistan is very clear that they award party nominees to their relatives from very safe constituencies of party. There are certain political constituencies of all political dynasties in the country which are reserved for the royal members of these dynasties.

Lahore remained as a safe haven for Sharif dynasty since 1988. Most members belonging to Sharif dynasty contested elections from Lahore and won with ease. Umar Sohail Zia Butt member of provincial assembly from Lahore is another member of Sharif dynasty. Umar Butt's father Sohial Zia Butt (cousin of premier Sharif) also remained as member of national assembly from Lahore during 2008-2013. Mohsin Lateef another nephew of premier Sharif is member of provincial assembly from Lahore. One can imagine when too many members of one family are holding party and government offices what would be the condition of country and masses. Is this democracy or monarchy? While doing the research for this chapter I visited the social media to see the reactions of youth about the political elite of the country. It was astonishing to watch the frustration and anger among youth of the country against the political dynasties. Some senior journalists of the country are also utilising social media as a tool to interact with masses. Amir Mateen a senior journalist wrote his comment on a social media network before the general elections of 2013 in these words "Sharif family continues to grow. About thirty relatives contesting polls including sons, brothers, in-laws. Is it monarchy?"

- **Bhutto-Zardari Dynasty Pakistan People's Party**

Pakistan People's Party commonly called as PPP possesses an important position in parliamentary politics of the country. PPP was founded on November 30, 1967 in Lahore by Zulfiqar Ali Bhutto on the bases of social democracy and populism. Z.A. Bhutto commonly called as Bhutto was a feudal lord from interior Sind who started his political carrier with the help of military ruler Ayub Khan in late 50's. In 1958, Bhutto led Pakistan in United Nations on a conference related to law of sea. Same year Bhutto became the youngest cabinet minister. Military dictator Ayub appointed him as a minister of state for water and power. In 1960, Bhutto was prompted as senior minister in the ministry of commerce and trade:

Z.A. Bhutto is an important character of Pakistani politics who has held important portfolios like Civilian Chief Martial administrator (Bhutto probably the only civilian in the world to hold this office), President and Prime Minister of the country during 1971-77. Bhutto is still alive among the masses even after his death. After his execution on April 4,1979 by a military dictator Zia-ul-Haq politics in Pakistan got divided among two ideological groups i.e. Bhutto and antiBhutto. Bhutto was among the closest companions of military ruler Ayub due to his feudal background and influential personality during the 1960's. Bhutto served as minister of communication and industries during 1960-63 before joining the important portfolio of foreign minister. Z.A. Bhutto served as foreign minister of Pakistan from June 15, 1963 to August 31, 1966 in the cabinet of Ayub Khan. Being a closest aide of military ruler Bhutto was very much aware from the mounting social pressure against military regime. Massive fraction of population was demanding resignation of military ruler and restoration of democracy in the country. Bhutto being a very keen observer closely watched the sociopolitical situation and decided to separate himself from military rule. At that movement Bhutto proved himself as wise and vigilant person and resigned from the office of foreign minister on August 31, 1966.

Bhutto was aware that regime of Martial laws in the country was leading it towards leadership vacuum, in order to fill this vacuum Bhutto decided to interact with the masses. Following his resignation a large crowd gathered to listen to his speech upon his arrival in Lahore on June 21, 1967. Sensing a wave of anger and frustration among the masses against Dictator Ayub Bhutto began travelling across the country to deliver political speeches. Bhutto being very vigilant sensed his popularity among the masses and decided to establish his own political party. On November 30, 1967 at the residence of Dr Mubbashir Hassan in Lahore alongside with J.A. Raheem a Bengali communist, Bhutto founded Pakistan people's party.

Islam is our faith, democracy is our politics, socialism is our economy and all powers belongs to masses was the manifesto of PPP drafted by J.A. Raheem and Dr Mubashir Hassan (later finance minister of Pakistan). Both these intellectuals played a vital role for making PPP a widespread and deep-rooted political power of the country by introducing slogans of mass attraction. They also spent their energies for inducting educated middle class in the party during its early years. During its early span of time PPP showed lot of character regarding socialism and popular politics. It strictly followed democratic norms and values and in its initial years educated middle class and intelligentsia was inspired by its slogans and a massive fraction among writers, artists, human right activist and civil society joined it, though concept of civil society was very new in Pakistan at that time even then educated middle class could participate against doctorial regime and join PPP without any trouble. But very soon after attaining power in 1971, it started turning into a party of feudal lords.

Pakistan People's Party got 81 seats out of 300 and 18.6 per cent among total casted votes in country's first general elections held on December 7, 1970. Rival of PPP in that election Awami League of Sheikh Mujeeb-ur-Rehman (Founder of Bangladesh) got 160 seats and 39.2 per cent of total casted votes in those elections. Sheikh Mujeeb-ur-Rehman's Awami League after getting single majority in Parliament deserved to form the government. But the alliance of feudal political elite with the military establishment of the country denied the mandate of Sheikh Mujeeb and this resulted in the formation of Bangladesh on December 16, 1971. Just after fall of Dacca, Z.A. Bhutto took the office of civilian chief Martial law administrator but soon replaced it with office of president. Until formation of a new constitution (Introduced on August 14, 1973) Bhutto remained as president of Pakistan, after the induction of constitution he took the office of prime minister.

Z.A. Bhutto was much inspired by the socialist democratic movement of USSR some sources said that PPP was founded by former members of Pakistan

Asif Ali Zardari Custodian of Bhutto Dynasty after the Death of her Wife Former Primer Benzair Bhutoo

socialist party banned by the then prime minister Liquate Ali Khan. Dr Mubashir Hassan once a close aide of Mr Bhutto played a vital role for the induction of socialist influence in PPP. Dr Mubashir Hassan at the age of ninety two, emerged as effective policy-maker in the early era of PPP but later he lost his influence in the party and intellectuals like him were replaced by feudal elite of the country. Initially Mr Bhutto tried to induct educated middle class (In the first general election of 1970) in parliament through his party but later he realised that politics in the country is only possible with the help of feudal elite. Feudal lords of interior Sind and South Punjab became an integral part of PPP very soon, since then it's a largeWadero (A terminology used to describe feudal lord) party of the country. PPP emerged as a different political party during the second general elections in the country held on March 7, 1977. Majority among the contestants of PPP were the representative of feudal elite, some among them were involved in rigging and manipulating election results which produced severe repercussion on democracy in Pakistan.

Though PPP won the 1977 general elections with an absolute majority but opposition denied to accept the results and started a mass movement against newly formed government, this movement led to implementation of Martial law in the country on July 7, 1977.

Z.A. Bhutto considered among most popular and intelligent leaders in Pakistan was trapped by the feudal elite of the country before general elections of 1977. Bhutto was willing to get an absolute majority for his second term of prime ministership, feudal elements (who are still integral part of PPP) convinced him for maximum numbers of party nominations. Bhutto collected massive party fund from this immense fraction of the party but this action proved very expensive for him later. Feudal candidates of PPP had no such tolerance to accept defeat like the middle class minute fraction of the party. Some among these feudal candidates were involved in pre-and-post pool rigging which provided an opportunity to the very weak opposition for raising an agitation. Election of 1977 was not fully rigged or manipulated but opposition started a continuous agitation for a re - election which ended on imposition of Martial law. Z.A. Bhutto was later arrested in a suspected case of murder and executed on April 4, 1979 through a biased trial in Supreme Court of Pakistan. Pakistan People's Party declared Bhutto's execution as a judicial murder.

After death of its founding chairman PPP faced a series of victimisation by the military establishment of the country. Feudal elite who became an integral part of the PPP during early 70's left it (massive fraction of it, only minute fraction remained loyal) in a hurry and rushed towards the dictator. In these circumstances Begum Nusrat Bhutto wife of Z.A. Bhutto led the party

Bilwal Zardari Chairperson of PPP Adressing a Public Meeting in Karchi

until 1982. Benazir Bhutto the eldest among the four children of Z.A. Bhutto was trained and groomed by her father for the chairpersonship of PPP for the next generation of Bhutto dynasty. After unnatural death of Z.A. Bhutto PPP faced a vacuum of leadership, though Mrs Bhutto took charge as a party chairperson but she remained ineffective among the workers. She was a foreigner who belonged to Iran, some sources say that she was a part of an ordinary family (Peter Paul Anatol Leven wrote in his book *Pakistan: A hard country,* that Mrs Bhutto was a club dancer before her marriage) being married to Mr Bhutto. She was considered a notable personality to run Bhutto's party in successful manner that's why Benazir Bhutto took charge of the party chairpersonship. Some sources also say that Benazir Bhutto sacked her mother from the office of chairperson with the help of senior leaders of party at that time. Benazir Bhutto commonly called as BB formerly took the office of chairperson of PPP on November 12, 1982 which remained intact until her death on December 27, 2007. She got the life time chairpersonship of the party without any election.

Benazir Bhutto being an active politician played a vital role for both PPP and the country. She took the office of prime minister in her life during 1988-1996. BB being a feudal lady supported and inducted feudal lords both in PPP and government offices. Feudal families of Sind and South Punjab remained as an integral part of PPP during her long regime of fifteen years. Yousaf Raza Gillani (later prime minister of Pakistan) a feudal politician from Multan got important portfolios twice during the Prime Ministership of Benazir Bhutto, similarly some other feudal families of interior Sind and South Punjab remained power centers of PPP during this era. PPP which was familiar for raising voice in the favour of labourers in 60's and 70's lost the aura of its socialist political party during early 90's. Second term of Benazir Bhutto as a prime minister proved as last nail in coffin when feudal elite of the party completely destroyed its socialistic image. Massive fraction of population was very much annoyed with the corruption, favouritism and nepotism of PPP leadership during the second regime of Benazir Bhutto (1993-1996) this was the major reason for its massive defeat in general elections of 1997.

PPP got only 18 seats of national assembly in the general elections of 1997, these elections restricted PPP in lower Sind only. But nine years of dictatorship in the country (1999-2008) once again diverted the minds of masses towards PPP and it got 124 seats of national assembly out of 342 as a result of general elections held on February 18, 2008. Murder of party chairperson Benazir Bhutto on December 27, 2007 generated a wave of sympathy for PPP in the general elections of 2008 and led the party towards a coalition government in a hung parliament formed as a result of this election.

Leadership of PPP was transferred to Asif Ali Zardari and Bilawal Bhutto Zardari, husband and son of Benazir Bhutto respectively, through a will just after her assassination. A much suspected will of BB was revealed after her death in which she nominated her nineteen years old son Bilwal as party's chairperson while her husband Asif Ali Zardari (later president of Pakistan 2008-13) was nominated as PPP co-chairman. PPP came to power after a long span of time in 2008 (after 1996) but it failed to make any impact in the minds of the masses in its last five years and this was the major reason for its massive defeat in 2013 general elections. Both of its prime ministers Veteran Yousaf Raza Gillani and non-experienced Raja Pervaiz Ashraf alongside several other ministers from their cabinet, faced severe allegations of corruption, favouritism, nepotism and abuse of power during the last government of PPP. Dozens of scams including mega corruption scandals of National Insurance Corporation Limited, Ministry of Religious Affairs (for looting Hajj pilgrims) and Oil and Gas Regulatory Authority were revealed during this span of time.

Due to massive allegations of corruption and bad governance PPP faced heavy criticism in media through its opponents and political pundits before the general elections of 2013 which impacted its election campaign adversely. As a result PPP lost its numbers in national assembly and PML (N) got another chance. PPP was able to fetch only 35 seats in lower house of parliament but sustained its position in provincial assembly of Sind. PPP got 92 seats in the house of 168 in the provincial assembly of Sind and Old Qaim Ali Shah took the oath for the office of chief minister for third term. Mega corruption scandals both in federal and Sind governments during 2008-13 remained a great matter of concern for PPP's young chairperson Bilawal Zardari Bhutto. The performance of the eighty two years old chief minister always remained a question mark throughout his term (2008-13) but he remained intact due to favours of Asif Zardari the co-chairman of the party. After completing his education and qualifying for the electoral politics (at the age of twenty five), party's young Chairperson Bilwal Bhutto Zardari has been showing more interest in party affairs as compared to its past leaders. Now he is involved in both internal affairs of party and governance issues of chief minister and his cabinet ministers. The old chief minister of Sind alongside similar faces of cabinet ministers (who were also part of cabinet during 2008-13) are now showing little bit more responsibility and relatively mature attitude as compared to the past. But time is quite cruel; influence of heredity has done much damage to PPP and has restricted it within the four walls of feudal occupied part of Sind.

- **Awami National Party**

Awami National Party commonly called as ANP is political dynasty of Khan Abdul Ghaffar Khan (Bacha Khan). Khan Abdul Ghaffar commonly called as Bacha Khan (February 5, 1890-January 20, 1988) was an independent activist of Pashtun descent, he also received the title of *The Pride of Afghans*.

Being an important part of Indian National Congress Khan, strongly opposed partition of India and creation of Pakistan. When referendum over accession to Pakistan was held Khan boycotted the referendum. After partition Ghaffar Khan took the oath of allegiance to the new nation on February 23, 1948. Eldest son of Baacha Khan (Ghani Khan) was a poet and was not able to carry his political legacy. But his younger son Khan Abdul Wali Khan commonly called as Wali Khan had a great interest in politics and became an important part of National Awami Party (NAP). NAP was founded by Abdul Hameed Khan Bhashania Bengali nationalist in 1957 at Dacca. All fractions of opposition gathered with NAP at that time and Wali Khan played an important role as a leader of opposition. Bachchaa Khan formed Pakistan's first opposition party within one year of independence on May 8, 1948 by the name of Pakistan Azad party. Baacha Khan proved himself as a Pukhtun nationalist and suffered a lot. He was arrested many times during 1948-56 by different governments due to his Pukhtunnationalist attitude.

Awami National party was founded by Abdul Wali Khan in 1986 after his long political journey in NAP. Possessing the ideology of secularism, democratic socialism economic equalitarianism and civil liberatinism Awami national party showed the legacy of Baccha Khan. But it too adopted the culture of heredity and influence very soon like other political parties of the country. Currently possessing two seats in national assembly and twelve in provincial assembly of Khyber Pukhtunkhawa ANP ruled the KPK province through a coalition government during 2008-13.

Forty two years Hadir Khan Hotti (currently member of national assembly) the great grandson of Dr Khan Sahib (Khan Abdul Jabar Khan commonly

Asfandyar-Wali-Khan

called as Dr Khan Sahib was the member of legislative assembly of Delhi in 1935 from North western frontier province now KPK) served as the twenty fifth chief minister of KPK during March 2008-13. Father of Hadir Khan, senator Azam Hotti also remained as federal minister twice in the coalition governments during 90's. Hadir Khan is also maternal nephew of party's president Asfand Yar Wali. Follower of Bachchaa Khan came under heavy criticism when ANP led government of KPK was criticised for its alleged corruption, favouritism and nepotism by its political opponent and mainstream media. Government of KPK was called as easy load government (If you load it with bribes you will be able to get your desired results easily) by its political opponents during 2008-13. ANP showed full trust on influence of heredity by rewarding all important party and government offices on the basis of kinship.

Bilour family of Peshawar is another dynasty in ANP. Haji Ghulam Ahmed Bilour member of National Assembly from Peshawar (NA-1) was federal minister for railways in PPP led coalition government during 2008-13. Despite severe allegations of corruption even by his party fellows Bilour enjoyed the office for five years but his opponents and major fraction of media claims that his period as a federal minister was worst in the history of Pakistan railways. Ghulam Bilour is a transporter of busses and goods and his opponent claims that he has destroyed Pakistan railways in order to enhance his business. Brother of Ghulam Bilour Bashir Ahmed was senior minister in KPK government, Bashir died in a suicide attack in 2012. Another member of Bilour family Ilyas Ahmed is a senator from KPK. Above mentioned examples are enough to assess that ANP is revolving around two families and influence of heredity is playing a vital role in politics of ANP and KPK province.

- **Some Other Political Groups**

Influence of heredity is not only widespread in mainstream political parties of the country but it also has produced severe repercussions on regional and minor political groups of the country. These political factions are also following the same norms and traditions of heredity which are followed by major political groups in the country. Jamet Ulmay-e-Islam (F) is an orthodox Islamic political group of the country led by Moulana Fazal-ur- Rehman a sixty years old cleric from Dera Ismile Khan District of KPK. Fazal is carrying the legacy of his father Mufti Memood, founding member of Jametulemay-Hind (mother party of JUI (F)) in 1945. Memood remained as chief minister of North Western Frontier Province (new name KPK) from March 1, 1972 to February 14, 1973. In the year 1988, Fazal founded JUI (F) by separating it from other fractions of JUI. Fazal carried the principles of conservation and cleric attitude as a legacy of his late father and is playing an important role in the politics of federation and province through his regional political group.

Some fractions of media heavily criticised Fazal for keeping a non-democratic and favouritism-based attitude. According to a senior politician who is part of another Islamic political group of the country, attitude of Fazal is very autocratic with his workers. Fazal has also faced severe allegations of corruption and nepotism throughout his whole political career. Fazal alongside with some other groups is flag carrier of religion based politics in the country which has produced severe repercussions on the whole political system of the country. Overall public opinion although is not in favour of religion-based politics but even then religious political groups possess reasonable support in KPK and Baluchistan province. Some political workers and commentator believe that religion-based politics is no more different than traditional politics of the country.

"Islamic political groups are also doing politics of heredity", said Attulaah Sial, former senior leader of JUI(F) and now president of JUI (Ideological) Punjab chapter which is a split group of JUI(F). Fazal is practicing politics of corruption and commissions like other political groups in the country, "You can't call his action as service of Islam", Sial continued. "We are willing to serve both Islam and masses that's why we separated our way from JUI(F)", he added more.

- **Pakistan Tehrek–e-Insaf (Pakistan Justice Party)**

Pakistan Tehrek-e-Insaf (Pakistan movement for justice) commonly called as PTI is a very important political party of modern day Pakistan. PTI founded on April 25, 1996 by former captain of Pakistan cricket team, Imran Khan. After the general elections held in May 2013, PTI emerged as a third largest political force in the country while it stands second in proportion of votes. It possesses 35 seats out of 342 in national assembly and 55 numbers out of 124 in provincial assembly of KPK. Pervaiz Khuttack a veteran politician, is leading the coalition government of PTI in KPK. PTI also has a minute representation in provincial assemblies of Punjab and Sind containing 27 seats out of 372 and four out of 168 respectively. Leadership of party claims that their party is a dear darling of youth in Pakistan and it looks true to a great extent, massive fraction of youth in Pakistan voted for PTI during general elections of 2013. PTI also claims that it is the only non-family political party in the country but time is required to prove this theory as it is still very new in mainstream politics, secondly, it is still working under the chairmanship of its founding chairman but nevertheless it also comprises of many traditional faces in its mainstream and second class leadership.

PTI claims to work for justice, humanity and self-esteem. Its slogan is "Break the status quo and traditional politics". Imran Khan the sixty two years old cricketer-cum-politician has shown a character in social services. Shukat Khanum, a cancer hospital in Lahore (a charity-based organisation) is considered among the big achievements of Khan before his entrance in the arena of politics. Supporters of Khan claim that he is energetic and a visionary and has raised himself as a change agent against traditional political dynasties of the country. Some political commentators believe that sociopolitical activism of Khan, his charity work and vocal attitude against corrupt political mafias acted as a driving force to bring youth voters in his favour during general elections of 2013 but this support of youth was not enough to bring power for him in centre as some other fractions of the society were in favour of PML (N), the ruling party. PML (N) though won the general elections of 2013 but PTI gave it a tough fight, it stood second in many of the constituencies in the country by getting reasonable votes alongside its 35 victory seats in the national assembly. PTI introduced itself with massive vote bank even in traditional constituencies of PML (N). The defeat of some of its candidates was with a very narrow margin in Lahore, the hub of PML (N) power.

It was autumn of 2011(month of October) when very first time PTI in a public gathering in Lahore proved itself as a massive mass movement. This public meeting held near Tower of Pakistan in Lahore opened the door of parliamentary success for the very first time in its history (Before PTI participated in two general elections of 1997 and 2002 and it got only one seat in 2002). Imran Khan the chairman of PTI is very vocal against corrupt mafias in political parties of the country. In his earlier political career he showed a reluctant attitude for the induction of traditional politicians in his party and claimed to bring in some new faces. His political opponents are not in agreement with this theory as according to them Imran's earlier failure to get popular mass support for his party had kept away the familiar political families from him but later these parties started approaching him when his mass appeal began to increase. After his mass following in politics a flood of traditional politicians joined hands with PTI and captured all important offices.

Induction of educated middle class in the parliamentary politics was the prime focus of Imran Khan when he entered the arena of politics. Khan sometimes was called as angry young man in his youth as he showed lot of anger towards traditional feudal and industrial politicians of the country. According to him the political system of the political dynasties has been delivering nothing for the more than 192 million faces of the country and is only working for the protection of super elite and elite classes of the country. Due to his clear intentions against old and corrupt mafias in the country, a massive fraction of educated middle class youth got attracted towards him but the ideology of inducting middle class in the mainstream politics is yet to become a Tsunami. Imran Khan even at the age of sixty one feels like a young and energetic man that's why he declared his movement as a Tsunami which will destroy the corrupt mafias of the country.

Khan had a clear point of view regarding change in the political system of the country and thousands of times before October 2011 he claimed that he will introduce fresh, educated, young and middle and lower middle class people in the parliamentary politics of the country if he got the support of masses. But after witnessing a massive mass support in Lahore while public addressing he opened the flood gates of his party for corrupt and traditional political families of the country due to their wealth and influence. Now truly speaking PTI is also representing traditional fractions of the society. Khan's political journey though started in 1996 failed to produce any impact on political scene of the country up till 2007.

Lawyer's movement for the restoration of judiciary (2007-09) was the movement during which Khan showed his street power for the very first time. This movement is an integral part of sociopolitical struggle for the basic human rights of the masses of the country during the recent past. Iftakhar Muhammad Chudhary the former chief justice of Pakistan (retired on December 13, 2013) was the key focus of lowers movement who was forced for resignation by military dictator Pervaiz Musharraf on March 3, 2007 but Mr Chudhary denied resigning. Later Musharraff sent a reference against Chudhary in supreme judicial council but council restored him as chief justice of Pakistan. Musharraff being a military dictator wanted to get rid of Mr Chudhary at any cost as he was involved in judicial activism to disturb military rule. At last dictator imposed an emergency on November 3, 2007 and sixty judges of superior court alongside Mr Chudhary were removed from their offices. Lawyers started a mass movement for the restoration of the judiciary supported by some political fractions including PML (N) and PTI. A long march was launched by lawyers led by PML (N) leader Nawaz Sharif on March 19, 2009 which ended on restoration of all the judges in their offices.

Imran Khan was very vocal in the favour of former CJP against military ruler Musharraff which not only gave a boost to his political party but due to this he also attained respect among different fractions of society including civil society, lawyers and youth of the country. But he turned against the CJP Mr Chudhary just after the elections of 2013 and declared that judiciary was involved in rigging to support PML (N). Judiciary issued him a notice of contempt of court and he (Imran Khan) apologised for his attitude. Just after the end of lawyer's movement a massive fraction of educated middle class joined PTI hence PTI progressed a lot during and after the lawyer's movement but it failed to test its power during 2008 general elections as Chairman Khan denied to participate in those elections conducted in the regime of dictator Musharraff. It proved to be a grave mistake later as two mainstream political parties of the country PPP and PML (N) faced severe repercussions during the dictatorship of General Pervaiz Musharraff. Ruling PML (Q) had lost its trust among the masses before the general elections of 2008, so Khan had a chance to get reasonable votes but he failed to catch the opportunity. Some veteran and loyal workers of PTI still believe that Khan had a chance in 2008 to get seats in parliament without the help of the feudal and industrial elite who have now become an integral part of the party.

"We started our journey with the Captain (Khan is familiar by the name of captain among his workers) in early 2000 era when no one was with him" so said an old worker (name not mentioned on his request) of PTI from Faisalabad. "We struggled a lot during early years of the party to introduce it as a mainstream political party among the masses. I am an advocate by profession when I started to introduce PTI among the lawyers of the city (most among them were PML (N) supporters during early years of PTI and they used to laugh at me but when party progressed a wave of feudal and industrial Tsunami swept out all loyal but middle class workers like me. We were promised the allocation of party nominations for national and provincial assemblies but at the end of the day feudal and industrial elite captured all. Was this the change for which we struggled so much?" He added more.

It was the month of October in 2011 when Khan finally realised enough public support for party, he decided at once to induct traditional politician possessing wealth and influence in his party. When some fractions of media described this action against his promise of inducting lower middle and middle class workers in parliamentary politics, Khan replied that these new comers (industrial and feudal elite) will not be given the party nominations for general elections without the permission of party's central committee which comprised of old party workers. But at the end of the day more than 99 per cent party nominations were given to the candidates belonging to the feudal and industrial classes. Some factions of media once again raised the issue of neglecting old party workers driven by financial circumstances, to this Khan had replied "I can't find angels", indicating that PTI too had to adopt the same culture followed by the other political parties of the country.

Shah Memood Hussain Quershi former foreign minister and then key figure of PPP was the first one to join PTI from the feudal class of the country. He was at once appointed as Vice Chairman of PTI by Chairman Khan which was heart breaking for the loyal workers of PTI. After Quershi's massive flood (Tsunami) of elite entered in PTI which destroyed the wishes of loyal but middle class workers of Khan. These old fashioned political elite who have unique and modern approaches to loot and corruption at once captured all important offices in PTI. After the elections of 2013, PTI founded a coalition government in KPK and most of the key offices were awarded to newly inducted faces in the party from other political parties.

Javed Hashmi then Vice President of PML (N), Khursheed Qassori and Saradar Asif Ahmed Ali former foreign ministers of the country (were part of PML (Q) and PPP respectively), industrialist Jahangir Tareen and many other feudal and industrial politicians joined PTI just after October 2011. Opponents of PTI claimed that so much induction of traditional politician in PTI during 2011-12 was due to favour of military establishment which has always been considered as a key player in the politics of Pakistan. A major fraction of media still believes that establishment was involved in destabilising the government of PML (N), PTI refused to accept the results of 2013 elections and started a blame game against the judiciary and media for their alleged involvement in rigging.This action of PTI produced severe repercussions and its relations with Jang/Geo group, the largest media house in the country came under strain. PTI also blamed Iftkhar Muhmmad Chudhary the former chief justice of Pakistan for the provision of support to PML (N) to which the judiciary showed a great reaction.

When PTI formed a coalition government in the province of KPK after the general elections of 2013 it neglected its lower middle and middle class workers who were struggling hard for the party for many years. It produced severe impacts and divisions started showing up in PTI's KPK chapter in a very short span of time. Chief Minister of KPK Pervaiz Khuttuack belongs to the same ruling elite class to which Shabaz Sharif and Qaim Ali Shah, chief ministers of Punjab and Sind respectively, also belong. Major fraction of media in Pakistan now believes that PTI too now has become a part of the traditional political system of the country which has no space for the lower income groups of the country. According to senior worker of PTI from Lahore more than 95 per cent of party nominations for the general elections of 2013 were given to the candidates belonging to the ruling elite. "Is this the change for what we were struggling from the last seventeen years! If this is a change we don't need this anymore," said he.

Some senior political commentators have indicated the harsh reality that the ruling elite influence is now very deep rooted and widespread in PTI too like other mainstream political parties of the country. They believe that top leadership of PTI received heavy bribes from the traditional political families of the country before the general elections of 2013 to ensure nominations for their own parties. Multan the largest city of South Punjab holds importance for PTI as its two key office holders (President and Vice Chairman) belonging to Multan remained in lime light till the general elections of 2013, media reported many scandals that indicated paying of bribes to key persons of PTI in Multan. According to a senior columnist from Lahore, a feudal member of provincial assembly from Multan paid heavy bribes to both the senior leaders of PTI belonging to the city to confirm his party nomination from the specific constituency. To recapitulate all about PTI we conclude that PTI is no more different political party than any other traditional political group of the country. PTI though claimed itself as a change agent but change is still too far away from the range of the unfortunate Pakistanis.

- **Influence of Heredity in Public Sector Organisations**

Influence of heredity is not only the dilemma of Pakistani politics but it has also produced widespread and deep-rooted impacts on public sector organisations of the country. All types of public sector organisations including semi-government and autonomous organisations which possess infrastructure and board of directors under the shelter of federal or any provincial government are facing severe repercussions of influence of heredity. It is a matter of fact that influence of heredity is very strong in organisations under full government control and their setup is made to especially support the heredity, as compared to this semi-government/autonomous organisations in the country possess relatively lesser influence of heredity and is under lesser pressure to support only heredity-based claims. Chairmen, board of directors or heads of semi government/autonomous organisations in the country are enjoying more administrative and appointing powers as compared to pure government organisations who are working like dictators and are spreading massive corruption and nepotism, due to this abuse of power there is conflict among the educated youth of the country. This gang of BODs is not only discouraging the culture of merit and calibre but is also shaking the very fabric of the country through brain drain which is going on large scale for not appointing on the basis of merit in more than 99 per cent of appointments.

There are fixed quotas for the sons/daughters of public servants in government jobs (in their relevant departments) and this system is already a question mark on the system of merit, but this does not stop here, large scale violation of quota system (through excessive appointments) is a common practice in Pakistan. Civilian and military bureaucracy is utilising it as a tool for the induction of their children in key positions. There are many loopholes in the civilian and military bureaucratic system of the country which and are used as opportunities by the bureaucratic elite of the country for the induction of their children alongside their fixed quotas. Armed force officers have a massive quota in medical colleges, public universities and other top level educational institutes for their children, similarly jobs in top public level institutions are granted to children of military bureaucrats. So we can say that for the fixed quota candidates there exists an immense opportunity under this system, whereas the people who do not have quotas have very limited opportunities, even if they are meritorious and deserving.

Influence of heredity is a very common practice in armed forces of Pakistan. Like political dynasties there are certain military dynasties in Pakistan as well which transfer their legacies to next generations. Current Chief of Army Staff, General Raheel Sharif like many other high ranked officials of the force is also a member of a military dynasty. According to a senior defence analyst, General Sharif was promoted to the office of COAS just because of solid family military background as many of his family members are or have been renowned officers in the Pakistani army. Lieutenant General (retired) Haroon Aslam, the senior most officer after Asfaq Pervaiz Kayani (then chief of army staff, November 2013) was neglected for the important office by prime minister Sharif as Aslam had less influential family ties as compared to General Sharif. Prime minister Sharif had once committed in a public address (in 2012) that if he came into power after 2013 general elections he will make appointments for all key positions based on merit and seniority. It is a matter of fact that General Pervaiz Musharraff (military ruler during 1999-2008) was also prompted by Primer Sharif by overriding the seniority issues, during his second regime in1997-99. Musharraff's place was third among all Lieutenant generals at that time with respect to seniority, but premier Sharif promoted on the basis of personal liking. According to a senior journalist of the country preference for promoting sons/daughters of serving and retired military bureaucrats is an unwritten law in Inter Service Selection Board (commonly called as ISSB, is a board for the selections of officers in the armed forces of Pakistan). Some sources also claim that there are favouritism issues among the children of low ranked and high ranked officials and we have many examples to prove this.

Kashif Mehmod was my (writer's) class fellow in intermediate and considered among low profiled students of the class. After completing intermediate he was immediately selected as Second Lieutenant in Pakistan army which was astonishing news for all of his class fellows including me. In a very first meeting with his old mates after his selection he proudly declared that his uncle is a serving Brigadier who supported him a lot and his success belongs to the efforts of his uncle. Similarly, another class fellow of mine from the University of Agriculture Faisalabad also fulfilled the same criteria and was also selected as Second Lieutenant during his studies (he left the University in his second semester). Rao Sabeeh -ur- Zaman Khan my friend and class mate during the graduation programme in Agriculture Engineering also appeared twice for ISSB. Rao (currently serving as a production engineer in sugar industry) being a son of an ex-military man (his father served as a low rank official in Pakistan army) was passionate about serving in the army. He was talented enough, very well groomed but was still rejected twice by the selection board. Describing his experience Rao claimed that he was rejected because his father had retired from an ordinary post. "Listen I am telling you the criteria" he got my attention, "First of all preferences are given to sons of currently serving high ranked officials, then comes the turn of children belonging to retired bureaucrats. Even then if seats remain vacant then junior serving bureaucracy and at the end children of low ranked serving and retired officials are considered. If you do not fall in any of the above mentioned categories (that is if one belongs to ordinary civilian class) then it is better not to waste your time and energy in applying to ISSB", Rao added more.

Civilian bureaucracy as we discussed earlier is familiar for corruption and favouritism it is also under great influence of heredity like the military in Pakistan. The combined competitive exam commonly called as CSS (Central Superior Services) held every year for the selection of civilian bureaucracy in the country, is also fraught with many weaknesses and by utilising these only a privileged class candidate is able to attain their benefits. A story was unveiled by an investigative journalist Anasr Abaasi (editor investigation of "Daily The News"), he uncovered the scam in 2013 civil services exams. According to his report many officials of federal public service commission (authority responsible for conducting civil service exam in the country) alongside with Pakistan post officials (responsible for delivery of examination material in the examination centres from the offices of FPSC and to examiners as well) were involved to support dozens of candidates for solving papers. These candidates paid heavy bribes to both FPSC and postal officials for allowing them use of illegal means in the examination. The report stated that specific candidates were allowed by FPSC officials to submit their papers unsolved during examination time in their respective centres, these candidates were then allowed to collect their unsolved papers from post offices for a certain period of time. After correctly filling the answer sheets these candidates returned their solved papers to the post offices again. This scam was unveiled due to unusual delay of some papers and concerned authorities showed a reaction when they were not able to collect papers of certain candidates who appeared in the exams according to record. But the authorities failed to trace and trial the specific candidates who were involved in the scam. Repercussions of this were severe for ordinary candidates when FPSC cancelled result of all papers conducted in Faisalabad region and examination was conducted again from those candidates as well who were not involved in any rigging.

Above mentioned example suggests clearly the illegal use of wealth and influence even in the highest level of recruitment examination of the country, this example also reflects the shaken state of the very fabric of organisational structure of the country. This also impels us to question that if influence and wealth is polluting the top level recruitment examination what would be the standards of recruitments at the lower levels? Now have a look at some other aspects of civil services exams in Pakistan. After qualifying written part of exam candidate for civil service appears in psychological and viva voce which determines the fate of a candidate as to whether he or she is going to be the part of civil services class in Pakistan or not? According to major fraction of candidates the examiners at viva voce show a clear bias and favour the candidates from bureaucratic backgrounds. Members of FPSC (responsible for conducting interviews on the basis of psychological results) belong to the bureaucracy (both civil and military retired officials) and the judiciary, one psychologist usually a woman is also part of the selection board of FPSC. Many candidates who appeared in interviews of FPSC during 2008-13 claimed while talking to me (Writer) that they witnessed undue favours from the FPSC members for the sons/daughters of serving and retired bureaucrats. According to them this type of attitude has made the entire procedure of recruitment very doubtful.

"Irfan, a guy from Lahore got 224th position in 2012 civil service exam but he failed to secure any job even after putting in a year of extensive hard work and preparation. While talking to me (Writer) Irfan showed lot of bitterness and harsh attitude towards the quota system in civil services of Pakistan. "I qualified the exam and secured 224th position in the country but I am not able to get any job but there are candidates belonging to Sind and Baluchistan who ranked more than 500 and still got jobs in higher groups (Police services, DMG etc). People like me are pushed down due to our non influential, non-bureaucratic and non-political backgrounds. Many among the sons and daughters of federal secretaries, IGs, (Inspector General of Police) and feudal lords have been inducted in the top groups of civil services in Pakistan during recent years with lot of ease just because these candidates were familiar with members of FPSC. I still remember a daughter of a DIG (Deputy Inspector General of Police) who got allocation in a very good group as she in spite of scoring much less than me in the written examination was awarded excessively high marks in the interview by the biased interviewers." Irfan added more.

Influence of heredity is not only the dilemma of Civil-military bureaucracy in Pakistan but it has produced severe impacts on all Public Sector organisations of the country. This fashion has produced severe impacts on the very fabric of all public sector organisations in the country and these organisations have been going through massive administrative and organisational collapse during the last few decades. There is a prevalence of massive killing of merit in public and semi-government organisations and allocation of all important offices to incompetent and corrupt individuals. Brain drain is another severe impact of influence of heredity in the public sector organisations of the country. Massive fraction among educated middle class is leaving the country at a rapid rate or thinking of settling abroad for the better future of their children. Feudal and industrial elite of the country already carry their wealth with foreign banks. This fraction of the society also hold agricultural and commercial lands, industries and real estate businesses in USA, Canada, Australia and other countries of EU. More than 200 billion US dollars of Pakistani political elite are deposited in the banks of Switzerland, according to media reports. The educated upper middle and middle class of the country possess knowledge and skills and they are increasingly utilising it to settle aboard.

"Influence of heredity has multidimensional impacts on public sector organisations and on the psyche of nation as well", said Tahir Ali - a sociologist from Islamabad, the capital of the country. If some deserving person is not able to achieve his/her right through legal means the first reaction would be an absolute distrust of the whole system which is not a good sign for any system in the world, moreover that individual is likely to find a wrong path (through bribe, influence etc.) to achieve his or her desired destination which will enhance the socioeconomic injustice in the country. Lastly, that individual will also work as an agent of socioeconomic injustice for his/her whole life. When people are hopeless in a cruel society like Pakistan either they use their powers to avenge and destroy others (through suicide bombing, killing, rape, etc.) or try to quit that place or country through immigrations. Those who are not able to do anything at all live their whole lives in a psychological turmoil and major fraction of the population in the country is going through such turmoil." he added more.

Influence of heredity is applied through various means in public and semi-government organisations in the country and one among all methods one very familiar and applicable way is to avoid advertisement. Most employments among the public and semi-government organisations are not advertised or advertised partially with the utilisation of specific methods to destroy merit. Some bigger public sector organisations like Railways follow the dual system of recruitments; these types of organisations are utilising both federal public service commission and their own internal system of recruitment as well. Appointment through FPSC (we have discussed its faults and failures already) is relatively transparent as compared to internal system of recruitment in different departments like railways and WAPDA (Water and power development authority, and other massive public sector organisation in the country).

Pakistanis are unfortunate enough that they are bearing corruption, favouritism and nepotism in almost all public sector organisations as the heads of these organisations are appointed politically. It requires no qualification and calibre to become a head of public sector organisation in Pakistan other than political influence and loyalty with ruling party's chairperson. Former Prime minister Yousaf Raza Gillani (considered as the most scandalised prime minister in the history of the country) appointed his jail fellow (Gillani was convicted for corruption charges during the military regime of Pervaiz Musharraff) Adnan Khawaja as a chairman of Oil and Gas Regularity Authority (OGRA is among the largest public sector organisations in Pakistan). Mr Khwaja was only qualified till secondary school level and possessed no professional qualifications to hold such an important office other than the beneficience of a federal minister (later prime minister) in jail. Above mentioned example is a little glimpse of the methods applied in the appointments of public sector of Pakistan. One can easily find hundreds of thousands of more such examples of favouritism and nepotism and this is further increasing socioeconomic injustice in the country at a rapid rate.

Now we will discuss some public sector organisations which are performing miserably and causing great deficits to government for many years. Corruption, favouritism and nepotism in these public sector organisations has produced severe impacts not only on the economy of the country but has also put under immense strain the very fabric of the country as well.

- **Pakistan Railways**

Though newly appointed federal minister for Railways Khwaja Saad Rafiuqe is trying hard to reshape his destructed organisation and he has achieved success to some extent but even then Pakistan Railways is among the most corrupt organisations of Pakistan. Founded in 1947, Pakistan Railways emerged from the Indian Railway, rail-road system in the sub-continent was founded in April 16, 1853 during the *British Raj* in this part of the land. It was 1861 when the first railway line started its operation between Kotri and Karachi covering a distance of 105 miles.

With more than 90,000 employees and a deficit of 40 billions PKR (Statistics of 2012) Pakistan Railways is considered among the most extensive public sector organisations of Pakistan. Possessing annual revenue of 18,612 million PKR and with assets of hundreds of billions it is a great hub of corruption, nepotism and favouritism. According to a report of *Daily Business Recorder* published on January 1, 2013, the year 2012 was the year of most deficits in the history of Pakistan Railways. More than 40 billion budgetary deficits along with several corruption cases, abuse of authority, operational inefficiency and violation of public regularity authority were reported in the report. Above mentioned facts are enough to prove that Pakistan Railways is the most corrupt and disorganised public sector organisation in the country but we will also look into some more details. Recently National Accountability Bureau (NAB) arrested Saeed Akhtar-the General Manager Railways for his alleged involvement in a multi-billion scam.

Pakistan Railways has been the easiest victim of influence of heredity during the recent past. Not only the political elite of the country but also the bureaucracy of the department were fully involved in using it as a tool to induct their near and dear ones in the already deficit making organisation. High ranked officials of the Pakistan Railways have completely sabotaged the merit basis in recruitments and promoted nepotism during the last few decades. Political appointments have always been a great dilemma for the organisation since many years. Yousaf Raza Gillani, former minister for railways (later prime minister of Pakistan 2008-12) was charged with corruption and abuse of power during his regime in the organisation. One officer from South Punjab (on the request of not disclosing his name) told me (Writer) that regime of Gillani in railways was worst among all, with the freedom of absolute abuse of power, Gillani appointed hundreds of non-professionals from his political constituency which created a great financial burden for the already destructed organisation.

Maryam Gillani, one lady officer of Pakistan Railways admitted in a talk show in 2010 (Capital talk with Hamid Mir) that minister of railways Ghulam Ahmed Bilour pressurised her for political appointments in regional headquarters of Pakistan railways in Peshawar. While talking to Hamid Mir, She said " Haji Ghulam Ahmed Bilour federal minister of railways sent me a list of dozens of political workers of his party for their appointments against lower ranked advertised employments in railway of Peshawar division. When I denied fulfilling his desire he victimised me" she added, "I was demoted from BPS 18 (Basic pay scale, used to describe bureaucracy ranks in country) to 17 on orders of the minister". Currently Abdur-Rauf Tahir a political activist cum columnist is working as the Director General Public Relations (Post of BPS 21) in Pakistan railways headquarter Lahore. Tahir, a freelance journalist ranked among third grade column writers in the country has only the qualification of loyalty with premier Sharif family. Tahir possesses no experience of public service but during his freelance carrier of journalism he worked for promoting the agenda of PML (N) and thus was his reward.

With too many annual deficits it's too difficult to run such an organisation of heavily over loaded employees. Continuous induction of employees on political and heredity basis has weakened the very fabric of the organisation badly and directly and severely affected the ordinary citizens of the country who depend on the railways to commute. Fares of rail in Pakistan are highest in Asia, as compared to its neighbour India, railways in Pakistan is lagging far behind. Indian Railways is now considered comfortable, organised and the cheapest source of travel by most of its1250 million people. In Pakistan, masses are demanding reforms since many years, for the riddance of corruption, favouritism and nepotism in this old and prestigious organisation of the country. Some fractions among the masses are demanding the privatisation of railways in Pakistan alongside with some other public sector organisations. But privatisation in some sectors of Pakistan including railways has not been able to deliver any result.

Shailimar express (a super express train) alongside with few other trains were handed over to the private sector during the regime of Ghulam Ahmed Bilour, the purpose was to enhance revenues of the railways through public-private partnerships, but this endeavour went in vain. Utilisation of influence and power here too rewarded few individuals at the cost of economic destruction of organisation and masses (who are paying taxes to run these organisations). Federal minister for railways Khawja Saad Rafiuqe has announced in his recent press conference that Railways is willing to regain trains from private sector that have done enough damage to the organisation. "Trains handed to private sector during regime of PPP (2008-13) are not returning proper revenues to Pakistan railways", said Khwaja, "These trains were given on lease to few individuals on political basis. Railway has lost more than 1000 million PKR during the last few years just because of these trains", he added more.

Employees working in Pakistan Railways are enjoying more benefits as compared to some other public sector organisations. Alongside big bungalows, (officers of Pakistan Railways enjoy the largest residences among all public servants) bureaucrats and workers of Pakistan Railways are enjoying electricity, gas and telephones almost free. Moreover, they also enjoy free travel with their families the cost of which is too much for this miserable organisation to bear. Massive hiring on political basis puts much burden on the organisation in terms of salaries and privileges.

It's almost impossible for a non-influential and non-political person to get an employment in Pakistan railways. Serving officers and workers have reserved their seats for their next generations, with their specific quotas they ensure the appointments of their sons/daughters before their retirements. Like the political dynasties, organisations like Pakistan Railways are following the same principal of heredity for promoting next generations of public servants.

It is almost a tradition in Pakistan Railways that every minister inducts his party workers in the organisation; these political appointments are responsible for multidimensional losses to railways. Politically appointed employees are not only responsible for over burdening the department (as most of the political appointments are made without advertisement, not against vacant seats) but they are inefficient as well. They don't like to work as they feel secure due to their influences. Major political parties are directly involved in affairs of Pakistan railways due to bulk of their workers working as employees in the organisation. "Pareem" is a big labour union of Pakistan railways working under the shadow of orthodox Islamic political group Jamat-e-Islami. Hafiz Salman Butt, a former member of parliament (National assembly) is the president of Pareem labour union of Pakistan railways. To the civilised countries of the world it may seem queer that a non-labourer (Member of Parliament, Butt was president during his membership of parliament as well) can hold the office of president of a labour union. Similarly some other political parties are also involved in labour unions like Jamat-e-Islami in Pakistan Railways. Leaders of these labour unions are familiar for not utilising their powers for benefits of labour, instead of that these leaders are involved in large scale corruptions. Salman Butt too, faced severe allegations of corruption from different fractions of labour people.

- **Pakistan International Airlines**

"Great people to fly with", is the logo of the great deficit bearing Pakistan International Airlines commonly called as PIA. PIA came into being from Orient Airways in 1955- founded on October 23, 1946 in Calcutta by some renowned Muslim industrialists on the advice of Muhammad Ali Jinnah (Founder of Pakistan). Jinnah being a visionary leader had foresighted the creation of a new Islamic state so he wanted the formation of new Muslim airline before the creation of the new state. A fraction of Muslim industrial elite of that time accepted Jinnah's advice and Mirza Ahmed Isphani alongside with Adam Jee group provided initial investment for the formation of Orient Airways which flourished within a very short span of time and after the partition of the Sub-continent into India and Pakistan, Orient Airways shifted its headquarters and assets from Calcutta to Karachi – the capital of Pakistan at that time.

On March 11, 1955, Government of Pakistan formed a new airline by merging Orient Airways with other small airlines and thus was formed Pakistan International Airlines. PIA was considered among the top airlines of the world during 1960-90 but now like the other miserable public sector organisations of the country this organisation too is passing through its worst period. "Great people to fly with" is no more able to carry great people with it due to the worst crises in its history, majority among the air passengers are now utilising other international airlines as they are more organised, less expensive and disciplined. Ordinary citizens in the country are unfortunate enough that they are paying from their taxes for the 152 billion deficit of PIA without even travelling in it. In fact massive majority among the masses is not able to travel in any airline due to their poor economic circumstances. Massive fraction of population in the country is not able to travel by plane not even a single time during their entire life span. Only the upper income groups (more than middle class, elite and super elite) are able to travel by planes.

Due to massive corruption and great influence of heredity PIA has proved to be a true white elephant for the government of Pakistan since the last two decades. Prime Minister Sharif has shown much interest in its privatisation but still has not been able to make any progress regarding this due to different pressure groups. According to the corporate sector, the performance of the officers and workers of PIA is much lesser when compared with that of even the ordinary workers of the public sector organisations, and yet they enjoy highest level of privileges. They lead a lavish life style on the taxes of the ordinary citizens of the country but in return the ordinary masses get nothing from the organisation. With only thirty two operational fleets, PIA possesses the highest number of employees in the world according to proportion of per fleet and passengers. Having more than four thousand six hundred employees it is comparable in size with The South West Airline of United States but stands nowhere near to it in performance. PIA is bearing the load of a massive staff without any work and repercussion of it is very severe –deficit of more than 40 billions every year which is now unbearable for the government of Pakistan.

According to a report of *Pakistan Today* published on February 11, 2013 Ministry of Defence and Pakistan International Airlines saliently raised the salaries of its employees by upto 45 per cent in recent days. This decision shocked many economic experts as officers and workers working in PIA were already taking handsome salaries. According to media reports, one former deputy managing director of PIA, who was later sacked, was taking 55 lakhs (5.5 million PKR) per month, a salary which was several times higher than that of the head of multinational companies of Pakistan.

Like Pakistan Railways, influence of heredity is widespread and deep rooted in PIA as well. Former PPP led coalition government (2008-13) faced severe allegations for promoting corruption, favouritism and nepotism in PIA. More than three thousand employees were hired in this time span in PIA and most among them were the workers of PPP according to media reports. Yousaf Raza Gillani and Ahmed Mukhtar (the then prime minister and defence federal minister respectively) alongside a senator (now deceased) from Multan faced severe allegations from their political opponents and media for massive corruption and nepotism during this span of time in PIA.

Many among the ordinary youngsters showed their concerns about ongoing corruption and appointments in PIA during 2008-13. It was during this period that I too who was quoted a very talented youngster, applied for an employment in PIA but was rejected due to poor economic and non-political background.

"I applied for the post of Electrical Engineer in PIA but was not able to fetch a seat as neither was able to search any link with the political elite of that time nor I had enough money to pay bribe to the bureaucracy of the organisation", said Salman Ali, a guy from Multan. "One among my friends was able to establish contacts with a PPP senator and was selected for the same post, I do not know what deal was finalised between them, but I guess it was around two million PKR", he added. "One among our common friends told me that after giving money to particular person (front man of senator), the senator gave the applicant a letter addressed to the Defence Minister, after having a meeting with the secretary of the defence minister the applicant was assured of selection and was later on selected", he added more.

- **Water and Power Development Authority and its Associate Organisations**

Water and Power Development Authority commonly called as WAPDA and its sub-ordinate organisations (power distribution companies) have been in lime light since a long period for their ongoing corruptions and bad governance. WAPDA was formed on February 12, 1958 by government of Pakistan for the managements of water and power in the country. Since then it has been involved for the constructions of water reservoirs and distribution of power (Electricity) in the country with the help of its distribution companies. For a long span of time (until late 90s) production and distribution of power was managed through one department but later with expanded infrastructure and employees WAPDA was divided among many organisations.

Initially production of power from water and oil was supervised by WAPDA but in October 2007 thermal power management was separated from WAPDA and handed over to Pakistan Electric Power Company (PEPCO) – an organisation linked to WAPDA. There are several electric supply corporations in the country like Lahore Electric Supply Corporation (LESCO), Multan Electric Supply Corporation (MEPCO) etc, working under the supervision of WAPDA. This widespread network of power distribution companies take electricity from power generation companies and distribute to consumers. Different sources like water, oil, coal and nuclear technology are utilised for the production of power in Pakistan even then power generating companies are not able to produce required amount of electricity for their consumers. System of generation and distribution of power consists of many loopholes and mafias involved in it have made it a hub of corrupt practices.

Pakistan is facing the worst energy crises of its history though it possesses mega infrastructure and resources for the provision of energy. Water, natural gas, wind, sunlight, coal and nuclear technology are the important means for the generation of power in the modern world and the country possesses all these resources but is still not able to produce enough electricity for its citizens while its neighbour India with squeezed resources is producing more than 2,00,000 MW electricity with ease. It would be very astonishing for the world that engineers and technicians of the sixth most populated country which is a nuclear power as well are not able to produce electricity of more than 10,000 MW. Due to shortfall of 6000-7000 MW there is massive ongoing load shedding of twelve to fourteen hours per day in Pakistan since the last decade. This massive power failure has done immense damage to the economy of the country during these years. As we already know that more than half of its total population in the country is living below the poverty line and we know this as well that there has been massive increase in this category during the last few years. Power failure in the country has played a vital role for the increment in unemployment and poverty during last five years as it has produced immense losses to the industry of the country.

Unlike some other public sector organisations there are equal opportunities of corruption for both high ranked and low profile officials in the power sector of the country. If a minister or a federal secretary is involved in money making though *Kickbacks* and commissions then at the same time a meter reader (meter reader is an important part of corruption in power sector of the country though a very low ranked official but without him power theft is not possible in traditional electric system of the country) of BPS 6 has an equal opportunity of being involved in corruption. According to a report of *Daily the News*, public sector power companies have lost more than hundred billion rupees during the last five years. Recent incident is that of the failure of Peshawar Electricity Corporation, as the company failed to disconnect the connections of defaulters it entered into a humiliating deal with the mafia of the province involved in electricity theft. This deal allowed electricity stealers to steal electricity on regular basis; electricity which they were using directly without meters was continued on the payment of only 700 PKR per month. PESCO agreed not to raise any hurdles for their unlimited consumptions of electricity at this very small amount. Contrary to this an ordinary user of electricity in the province of Punjab (consuming 200-250 units per month) is paying a bill of 4000-5000 PKR per month to the government owned power companies.

A report published in *Daily the Dawn* in the year 2010 by the name of 'Kunda Culture' (theft of electricity through hooks) described the miserable conditions of the electricity controlling and managing departments. The report stated that specific areas in the country including Karachi (the largest city and commercial hub of the country), Hyderabad, and interior part of Sind, FATA and Peshawar and some districts of Baluchistan are involved in serious thefts of electricity. As compared to these above mentioned areas of the country citizens of Punjab have relatively better repute in this regard.

Pakistan is the most strange and probably the only country in the world which is providing absolutely free electricity to the employees of power generating and distributing public companies. More than two lakh (0.2 million) employees of WAPDA and its allied institutions like LESCO, FESCO, MEPCO, etc. are providing absolutely free electricity to their employees which is a great burden on the poor economy of the country. Massive number of employees in these organisations further exploit this corrupt opportunity for commercial purposes and money making by selling the unused part of their quota of electricity to their neighbours.

According to a recent statement of Khawaja Muhammad Asif, federal minister for water and power, employees of power distribution companies in the country are involved in power theft. While talking to journalists in a press briefing he said that without the cooperation of company employees it is not possible for the consumers to steal electricity. Mr Khawaja is very right to say so as theft of electricity in the country is going on with the mutual understanding between thieves and public servants. Somehow feudal and industrial class of the country is committing this crime without any internal help because of their own influence. Now the question arises that why does the ministry of water and power feel so disabled for taking any action against this mafia? There is absolutely no answer to this question like so many other questions in this country. Unfortunate Pakistanis have to put up with injustice and discrimination in this regard too like in almost all and every other matter.

- **Discriminations in some other Public Sector Organisations**

Influence of heredity, discrimination and injustice is not only the dilemma of few public sector organisations in Pakistan but it is widespread and deep-rooted in all types of public sector organisations in the country. It is a fact of the day that public servants are involved in the promotion of favouritism and nepotism. Abuse of power is practised among most of the semi-government and autonomous organisations working under the supervision of federal and provincial governments respectively. Induction of sons, daughters, nephews, and son-in-laws in high ranked positions is very easy in these organisations. It is relatively a little bit more difficult for the heads of some public sector organisations to induct their favourites in important positions as compared to semi-government and autonomous pubic organisations (though for them too it is quite easy yet prescribed rules are a little bit stricter as compared to the semi-government organisations).

Semi-government organisations like Oil and Gas Regularity Authority (OGRA), Sui Southern Gas Pipe Line Limited Corporation, National Engineering Services Corporation (NESPAK) and many more possess many loopholes that support favouritism and nepotism. NESPAK possesses a very notorious reputation in this regard among all semi-government companies. Its highest level officials are involved both in corruption and nepotism.

"I was interviewed for the post of field engineer and was very hopeful for the selection in water and agriculture wing of NESPAK", said Ahmed Khan (name disguised). But the head of water and agriculture department was seeking to appoint his son-in-law in the same position. After completion of interviews HOD delayed the procedure until the managing director of the organisation (who was the part of interview board and was impressed by my performance and was not satisfied with the interview of son-in-law of the HOD) retired from his post. Just after the Managing Director retired, the HOD appointed his son-in-law in the desired post with the approval of the new MD", Ahmed added more. Ahmed further told me (Writer) "The son-in-law of the specific HOD held a very bad academic record as compared to me, he was also expelled twice from the university due to his bad character. He took eight years to qualify a four year engineering degree course (1996-2004) even then he was preferred over me. Do you think this is not enough loot and favouritism?" Ahmed questioned me.

"Accountability is almost none or very rare on favouritism issues in all public, semi-government and public sector autonomous organisations", said Salman Azeem, a member of civil society. "Reason for this liberty is immense administrative powers, when high ranked officials possess too much administrative and appointing powers without the need to consult the result will be same like as is now. Abuse of power has always been a great fortunate factor for the families and relatives of these high profile officers". Azeem added more.

- **Influence, Discrimination and Injustice in Public Sector Educational Institutes**

Education is a premier focus of human beings in today's modernised and globalised world, but Pakistanis are not fortunate enough like the citizens of United States and Europe to get equal and non-discriminatory opportunities for basic and higher education. As we already know that there is a multi dimensional system of education in Pakistan i.e. Religious schools or Madarsas for the population ballooning to below the poverty line, Urdu medium school and colleges for the massive fraction of population belonging to lower income groups, Partially English medium schools and colleges for middle class of the country and lastly modernised educational institutes for the elite of the country. In previous chapter we discussed the miserable conditions of public schools in Pakistan as compared to the modernised private sector educational institutes of the country.

Issues related to conditions of the staff and proper provision of funds in the public sector schools and colleges of the country has always been and continues to be a great matter of concern for all the previous governments in the country. It's in our knowledge that due to lack of funds public schools and colleges are going through worst period of their history. Lowly paid teachers, lack of basic necessities and administrative issues has caused some severe repercussions on the basic infrastructure of public schools in Pakistan. Public sector colleges are also facing some severe problems and are not able to deliver the desired results. Now let us move ahead and discuss about the heredity influence, discriminations and injustices in the highest level of educational institutes of the country that is the public sector universities.

- **Public Sector Universities in Pakistan**

Universities are considered as the highest level of educational institutes in the world, similarly in Pakistan, but there is a massive difference between renowned universities of the world and the highest level educational institutes of Pakistan. None among the top level public sector educational institutes in Pakistan is comparable in quality and character with any top university of even Asia. Names of Harvard, Cambridge, MIT (Massachusetts Institute of Technology ranked as number one in the world) are ambassadors of not only quality education but research as well in the world. On the other hand, Pakistani universities are nothing but a symbol of corruption, favouritism and nepotism. Influence of heredity exists in Pakistani universities as well and it has produced worst impacts like in the other public sector organisations.

It is a matter of fact that educational institutes are directly related with the future of the nations but here again Pakistani's are unfortunate enough that politicised and corrupt atmosphere of highest level public sector educational institutes is putting black spots on the future of the youth. After the 19th constitutional amendment, subject of education is now the responsibility of the provinces, so local politicians are now interfering massively in the affairs of public universities which are considered as autonomous organisations as compared to schools and colleges. Governors of provinces are the chancellors of universities in Pakistan but role of governor is now limited to the universities after the constitutional amendment, so chief ministers who are the political heads of the provinces have now got the authority to interference in the affairs of the universities. Though the influence of the political elite was already part of higher educational system of the country but after the 19th amendment in the constitution it has gone up to a great extent as compared to the past.

Appointment of Vice Chancellor of any university in the province is now the principal power of concerned chief minister, this power has been taken off from the governor and this action has enhanced political appointments in the universities to a great extent. As we know that governors are the constitutional heads of provinces and until lately were responsible for appointing Vice Chancellors to look into higher educational matters but in the recent past the political elite have become directly involved in the affairs of higher educational institutes of the country. According to some educational experts governors too were involved in political appointments in the universities but chief ministers are involved in massive killing of merit by promoting only their dear and near ones to very important portfolios. The experts claim that in the recent past only those candidates with strong political connections with ruling parties were promoted to the posts of Vice Chancellors.

Dr Iqrar Ahmed Khan, Vice Chancellor of University of Agriculture Faisalabad is a close relative of Punjab law minister and was appointed at this post just after the formation of PML (N) government in Punjab in the year 2008. After completing his four-year term in 2012 he was given a term extension of another four years by the chief minister as his two cousin brothers Rana Sanaullah Khan and Iftkhar Muhammad Chudhary (then Chief Justice of Pakistan) were intact at their posts. The then PML (N) leadership in Punjab took a very harsh stance against officers working under extensions and abolished contracts of dozens of retired officers who were serving in different government departments on contracts.

According to a retired Professor of above mentioned University most among the appointees on senior positions in public sector universities are dear and near ones of political elite of the country. Influence of heredity and kinship are major qualifications for the appointments on key positions in top universities of the country and University of Agriculture Faisalabad has a very notorious record in this regard. Former Vice Chancellor of UAF

Dr Bashir Ahmed was from Jatt clan and appointed in 2004 when Ch Pervaiz Elahi (who belongs to jatt clan as well) was the chief minister of Punjab. Similarly Dr Iqrar Ahmed Khan (current Vice Chancellor) is Rajput and is able to hold such a prestigious post due to the support of his cousin who is also a minister. 'Let's stop corruption in Pakistani Universities' is the article of Prof Dr (Retired) Pervaiz Hood Bhai published on January 4, 2013. Hood Bhai is a former Professor of Physics in Quied-Azam University Islamabad. Mr Hood Bhai is very much disappointed with the ongoing corruption, favouritism and nepotism in Pakistani universities and he has often discussed his opinion through his articles. According to his recent article more than 99 per cent publications of Pakistani professors (published in research journals and papers) are based upon plagiarism. Hood Bhai indicated two professors involved in this shameful act but who faced no punishments and remained intact in their positions.

To me plagiarism seems a very ordinary crime after witnessing many other heinous and shameful actions of faculty members working in Pakistani universities. Most among the faculty members and other high ranked in Pakistani public universities are involved in corruptions, favouritism, nepotism and sexual abuses. They feel free and unaccountable after doing such crimes as there is no system of real accountability to counter these types of activities in the educational institutes of the country.

A long list of crimes ongoing in public sector universities of the country being committed by faculty members and other top ranked office bearers has been mentioned above which can now be discussed one by one. Deans, directors and some other high ranked officials in the universities enjoy immense powers and benefits in the public sector universities of the country. Result of this abuse of power is massive corruption, favouritism and nepotism which has been ongoing since many years with ease and comfort. .

High ranked officials in the universities including vice chancellors, deans, chairpersons of different departments and directors are allotted billions of rupees as funds for various research projects and other projects such as constructions of new faculties, administrative blocks, hostels, etc...It's a harsh reality that research projects are a great source of corruption in the universities of Pakistan. The article of Perviaz Hood Bhai, discussed earlier indicated on plagiarism in research publications, imagine if research publications and thesis are based on plagiarism what would be the standard of research? It's very clear that with ongoing massive corruption in research projects no new innovation can be achieved through this system.

It is a great dilemma that most among the allocated funds for research in universities are used for purchase of luxury cars, furnishing offices lavishly, foreign visits, daily allowances and other luxuries of concerned officers. Junior officers working on these research projects have to put up with a lot of sufferance, they are not only very lowly paid but are treated inhumanly by the Senior Professor-bosses.

It's a great dilemma in Pakistan that most among the research projects belong to Senior Professors- the serving deans/directors of faculties. Due to academic engagements of these deans/directors it's not possible for them to have complete focus on research only so they take up research as a part time job. The provision of less than the requisite time and efforts required for research is showing severe repercussions. Less experienced and junior scientists and researchers are involved in the important phases of research in universities and they do this for pleasing their bosses. Many among the junior scientists working on research projects of senior professors are their students of PhD and M Phil. It indicates that senior professors in Pakistan working on research projects are involved in massive corruption by saving staff funds as they are not hiring staff and are utilising their PhD scholars as a staff instead. Senior professors are also involved in other money-making activities for which they are using their academic offices and equipments allotted solely for research purposes.

I asked a PhD scholar of a renowned university of the country in 2010 who was working as a research associate with a senior Professor as well as to how much he was earning from his research job. The reply astonished me very much the student replied with ease in these words "He (Professor) is my supervisor in PhD and I am still happy if he denied to pay a single penny to me as I have to complete my degree under him. Any sort of hesitation while doing his work can delay my degree for an unlimited span of time. But he is kind enough as compared to other supervisors and is paying me 8000 PKR per month and I am quite happy with his gracious attitude." To this I replied to him that as per my knowledge the project on which he was working was of high worth so then why is he getting paid so less and does this imply that all the allotted money for the research project is going into the kitty of the professor. To this once again he replied softly, "I want to get my degree and you know that the degree is in the hands of the Professor so even if he is taking all the money it should not be my concern".

Favouritism and nepotism have always been the great concerns of the ordinary Pakistani university students. As teachers possess absolute powers about the fate of students in semester system so teachers are using this absolute power for promoting favouritism and spreading injustices and discriminations through their actions. Semester system has given maximum authorities to teacher in the modernised system of education and this system is working in excellent way for the better assessment of students with the exception of Pakistan. Influence of higher fractions of society on teachers and their personal favouritism has created too many evils in this system of semesters.

Influence of heredity is utilised as a tool of discrimination in semester system of education in Pakistan. Student who is the son/daughter of University Professors/deans/directors treated as special human being by the most of teachers. Both high ranked and even low ranked university officials follow the teachers of their children for their higher grades. Most among the children of University employees get good grades and jobs in the university with the help of their parents. It looks astonishing but it's a very harsh reality that students possessing poor academic backgrounds (In schools and colleges) are getting higher grades in universities because of their parents who are serving there as Professors.

Influence of heredity is a great cause behind the sub-standard quality of education in the public sector universities of the country. There is a certain criteria of merit for ordinary citizens' children for admission in public sector universities of the country but there is absolutely no criteria of merit for the children of university employees in Pakistan. Though there is a specific quota for both the children of academic and non-academic staff of university but violation of this quota is very common. This massive violation of quota has produced severe repercussions on the academic fabric of the universities.

I (Writer) got admission in the University of Agriculture Faisalabad in the faculty of Agriculture Engineering & Technology for a four-year course. There were only two seats that were reserved for the children of the University employees that year but at least one dozen got admission against reserved seats of university employees in the undergraduate programme of Agriculture Engineering. University authorities however feel no accountability for the occurrence of these illegal actions.

Now we will discuss how influence of heredity is sabotaging the merit on the basis of favouritism. Most among the public sector university teachers like to promote sons/daughters of their colleagues. This kinship fetches high grades for these underrated students. I will give you two examples to understand this fact. Abdul Nabi (son of former vice chancellor of UAF) got admission in the University of Agriculture Faisalabad in 2003 on reserved quota due to being the son of dean of faculty. Abdul though was a hard working guy (now settled in Canada) but was not such a highly talented as to become a candidate for gold medal. After the end of first semester, Abdul was on tenth position, many among his class fellows claim that his ranking within the top ten was just because of his father who was the dean of faculty of Agriculture Economics at that time. Abdul was fortunate enough that after the completion of has first semester his father Professor Bashir got the prestigious office of vice chancellor due to his political connections, and from here started a new journey of success and glory for Abdul.

Dr Bashir Ahmed took the office of vice chancellor in April 2004 when his son Abdul completed his first semester in Faculty of Agriculture

Engineering. From the very first day of his second semester he was the son of a vice chancellor. The student who was at the tenth position (that too with the influence of his father the then dean of faculty of Agriculture Economics), started to get highest GPA (Grade Point Average) in every semester and completed his degree with gold medal in 2007. Abdul who did not even get admission through merit seat but through special quota of the university employees got a scholarship of UAF in Asian Institute of Technology Bangkok just due to his father's contacts and arrangements. Abdul Nabi did his Masters in Engineering from Bangkok and is now settled in Canada.

I would like to give another example of influence of heredity in Pakistani universities though it could harm relationship between me and a very good friend of mine. Late Muhammad Ishtiaq was the registrar of Islamiya University of Bahawalpur during 2005-11 (until his unfortunate death by accident). Muhammad Hassan a very good friend of mine (nephew of Muhammad Ishtiaq) was an ordinary student throughout his academic career, he got grade B in Matriculation, D in intermediate and C in graduation but he completed his Masters degree in Business Administration with excellence (Got GPA 3.6/4) from the same university where his uncle got an important portfolio. Former registrar Muhammad Ishtiaq not only worked for the good grades of his nephew but he was also involved in massive abuse of power and appointed his younger nephew as lecturer in the department of business administration. Ishtiaq also inducted some more relatives of his family in important positions and faced severe allegations of corruption in different projects as well.

Recruitments in autonomous public sector organisations like in universities has always remained controversial in Pakistan due to various faults. Not only influence of heredity is killing the merit but political and bureaucratic pressure is also a great hurdle in the way of merit and justice in these organisations. Last governments of PPP (2008-13) have a notorious record in this regard. There was massive pressure on public office holders from the political elite of the country during this span of time to induct their dear and near ones on very important port folios. Both mainstream and local leaders of PPP faced immense allegations for massively interfering in the matters of the public sector organisations.

Bhau din Zikriya University of Multan and Islamiya University Bahawalpur remained in lime light due to interference of the political elite in these organisations throughout the PPP lead government during 2008-13. Top leadership of PPP was from south Punjab (Prime Minister and foreign minister were from Multan during this span of time) so its leadership was fully involved in political appointments and admissions of students by violating rules in all the higher education institutes all over Pakistan particularly in the southern part of Punjab. Yousaf Raza Gillani (former prime minister of Pakistan 2008-12) and his sons faced severe allegations of receiving bribes for appointments in public sector organisations particularly in the universities of south Punjab.

"I was the candidate for the post of administration officer in BZU Multan in 2010", said Saim Raza a young Master Degree holder from the city of Multan. "I did Masters in business administration with silver medal and had two years of work experience as well" Raza continued. "So I considered myself among the likely candidates for selection for the twelve advertised posts of administration officer, but I was highly astonished when I did not get any interview call even after two months. I waited, waited and waited for the call of interview for a long span of time but my call never came so I decided to contact university administration. They told me recruitments were done on merit and as my name was not included in the merit list so I was not eligible even for the interview. I thought that if I am not eligible then were all those selected gold medallists? I found the answer to my question within a week when I came to know that one of my friends who had applied for the same post had been selected, I wondered how come that guy with very ordinary academic record happened to get selected. To know this I contacted him, initially he claimed that he was selected on merit but when I quizzed regarding his academic records, (as he had studied with me in matriculation and intermediate and I was familiar with his later records as well and knew that he had always been a second division holder) he disclosed the fact that he had paid eight lakhs (0.8 million) PKR to a very renowned political figure of that time for being selected for the post."

Another candidate who also applied for the same post (Administration officer in BZU Multan) said that he contacted a senior journalist for influencing the then vice chancellor (as he was an active guy and was fully familiar with the fact that no one can get job without influence and bribe in BZU) Professor Dr Zafarullah, the vice chancellor told the aspirant in front of the intermediating journalist that he has now no authority for appointments as all the twelve seats had already been distributed among the favourite candidates of Yousaf Raza Gillani (then prime minster), Shah Mehmood Quershi (then foreign minister of Pakistan), Javeed Hashmi (then Senior vice president of PML(N) ruling party in Punjab) and Ahmed Hassan Dehar (then member of Punjab assembly of PPP from Multan). Dr Zafarullah also admitted in front of that journalist (in a private meeting) that he was facing immense pressure from the top leadership of PPP for political appointments in the University.

I (Writer) was once travelling by public transport between the two cities of south Punjab in 2010. Sitting beside the driver who appeared to be a neat and clean man to me as compared to other drivers running Omni pubic busses, I ventured into a little gossip with him. I started discussing the political situation with him (as it is almost a tradition in Pakistan that commoners discuss on politics in public places). The young driver (aged between twenty five to twenty eight) seemed very satisfied with the performance of PPP led government in the centre which was very astonishing to me as massive majority of his class (lower income groups) was very much against the government (as it always happens in a third world country like Pakistan that majority among the masses always hates the governments). I was highly shocked at his response as massive fraction of commoners were decrying the massive electricity failure, unemployment and hunger whereas he was satisfied with the performance of the government, but the secret was unveiled very soon. Considering me as an educated and decent guy (He was unaware that I was a journalist) he disclosed his reason for preference for the PPP government.

"I got appointment letter for the job in BPS 14 in BZU Multan and I am joining next week", he told me softly. I was stunned at his answer so I asked. "You are a driver what is your qualification?" he replied, "I have done Intermediate from private four years back and I was running my family business of transport, we own three twenty two seater vans, I am ruining this one and two other are in the custodies of our drivers". "But how you got this job?", I asked him. "Actually one of my uncles is a private secretary of Makhddom Shah Mehommod Querishi and I got this job as Shah Mehommod is foreign minister of Pakistan", he replied with ease.

Part II

Silence is a Crime

"Injustice anywhere is a threat to justice everywhere"
—Martin Luther King Junior

Being the follower of Martin Luther King Junior I feel it's my prime duty to raise myself against the massive, ongoing, widespread and deep rooted socioeconomic injustices with the ordinary masses of my country imposed by the minute fraction of the ruling elite. It's a great blessing of the Almighty on me that like my hero I too have spent an immense portion of my life in fighting against corruption, injustice, discrimination and cruel attitudes and behaviours though my writings and vocal communications from the very beginning of my life. These evils are very deep-rooted among the massive fraction of population in my home land but I am still hopeful and passionate that my extensive efforts since the very beginning of my life will have atleast some positive impact.

Martin Luther King Junior paid a heavy price for his vocal voice and dreams, among many of his dreams very rare came true in his very short life span of thirty nine years but his fight against discrimination and injustice produced very long-lasting and durable repercussions on the American society even after his death. He was against discrimination on the bases of religion, race, colour and clan and he had a dream to see United States as a country free from all biased attitudes and with regard for the freedom and rights of every citizen. I too have a dream today and I also want my country to be free from the culture of influence of heredity, discrimination on the bases of clan and cast, favouritism, nepotism and economic imbalance. Out of twenty eight years of my life massive portion has gone in cherishing such dreams and struggling immensely for making this dream to come true and unfold as reality as a happy, progressive and prosperous Pakistan. But I too am facing massive socioeconomic pressure like majority among the 192 million Pakistanis. It's a fact of the day that life is cruel enough for me and massive fraction of population in this part of the world and we do not know whether our dreams of timely justice, socioeconomic equality and political equilibrium will live or die before the end of our life spans in this so called land of pure but one thing we know that the struggle for betterment will continue, as my hero had said "If you can't fly then run, If you can't run then walk, If you can't walk then crawl but whatever you do you have to keep moving forward". Hence I too am moving forward and raising my voice as I feel that silence is a crime.

4

Triangle of Feudal, Industrial and Bureaucratic Elite

Truly speaking triangle of feudal, industrial and bureaucratic (Here we include superior judiciary also as a part of bureaucratic elite usually civilian-military bureaucracy is only considered part of bureaucratic elite) elite has captured the whole country the name of which is Islamic Republic of Pakistan. Here, life is life for only the above mentioned factions of the population. The remaining ones are living like reptiles. It is a fact of the day that in modern day Pakistan feudal lords, industrial tycoons and civil-military bureaucrats possess absolute and infinite powers which they have been exercising on the deprived factions of the society since the last sixty eight years with full ease and comfort.

Some people may find the above mentioned fact awkward that everything in Pakistan revolves around the three factions of the feudalists, industrialists and bureaucrats yet the political elite have not found mention, here one should keep in mind that the members of the parliament (upper and lower house) and even the provincial assemblies are none other than the representatives of the feudal and industrial elite of the country so whenever we discuss the latter the political elite would be included along with them. It is almost impossible for even the educated middle class of the country to attain presence in any fraction of parliament (fraction of lower middle class can't even think about it) as more than 95 per cent among the parliamentarians belongs to super elite and elite classes. Only a minute fraction (less than 5 per cent) belongs to more than middle class which is a very small fraction of population between the elite and upper middle class.

Above mentioned all factions of population are closely associated with each other in modern day Pakistan and support each other in matters of mutual interests. The traditional feudal elite of the country have close ties with the bureaucratic fraction as well as the emerging and established industrial tycoons.

The industrialist fraction of the society is also smart enough and it too maintains good relationships with the other two factions. Civil-military bureaucracy also attains its interests with the help of feudal and industrial factions of elite; hence all the three factions are working for their own mutual interests. Let's have a look on their mutual bindings and its repercussions.

- **Feudal Elite of Pakistan**

Feudalism (a system of land agreement between the vassals and land owners where the vassals providing military services were given rights to own land) has become a part of history in most parts of the modern world including Europe, Central and South East Asia even South Asia with the exception of Pakistan, though some form of it is still remaining in few parts of the world including Oceania and North America, yet feudals still present in the continent of America are not so cruel as their counterparts are in Asia. Europe which was considered as the home of feudalism during ninth to sixteenth century is now among the most civilised and developed part of the world.

Generally feudalism is a result of decentralisation of rule of law and empire, if we have a look on European feudalism it emerged due to lack of bureaucratic infrastructure. The feudals of medieval Europe attained powers amidst very weak and shaken fabrics of states which helped them to establish their monarchs. Feudalism started to flourish in sixth century AD in Great Britain and was an integral part of English society until 1660 but even in the era of feudalism there was a proper channel of land agreements between the landlords and the vassals. In Pakistan, Hari and Mazara are the terminologies used for feudatories.

Feudalism in the great Roman Empire was a politico-economic system established in the latter Middle Ages. This system was based on Roman client ship and social hierarchy of lords and retainers. The Lord was responsible for providing food, protection, and shelter to the vassals (a terminology for land retainers or feudatory). Relationship of lord and vassal was not such as that of a master and slave like in modern day Pakistan but it was based upon mutual cooperation and respect. Feudal system in modern Roman Empire was based upon two components of personal and material elements. The personal element helped sustaining mutual commitment and loyalty between lords and vassals while material element enabled fulfilment of mutual commercial interests.

Contrary to above motioned system of feudalism the Waderos, Sardars, Chudharies and Maliks (different titles for the feudal lords of Pakistan) of Pakistan are not familiar with the norms of humanity and piousness. The feudal elite in the land of pure is expert enough in following the traditions and norms based upon pure cruel attitude.

"Wadero or Sardar is the most important part of the rural society in interior Sind, southern part of the Punjab and Baluchistan after the Almighty", so said Salman Ali a human right activist from Islamabad. "Disobedience of a feudal lord in above mentioned parts of the country could produce very severe repercussions including death sentences, imprisonment for life (feudal factions of the country have their own private detention centres where they imprison their self created culprits) and corporal punishments, such practices are very familiar among this fraction of population which they impose on their bonded feudatories. Feudal elite in almost every part of the country have created their socioeconomic and political estates and have imposed certain sanctions on all the feudatories living within the premises of their estates", Ali added more.

Many among the renowned (more than 90 per cent) feudal families in the country are part of the political elite of the country as well. Feudal fraction of the society has shown its great presence in almost every political group of the country since the birth of the country and they are involved in continuously changing their political loyalties but their vote bank always remains intact due to the influence of their heredity estates which has been passed down their generations since hundreds of years. Great Britain which ruled the Sub-continent for about 200 years (Though the time span of direct rule is not more than 90 years from 1857-1947 but it prolongs due to indirect rule since 1757) with a small army and limited resources with the help of this feudal fraction which worked for the Englishmen against their own countrymen only for attaining their personal commercial interests. Division of Indians between the feudal lords (who provided support to the British rule in India) and ordinary masses proved to be a great benefit to the Britishers for sustaining their rule. A massive fraction of population (either deprived or not) possess an attitude of hatred against the feudal fraction of the society as they feel that the forefathers of these feudal elite played a vital role in strenghthening the foreign rule in the Sub-continent.

"It is a proven fact that group of criminals and other mafias provided their strengths for the sustainability of British rule in the Subcontinent and later above mentioned fraction was rewarded by Great Britain with massive pieces of lands", said Baba Nizam-Din an eighty two years old retired Head Master. "Above mentioned fraction ordered massive massacre of their country fellows whenever British rule in the Subcontinent faced any kind of danger. After the division of the Subcontinent the Britishers left but we are still slaves of that fraction which was imposed on us by the Englishmen. Partition of the Subcontinent brought massive relief for the Indians as India abolished all feudal estates through strict land reforms just after independence but nothing has changed in this miserable piece of land even after independence", Baba added more.

If we make an analysis about the nomenclature of feudalism in Pakistan its composition would be different in every part of the country. In most parts of the interior Sind and South Punjab most feudals are chief of the tribe as well. Tumandar is a specific word used in most parts of South Punjab and interior Sind to represent the chieftain. Most chieftains also hold vital positions in the mainstream political parties i.e. PPP, PML (N) and PTI of the country. Mazrai, Lughari (former President of the country Sardar Farooq Laghari was the chieftain of Laghrai tribe), Khoso, Mangi, Mugasi, Bhutto and many others….are the important tribes of South Punjab and Sind –occupying key positions in the politics of the country.

Having thousands of acres of land, harem of dozens of wives, army of thousands of servants, private militias and many such luxuries –the feudal lords in Pakistan possess the grander and style more than an ancient King. Feudal elite of the country is very unfamiliar for abiding the laws and regulations imposed by state for the provision of strength to very fabric of the state. Police and other law enforcing agencies find themselves disabled to a great extent in front of this fraction which considers itself above the law. As we discussed earlier massive fraction of feudal elite in the country have their own detention centres where they keep their feudatories and enemies. Some victims of the feudal elite spend their whole lives behind the bars and only their dead bodies came out after their deaths.

According to Ahmed Khan, a small framer from interior part of Sind, "The feudal elite of Sind and Baluchistan has made slaves of the masses generation after generation. If a feudal lord is being cruel with any of my fellow (even if he is not among the feudatories) I will not raise my voice in favour of my fellow as it will bring severe repercussions for me as well". According to Shujat Ali Rohi, an author working on bonded labour, more than 1.7 million people in Pakistan are forced to work as a bonded labour. Massive fraction of this labour is detained in the farms of the feudal lords of the country. Culture of private prisons is very popular among the feudal lords in Pakistan, landlords with more prisoners are considered of more worth among the feudal elite of the country.

According to Tariq Hussein, a human right activist from Lahore, "No government in the country ever provided any serious attention to the issue of bonded labour detained by the feudal fraction of the country. Ruling elite of the country consider this fraction of population lesser deserving than their animal pets hence what more can we expect from them for the deliverance of these miserable creatures", he added more...

- **Repercussions of Feudalism in Pakistan**

Feudalism has not only produced absolute authority of this fraction on their feudatories and ordinary masses living within the premises of their estates but it has produced severe socioeconomic repercussions on all factions of the society. It has been a great cause for increasing the level of poverty and for sabotaging the process of industrialisations-undertaken to enhance the economic growth of the country.

"Feudal fraction of the society is very much against the education of the masses especially of girls living within their territories", said Ayesha a twenty six years old lady - an active human right activist from Lahore. "One big reason for a large number of non-functional or ghost schools in most parts of the interior Sind and South Punjab are the feudal elites who want to keep massive fraction of the population ignorant and deprived. Civil society and human right organisations in the country are focusing enough on the education of girls of the rural deprived factions as it will be helpful to bring radical changes in the society, but above mentioned mafia of the elite is a great hindrance to it", Ayesha added more.

Feudalism in most parts of the country has not only put up a massive challenge for the writs of the state but it has also caused severe repercussions on the system of policing. As massive fraction of the feudal elite of the country is an integral part of the political elite of the country as well and leaders of most political dynasties in the country are the representatives of the feudal elite, so due to the high influence of the feudal lords in bureaucracy the Police is always fearful of them. Usually police heads of districts and divisions are appointed by the administration after consultations with the local lords and they always like to be in the good books of this feudal-cum-political elite of the country.

Police station known as Thana in Pakistan is a basic unit of policing which is commanded by an Inspector or Sub Inspector sometimes referred to as SHO (Station House Officer). Police Inspectors or SHOs belong to second category of police officers who are not recruited through the federal prime competitive exam but recruited either through internal exam of police department or via second level competitive exam conducted by the provincial governments are very much dependent on local feudal politicians for their appointments and postings. They also face lot of pressures during their postings in the specific territories belonging to the feudal factions so majority among this portion of police abides the feudal elite of the country for the sake of their job and promotions. As massive fraction of population in the country is deprived enough and it is very difficult to attain a government job for a commoner so Police officials (Public servants) want to readily oblige and obey the feudal lords for saving their jobs.

"It's almost impossible to get an employment in public sector of the country without giving bribe and using political influence", said Ali Bukhari a Master Degree holder of BZU Multan. I had given applications for dozens of jobs in public sector organisations but I was not on the receiving end (failed to get even an interview letter). I completed my degree with distinctions but there is no space for me in this system as I belong to the deprived fraction of the society", he added more.

During the process of writing of this book I (Writer) tried my level best to gather information from various sources. I collected the point of view of different socioeconomic classes and also reached out to the factions of different school of thoughts. During this process I keenly observed the lavish life style of super elite and elite factions of the society and their attitude towards the commoners. I also witnessed the conflicts and depressions among the massive factions of deprived population, wide gaps between the upper and lower factions of income groups which has produced severe repercussions on the very fabric of the state. Heinous increase in crime and dacoit groups in both rural and urban societies of Pakistan is a result of massive gulf between rich and poor.

One major repercussion of feudalism in the country is the attitude of hatred and harshness among different social classes of the country. One may easily observe a very tense and heinous attitude of both lower and upper income factions of the society towards each other. Relationships between land owners and feudatories are too different from above mentioned factions of the Great Roman Empire. Dictatorial attitude of the upper fraction (other than feudal elite) of population including tycoons of industry and business towards lower fraction of the society is also a repercussion of feudalism. It is a matter of fact that human beings have always been inspired with the surroundings of which he is a part so when fraction of industrial and business elite of the country witnessed the inhuman attitude of feudalists with their feudatories they too adopted the same behaviour with their detained (Industrial elite of the country also detain a massive fraction of deprived population working on very low wages for them) ones for attaining their own benefits and objectives.

Feudalism no doubt is responsible for spreading a sort of dictatorship in every powerful fraction of the society. Anyone from any fraction i.e. industry, business, bureaucracy or other factions of the society possessing wealth or authority behaves like a feudal. To understand it lets have a look at this example.

"This society has gone down to such extent that each one from the powerful factions of the society is involved in snatching everything from the deprived ones", said Shazia a twenty eight years old lady secretary of a Managing Director of a pesticide company. "My boss who already has two wives flirts with the girls working in the company, though I am her lady secretary but the frequent forced sexual relationship with him has categorised me in the line of his unofficial wives. I have been fulfilling his sexual desires since a long span of time and I will keep doing this for keeping my job which helps me to fend for myself in this cruel world", she added more.

- **Industrial and Business Mafias in Pakistan**

Before writing this book I studied many autobiographies of renowned leaders which have discussed the socioeconomic mafias in various parts of the world. The Malay Dilemma, written by Dr Mahathir Muhammad (Prime Minister of Malaysia during 1981-2003) published in 1970 was really a fabulous effort in this context and inspired me a lot. I do not feel myself so courageous as Dr Mahathir was but even then I will try my level best to be more vocal against the ongoing socioeconomic injustices and discriminations imposed by various kinds of mafia's including the industrial and business elite of the country in Pakistan. Let us now discuss some aspects about the above mentioned factions who are involved in the exploitation of commoners.

Though Pakistan is basically an agricultural country but industry and business (agro based industry and agriculture businesses are playing more part in the economy) are also going on side by side with its economy. Ease of doing business in Pakistan ranked 107th in the world but even then some industries and businesses have flourished here and are now playing their important part (though not accordingly) in GDP (Gross domestic product). We have discussed earlier that massive fraction of industry i.e. sugar, textile, oil mills etc. is associated with agriculture in Pakistan and accounts for 24 per cent of its GDP. Textiles possess key importance among all industries in the country and massive fraction of industrial exports belongs to the textile sector in Pakistan.

With more than 20.30 million industrial labourers, Pakistan is among the relatively flourished industrial estate among the deprived part of the world. Like many other lesser developed countries industry is not much beneficial for the lower income fraction who are an integral part of the industrial production. A massive fraction of technicians and even highly educated professionals are exploited badly by the industrial mafia. Majority among the labour working for the industrialists are in the same circumstances like the feudatories of the country as most industrialists are cruel like their rural counterparts (feudalists/feudal lords).

"Massive fraction of the industrial class in the country is like another type of feudalists, involved in the same sort of exploitations like the agricultural landlords of the country", said Tariq Kamal, an NGO worker from Faisalabad. "Fact of the day in modern Pakistan is that rural landholders are the rural Masters while urban tycoons are the urban Masters for the massive fraction of population in the country. Both suck the blood of the commoners by utilising their own tactics", he added more. Hashim a thirty eight years old manager of a cotton factory in South Punjab also looked very disappointed with the attitude of his boss (owner) and blamed him for massive exploitation. These beasts (indicating towards the industrial elite) do not consider us as a human being even if we perform 24/7 for them said Hashim. I am working for my owner for last twelve years even then he is not willing to support me in any difficult situation. My child was very ill and I demanded one salary in advance but he denied at once, that moment I felt that either I am still a stranger for him or he has no heart and emotions", Hashim added more.

It's a proven fact that in this civilised and modern world of today, industrial progress is mostly directly proportional to progress and prosperity of its common country folk. But the commoners of underdeveloped countries like Pakistan are suffering a lot even if these countries possess industrial infrastructure and only a small fraction of population is benefiting from it. Faction of industrial elite is making money at a very rapid rate with cunning tactics like tax evasions, artificial price hikes etc., this fraction is involved in the exploitation of the interests of both commoners and government. According to a latest report of Federal Board of Revenue (FBR) the tax evasion in the country is more than 1000 billion PKR and massive fraction of this theft is committed by the industrial and business tycoons of the country.

Sugar, fertilizers, steel, cement and textile industries are considered among the heavy industries and they belong to the giant industrial groups comprising of the political elite of the country as well. Ruling Sharif family (Premier Nawaz Sharif, CM Punjab Shabaz Sharif are the prominent members) is engaged in steel, sugar, poultry and medicine industries alongside with a massive business of real estate in Pakistan and abroad. Former President of Pakistan and now the co-chairman of PPP, Asif Ali Zaradari -c (the Bhutto dynasty party is currently the second largest party in parliament) is also running several other businesses in the major industries of the country. Mr Zardari being the chieftain of Zardari tribe also posseses thousands of acres of land but he has established himself as an industrialist as well.

It's a great concern of modern day Pakistan that above mentioned fraction of industrial and business tycoons are multiplying their wealths with the utilisation of public money. This fraction is writing off debts from public and semi-government banks and is involved in massive tax evasions, but the concerned accountable authorities have always failed to nail them as they (the industrialists) are the integral parts of the mainstream political parties of the country and hold political clout.

It is very astonishing that all the privileged factions i.e. Feudal, Industrial and bureaucratic elite of the society are closely associated with each other in terms of clan and kinship in Pakistan. Commoners in the country are deprived enough and massive fraction among them feels that coordination and relationships among the elite factions of the society is the cause of severe repercussions on the ordinary ones. Now let's have a look on what the commoners think about the above mentioned association.

- **Exploitations of Commoners by Industrial Fraction**

"There were only twenty two feudal-cum-politician families in the era of General Ayub (military ruler Ayub's regime was during 1958-69) involved in loot and corruption of national resources but now this has increased to five hundred", said Roshan Ali a secondary school teacher belonging to the deprived area of South Punjab. "We blame the feudal fraction of the society for these miserable circumstances but what would you say about the cruelty of industrialist and bureaucratic elite of the country? There is a sugar mill in my area and I am familiar with the tactics it utilises for looting the poor farmers during the sugarcane season but it will never come under the court's notice as bureaucratic elite in the administration and judiciary is supporting the industrialists of the mill to get their own share from them.", he added more.

Public and private banks support different types of industries through loans in most parts of the world, and similar is situation in Pakistan as well. Both public and commercial (commercial bank is a terminology used in Pakistan to represent private banking system) banks are supporting industrial and business factions of the society but this fraction is utilising debt as a tool to enhance their assets only. Heavy industries like sugar, steel, fertilizers, textile and cement needs lot of investments for their operations and massive fraction of this type of industrialists are financing their businesses and operations through above mentioned financial sources.

Concept of public-private partnership revolves around the participations of public money in private sector and vice versa. In most parts of the developed and civilised world governments are the shareholders in many private organisations for the protection of labour rights, reciprocally many factions of private sector invest in public sector projects as well. This mutual cooperation between governments and masses is helpful for the provision of strength to the very fabrics of the states. It was the year 2009 when General Motors, a giant industrial group of United States (largest automobile company in the world possessing assets of 167 billion dollars and twenty one thousand nine hundred employees) came under severe economic circumstances and was near to collapse. On July 10th 2009 above mentioned organisation was bankrupt and most of its plants stopped working and its brands Hummer, Pontic and Statrun were closed and Swedish brand Saab was sold out. At this juncture United States government involved itself in this affair and a bailout package of two billion dollars was approved by the Senate of United States for the provision of relief to the organisation and purchased thirty three per cent of its shares for the sake of survival of the company. Above mentioned action provided a great strength to the company and it got success in attaining its pervious prestige in the world market, currently General Motors is earning more than five billion net profit (5.32 billion dollars, 2013) annually. Above mentioned example describes the public-private partnership in a very good manner where public money was utilised for the provision of relief to both industrialist and masses. Bail out package for General Motors not only secured the employments of the twenty two thousand staff but it also helped the industrialists.

Massive fraction of Pakistani industrial groups are also gaining loans and financial assistances from public sector organisations in Pakistan but this practice is not providing any good repercussions on workers working in these organisations as benefits attained through this way is fetching only for the upper faction. Industrial mafias in Pakistan are involved in various types of corruptions like theft of electricity and gas, exploitation of labour etc. and writing off their loans. Writing off loans has been utilised as a smart tool for the loot of public money in Pakistan since a long span of time by this industrial fraction of the society. Massive fraction of industrial class attained loans of billions of rupees against their businesses which is never returned back, this has produced severe repercussions on the economy of country. According to a report of Daily The News (considered among the leading English Language Newspapers in the country) published on December 02, 2009, more than hundred billion PKR loans were written off during the regime of Military Dictator Pervaiz Musharraff (1999-2008). Report stated that massive fraction of written off loans during that era belonged to industrialists only. As we discussed earlier that industrialists, feudalists and bureaucrats are among the most privileged classes so other factions who are involved in writing off loans are feudal lords cum politicians and civil-military bureaucracy.

It is a great concern of modern day Pakistan that industrial groups running their outlets on public money treat the common public in a very inhuman manner. Labours working in big industrial groups of the country are not paid as per the labour laws and get meagre wages and facilities. In the year 2014, an ordinary layman was not able to earn more than seven or eight thousand PKR per month (US dollars 70-80) which is not sufficient for the expenditure of even a single human being in this period of massive inflation in Pakistan. Above mentioned fraction of deprived class is living in very miserable circumstances due to their extensive work and minute earnings. Faction of industrial elite is not exploiting the unskilled labours but it exudes a cruel attitude towards the qualified and skilled fraction of workers as well.

"There is enough exploitation of skilled and educated fraction of population in the industrial groups of the country", said Anjum Ahmed a twenty nine years old accounts degree holder from Multan working in a renowned industrial group in Raiwind (a town adjacent to Lahore). After completing Bachelors in Commerce I qualified the exam of ACCA (Association of Chartered Certified Accountants) but I am getting only 25000 PKR per month with the working experience of three years. A person of my calibre and class is getting 3000-4000 pounds in UK per month, I also want to go to UK as soon as possible as there is nothing for me in this country", Ahmed added more.

National Reconciliation Ordinance commonly called as NRO was a controversial ordinance issued by former military dictator Pervaiz Musharraff on 5th of October as a result of a political deal between military ruler and former prime minister (Late) Benazir Bhutto the then chairperson of PPP. Above mentioned ordinance provided amnesties to politicians (massive fraction of these politicians were part of industrial and feudal elite), bureaucrats and political workers against their accused crimes such as money laundering, corruption, murder, terrorism etc. registered during January 1, 1986 to October 12, 1999. Though this ordinance was declared null and void later (December 16, 2009) but its beneficiaries are still able to avoid the consequences of the orders of Superior courts. NRO no doubt enhanced the culture of loot, fraud and corruption among all factions of the society.

- **Business Mafias in Pakistan**

"Business mafias in Pakistan are involved in massive loot and frauds of commoners like other factions of their types", said Salman Sheikh a gazetted officer from Gujranwala. This mafia is responsible for artificial price hikes and inflation in the country to a great extent, apparently it seems that ongoing price hikes and massive inflation is due to the worst economic policies implemented by different governments in their regimes and this is true to a great extent but one can't neglect the role of above mentioned mafias as well as this fraction too is looting the commoners with both hands. Materialism and greed has become so much widespread in this fraction of population that they are growing at a rapid rate even more than the Sicilian mafia (belongs to criminal syndicate in Sicily Italia 1800) and a government officer like me is facing enough difficulties for survival due to this massive price hike and inflation in the society during the last few years", Sheikh added more.

It's a proven fact that business communities in Pakistan are enjoying nill or very less accountabilities and are rarely checked by concerned authorities. Ruling Sharif family also belongs to an industrial dynasty, father of prime minister (Late) Muhammad Sharif started his business in 1935 with a borrowed sum of five hundred rupees but now the Sharifs are among the richest families in the country. One massive fraction of population which is deprived enough strongly believes that the ruling Sharif family only likes to protect the interests of industrial and business class of the country, a fraction of the population even believes that these rulers (Sharifs) are giving hyper protection to the above mentioned business factions as massive portion of business and industrial community are supporting PML(N) - the political party led by Sharif.

"We support the Sharifs as they too are businessmen like us", said Sheikh Amir a leading cloth merchant in South Punjab. Zardari regime (indicating the government of PPP 2008-13) was not good enough for us as he (Asif Ali Zardari, former President of Pakistan) was not willing to facilitate the business community of the country. Feudal and the class of public servants were happy enough during the previous government as PPP favoured enough the civil servants and doubled their salaries, but now is our turn as we too want to gain something from this system", Amir added more.

Inflation has been a great matter of concern during the most part of the history but now it has become a great danger for the economy. Devaluation of Pakistani rupee vis-a-vis the United States dollar has produced severe repercussions on the economy during last few years. It's very obvious that when rupee is devalued prices go up and these circumstances are favourable for business mafias who are looting the commoners by using inflation against the commoners and in their own favour, so inflation has become a great source of surplus income generation for the massive fraction of business community in the country. This has been explained below through an example for better understanding.

Fuel price increment is responsible for the price hikes in Pakistan, currently premier oil normally called as petrol (used in most of the vehicles of the country) costs 104 rupee per litre which is very much higher than the other parts of the world according to price of per barrel in international market, Pakistani's are unfortunate enough that they are forced to pay heavy levy on oil goods which is a great source of income generation for the government. Even a minute increment in price of petrol can increase the price of everything in the country, let's suppose petrol price goes up to 107 PKR per litre then there would an increment (massive one) in fairs of transport and shopkeepers will charge much higher for cloth, grocery and many other ordinary goods of common human use by describing a counter effect of hike in petrol prices.

In the year 2014, inflation rate in the country has gone up too much and currently it is 11.7 per cent, as a result prices have also risen rapidly during this year. This has produced severe repercussions on both consumers and the economy.

"Inflation has produced price hike up to five hundred times during last five years in the country", said Mrs Hussein Shah a housewife from Multan. "Minute increment in salaries among the serving class is not able to bear the pressure of rapidly growing increment in prices that's why life style of middle class is going down every year. Being a housewife I have to manage all expenditures of my family and it seems now that salary of my husband is falling short in front of rapidly growing inflation. I used to do shopping every season in recent past but now I can hardly shop only once in year as prices are going higher every year. I purchased a suit (an unstitched cloth) for 2500

PKR in 2013 but the very next year price of the same fabric went up to 4000 and this seems very astonishing sometimes because such type of price hike is only possible in this part of the world," she added more.

This year (2014) inflation is much higher alongside there are some other factors as well producing severe repercussions on the economy and affecting the massive factions of commoners. Balance between demand and supply is another factor which plays a vital role for keeping prices under control but here in Pakistan exist certain mafias who excessively stock everything and later sell them at very high prices. For example, country is suffering from electricity crises since a long span of time so there is a huge difference between the demand and production of electricity so massive fraction of population is now heavily dependent on generators and investors for the provision of relief during the absence of electricity. Provision of electricity in Pakistan is totally dependent on government power production and distribution companies which have failed to deliver and there exists a massive shortfall of upto 10,000 MW causing ten to twelve hours of load shedding in every part of the country. Over and above, mafias operating in the power sector of the country decided to make loot from these miserable circumstances and there exists an artificial shortage of generators, inverters and batteries every year in summers which have enhanced their rates by hundreds of times during the last few years. The price of a generator of minute capacity was 55,000-75,000 in 2011 but now the price has gone up to more than 20,00,000 . Hence above mentioned mafia has earned billions of rupees during last three years. In a nut shell we can say that business mafias in the country are no different from their feudal and industrial counterparts and are also involved in loot and fraud.

- **Glimpse of Civil-Military Bureaucracy in Pakistan**

Composition of civil-military bureaucracy usually called as establishment in Pakistan is considered as the most important fraction of power here. Being the most important part of the very fabric of the state above mentioned fraction is considered responsible for every wrong and right as massive fraction of population believes that everything belongs to establishment. After Allah and America (Majority fraction of population also believe that United States is directly or indirectly fully involved in all important affairs of the country) in Pakistan. It's a fact of the day that in modern day Pakistan both military and civilian bureaucracies are enjoying infinite powers and privileges with nill or very rare fear of accountability and play an integral part in the power circle of country.

With more than 7,25,000 active troops, Pakistan army is the sixth largest in the world and consider as the largest and most expanded organisation of the country in every sense. Country is spending a lot (more than 24.5 per cent of GDP is allocated for army in every fiscal year) on its armed forces or is forced to do so due to its complicated geo strategic position. Military directly ruled the country for more than thirty three years during its short history of sixty seven years and even now in the present era the military still commands an important pillar of power game in the country. Apparently democratic process has been restored in the country since 2008 after the resignation of the last military ruler but still Pakistan seems much a far from being a truly democratic country. Military is still playing an active part (as it always did) by dictating foreign policy alongside with other matters of its interest and fraction of the political elite has not yet been successful in proving its supremacy in strategic decision making and policy issues.

Four military dictators including Ayub Khan (1958-69), Yahya Khan (1969-71), Zia-Ul-Haq (1977-88), and Pervaiz Musharraff (1999-2008) ruled the country for almost thirty four years in different intervals through their extra constitutional actions (by imposing martial laws and suspending the constitution). This fraction of dictators enjoyed more powers than any civilian ruler and ruled like Kings but even then they failed to bring any socioeconomic reforms or improvement in the living standards of the majority of the country folk. A massive fraction of analysts alongside the political factions and civil society of modern day Pakistan concedes that military rule has caused severe repercussions on the very fabric of the country. A massive fraction of journalist and intellectuals of the society also blames above mentioned military dictators for sabotaging the constitution to fulfil their personal interests. According to this fraction of intellectuals extra constitutional actions of military dictators are responsible for providing the base to ongoing corruptions, loot, fraud, injustice and anarchy in the country.

Fact of the day in modern Pakistan is severe enough about democracy when massive fraction of existing political elite in the country is still accepting the supremacy of military against the parliament due to its hyper active role since the very beginning of the country's history. Though during the tiny periods of democracy (between the intervals of martial laws) political fraction tried to build itself as a force against the conventional power of military but every time it failed due to many reasons, one such reason being that military leaders always thought themselves as superior and the political elite as incompetent and so always tried to impose their decisions and dictations even when the democratic forces were voted into power. Moreover, corruption and scams of political factions also provided the military an alibi to play its role through the back door even during the democratic regimes.

"Without the military and ISI (Inter Services Intelligence, the premier secret service working for national security of Pakistan-ranked among the top intelligence agencies in the world) no one can form a government in Pakistan and we look like their poodles sometimes", said a former minister (name disguised) cum feudal from South Punjab. "Politicians are considered responsible for evil here and in modern day Pakistan every Tom, Dick and Harry are talking about the accountability of politicians which is a very good thing and I appreciate it but there is no talk about the accountability of those who are responsible for the involvement in extra constitutional actions for their own personal interest. This fraction is not only sabotaging the constitution but is also dragging the political factions towards corruption in the name of national interest, astonishingly this fraction is declaring its own interests as a national interest but no one can ask them about anything", he added more.

In the year 2014 when premier Sharif of PML (N) had a two-thirds majority in parliament there was still a debate going on about another coup d'état in the country as PTI (Pakistan Tehrek-e-Insaf, the third largest political force in parliament) started a long march on August 14, 2014 against the alleged rigging in the general elections of May 2013. At the same time former military dictator Pervaiz Musharraff was facing a trial (first time in the history of country when a military ruler faced such a situation in Pakistan) for his extra constitutional action of imposing emergency on November 3, 2007, prior to this his first action on 12th October 1999 of overthrowing the Sharif government had been validated by the parliament chosen in 2002. According to a survey conducted by a large media outlet of the country, presently 97.5 per cent political factions of the country are in favour of trial of the former military ruler. Yet at the same time when the proceedings of the trial are ongoing, the government has fallen into a severe crises. PTI started a series of agitation and sit in in Islamabad against the alleged rigging in the general elections of 2013. A massive fraction of analysts believes that the military is trying to overthrow the current government by backing the agitations of PTI so as to sabotage the trial of its former chief Pervaiz Musharraff. Former military ruler has suspended the constitution of the country not once but twice, once in 12th of October 1999 when he dethroned Premier Sharif and second time on 3rd of November 2007 when the dictator imposed an emergency and declared massive fraction of judiciary as non-functional.

It is a very first time in the history of the country when politicians, civil society and massive fraction of media (though a minute fraction in media is opposing the trial of the former military ruler) is demanding the accountability of former Generals (General Musharraff alongside with his aides) who have been involved in the destruction of the constitution and also were the participants in loot and corruption during military regimes. Contrary to this massive fraction of population in the country still believes that military is a powerful institute in the country and it wants to save its former head from any sort of punishment and if this happens it would put a big question mark on the future of democracy in Pakistan.

Daily Guardian London published a detailed report on May 3, 2009 about the massive shares of the military in Pakistan in agriculture and businesses and described the role of the army in such affairs which are out of its professional premises. Let us have a look at what Mustafa Qudari (contributor in Guardian) was trying to expose about the role of military in Pakistan. "No institution dominates like Pakistan army in Pakistan, fraction of military has been unaccountable since the creation of country and formation of this organisation. Generals ruled the country directly during the short history of sixty seven years and during the remaining years out of this period (so called democratic period) it commanded through back channels. Military owns massive assets and businesses in the country and according to recent estimations, worth of military businesses and assets are more than ten billion pounds. Generals due to this are showing more interests in leveraging control over businesses and properties".

It would seem very peculiar to people of most parts of the democratic world that military is more involved in agriculture, trade and politics rather than its professional commitments. This practice is the cause of severe repercussions on its performance and moral. Massive increment in orthodox militant groups associated with Taliban and even with Al-Qaeda in Pakistan (which are responsible for the spread of religious militancy not only in Pakistan but in the surrounding region and the world as well) during the recent past has raised many questions about the abilities of Pakistani armed forces to fight against extremist factions. Armed forces officers (both serving and retired) in Pakistan are running many profitable businesses like transport (National logistic cell a military organisation involved in transport business), agriculture farms, petrol pumps (oil business) and many other cooperations which are diverting the attentions of this fraction from its core professionalism and dragging them towards materialism.

National logistic cell (NLC) scam was among the massive ones of recent days in Pakistan. National Accountability Bureau (NAB the highest level organisation responsible for checking accountability) and public accounts committee of National assembly exposed this mega scandal. Above mentioned scam was of more than four billion PKR and four Generals were involved in it. NAB chairmam (then) Admiral (Retired) Faseech Bukhari held three meetings with the then chief of army staff Ashfaq Pervaiz Kayani during July 2012 about the proceedings of the matter. Initially when scam came under spot light then COAS showed a hard stance towards the Generals belonging to his intuition and said that army will itself punish them and a proceeding of court martial will start sooner but later it was dragged under the carpet and no proceedings started.

According to a report of Daily Dawn published on 02-07-2012, chairman NAB announced in a press conference that three Generals implicated in this scam could face court martial by army as enough evidences have been collected against them. The Generals were Lieutenant General (R) Khalid Munir Khan,

Lieutenant General (R) Muhammad Azfar and Major General (R) Khalid Zaheer Akhtar. Report stated that the then COAS General Ashfaq Pervaiz Kayani ordered an inquiry about the matter and report of that particular enquiry was submitted to him in February 2011. According to Inter Services Public Relation (ISPR) COAS ordered in September 2012 that among the three alleged Generals two will face court martial and for this purpose they will be recalled in service but for what actually happened let's have a look at another report of Daily Dawn.

According to the report of Daily Dawn published on 20-10-2013 military officials has dumped the NLC scam against the three retired generals. Report also stated that army used delaying tactics in the trial of two civilians alleged in this scam case. Entire record of the NLC scam is in the custody of military authorities which has not been shared with National Accountability Bureau so the matter has been suspended for an indefinite time period. Above mentioned practice shows the double standards of justice in Pakistan and has produced severe repercussions on the minds of the sensitive fractions of the society, let's have a look at the following comment:

"There are many sacred cows in this so called land of pure and the military is most important among these all", said Syed Asfar Zaidi a human right activist from Islamabad. "Every fraction of society is accountable with the exception of military and judiciary but they (Generals) consider themselves superior among all factions of society. I am very sure that this very powerful fraction of the country will save their man (General Musharraff) from any sort of trial and political fractions will be no more than spectators", he added more.

Armed forces officers in Pakistan (even low ranked officials as well) are considered among the most influential and privileged fractions of the society alongside with feudal, industrial and civilian bureaucratic elite. Public servants other than army are unmatchable in the context of powers and privileges in comparison with the officials of armed forces. Military officers are offered with fertile agriculture lands (agriculture graduates of the country are deprived enough in this regard), residential plots in the posh colonies like DHA's (Defense housing authority in various cities) and higher designations in the civil service and other prime public sector organisations (after retirement and during service as well) of the country, alongside with many other financial benefits.

Defence housing authorities in Karachi, Lahore and Rawalpindi alongside with other posh colonies of this fraction are reserved for military officials. Ex-servicemen (terminology used for retired armed forces officers in Pakistan) are getting massive pieces of land in these societies at almost no prices (symbolic price is charged for these plots from the officers) in all colonies reserved for the armed forces. According to a report of BBC in 2006 residential plots belonging to three star Generals in DHA Lahore are worth 1.5 million

US dollars. According to the report a rough estimation about the incentives of a three star General after retirement are between thirty five to forty crores PKR (US dollars 3.5-4 million) in terms of agricultural land, residential plots and other benefits while a four star General receives benefits of more than fifty crores.

In the year 2009 the then chief minister of Punjab (he still is) Shabaz Sharif announced that 12.5 acres of barren land would be provided to the unemployed graduates of Agriculture, Forestry and Veterinary streams of the province on a lease of five years through a contract between Punjab government and this unemployed fraction. Thousands among the jobless graduates of these streams (indicating the very high rate of unemployment among the professionals of the country) submitted their applications for attaining even barren land on lease from Punjab government but even then many were not able to attain that. Vast portions of land announced for this provision in particular districts were already captured by feudal and criminal land grabbers. Few among the thousands of graduates who gained the contracts of lease also remained deprived (remaining were refused for non-availability of land in their districts) as they were not able to attain the custody from above mentioned mafias. Civilian bureaucracy showed a very hippocratic stance in this matter. Not only the bureaucracy hid the state lands and adopted a reluctant attitude for showing these as available but it also did not provide any help to those graduates who got the land contract but were unable to attain its custody from the grabbers.

Above mentioned lease contract was designed for only five years (could be extended if the graduates were able to fulfil the requirements of lease) on the payment of 1000 PKR per acre every year. Contrary to above mentioned fraction of deprived graduates the privileged armed forces officers are allotted (permanently) thousands of acres from state land every year. It seems very astonishing that the bureaucracy who denied the provision of state land to the Agriculture graduates provided the land to military bureaucracy in the above mentioned districts and same year massive pieces of state agriculture land were handed over to this faction. Every commissioned officer is awarded at least twenty five acres of fertile agriculture land after his retirement alongside with other incentives while the fraction of military top bureaucracy is getting more than it i.e. two, three and four star Generals can get fifty, seventy five and hundred acres respectively.

One major concern of Pakistani professionals is the access of retired military bureaucrats to appointments in top positions in civilian institutes with ease and comfort. During the regime of Martial laws in the country this practice becomes even more prevalent and top positions in civilian bureaucracy and other organisations of public sector are appointed to mostly retired and serving military bureaucrats. It's a matter of fact that when a General occupies the throne via extra constitutional actions he needs the support of his subordinates to strengthen his position against the political factions of the country and whenever this happens in Pakistan military dictators are familiar for rewarding their juniors. Two former military dictators Zia-Ul-Haq and Pervaiz Musharraff have given too many key positions in civilian bureaucracy to a massive fraction of military officials, above mentioned both dictators were generous enough in distributing top positions to their aides from military and this practice prompted corruption and nepotism in military and its allied organisations. During above mentioned both regimes many serving Generals were appointed on top civilian positions alongside with their retired aides. Massive fraction of former and serving Generals were appointed as heads of public sector organisations by violating the rules and sabotaging the merit even few retired Generals were appointed as vice chancellor in public sector universities of the country.

Former COAS Ashfaq Pervaiz Kayani was ordered to shift all serving military bureaucrats from civilian institutes to military again during his regime (2007-13), yet even at present many military officials are working in civilian institutes. In the year 2014, when Mr Sharif is enjoying his third term as a prime minister many retired military bureaucrats are still occupying the top positions in civilian bureaucracy, have a look at some among them. Secretary of defence is an important portfolio in civilian bureaucracy of the country and nomination for this post on the basis of military instructions is almost a taboo in Pakistan (if there exists an unwritten agreement between military and civilian government). Many top level civilian bureaucrats failed to gain the trust of the military during the recent past and retired Generals were appointed on this important civilian position, current secretary of defence - Asif Yasin Malik, is also a retired Lieutenant General. As we discussed earlier that not only retired Generals in Pakistan are capturing the key positions but this fraction is also involved in the exploitation of the rights of professionals of the country, current chief executive officer (CEO) of Pakistan steel mills (another state owned organisation) Zaheer Ahmed is also a retired Major General of Pakistan army. This practice of appointing retired military officials on top civilian positions is not only the cause of frustration among civil bureaucracy but it is also creating hindrances for the professionals of country in achieving top ranks in their fields.

It's a fact of day in modern Pakistan that above mentioned influential fraction of the society is fetching more than it's worth but so called civilian governments are not able to make it easier for the deprived ones as they are always in danger of their survival from the powerful elite of the military. Army being the most influential fraction of the society is considered not accountable to the political elite (parliament) but civilian bureaucracy on the other hand is more abiding of their political masters, but this political elite fraction has always been involved in massive corruption, loot, and abuse of power.

Generally bureaucracy is defined as "Body of non-elected people /officials responsible for administration and policy making". The term bureaucracy was not coined until mid of eighteenth century, though it is said that in ancient Egypt and Rome system of bureaucracy was in existence even during the era before Christ. This ancient bureaucracy was a hierarchy of regional officials and their deputies. Modern bureaucracy is different from the ancient Roman bureaucracy in many ways yet it possesses some similarities with it as well.

Modern form of bureaucracy evolved in United Kingdom during the mid of eighteenth century. According to Nail Ferguson - professor of history in Harvard University, British bureaucracy of eighteenth century was based on recruitment by examination and trainings, promotions and pensions were integral parts of this bureaucracy. Renowned social scientists and philosophers of modern era including Karl Marx, John Stuart Mills, Max Weber, Woodrow Wilson and many others presented their theories on bureaucracy. According to German theorists Max Weber bureaucracy is described as ideal and typical form of public administration but here in Pakistan bureaucracy is entirely different from ideal bureaucracy of public administration.

Massive fraction of bureaucracy is based on corruption, nepotism, exploitation and favouritism. Bureaucrats are generally called as God Fathers of the system in Pakistan blessed with the three P's of power, prestige and privilege. "Are bureaucrats the major cause of failure of the very fabric of the state?" This is the most frequently asked question in modern day Pakistan and reason for that is massive ongoing corruption, nepotism and favouritism of above mentioned fraction of the society. Truly speaking massive fraction of the population of Pakistan believes that many of their problems are due to corruption and incompetency of the bureaucracy in the country.

Bureaucrats in Pakistan normally called as CSP (Civil Servant of Pakistan who qualify the competitive exam of highest level) and possess the power and privileges given to ICS (Indian Civil Servant) during the British rule in United India–pre-independence era. Arrival of Englishmen in the guise of East India Company was completed up to mid eighteenth century and Great Britain completed the grip on massive fraction of Sub-continent but war of Independence of 1857 caused severe repercussions on the British Raj in India. After demolishing the rebellion with the help of feudal elite of the country Englishmen imposed a strict bureaucratic system for the provision of strength to their rule in this part of the world. Britain bestowed undefined powers and privileges to his fraction who adopted a very brutal attitude towards the masses in India and this practice produced heinous repercussions on the attitude of bureaucracy in India. After the division of Sub-continent into two sovereign states, Pakistan borrowed the similar system of bureaucracy from British Raj while its neighbour India did lot of ammendments in above mentioned system to make it more flexible according to new conditions. Indian political elite at that time was much aware with the flaws of British style of bureaucracy imposed in India during pre-independence era and they did expensive efforts for the formation of new system (constitution of republic) for the new circumstances, while their Pakistani counterparts were not able to establish such practices in a short span of time. Repercussions of above mentioned conditions were severe enough and bureaucracy got control of governance from the political factions very soon.

It's a great concern of modern day Pakistan that corruption is very widespread and deep-rooted in every fraction of life but fraction of bureaucracy is much involved in it as compared to other factions of the society. Generally the term bureaucracy is used for those officers who start their career of public service in Basic pay scale (BPS) of 17 after going through an extensive examination called as Central Superior Services Examination (CSS). BPS 17 is the first step of the stair for a CSP in Pakistan and he can attain maximum 22 grades (highest level of achievement in public service) within a span of service that goes up to sixty years of age. The general age for the recruitment of a civil servant in Pakistan is 21-28 years (Though age relaxation is provided in specific cases i.e. already working government employees and resident of some deprived areas are given the relaxation of age upto two years) and they are eligible to work upto 60 years (many among the civil servants have been given extensions of three to five years in their services throughout the history of the country). Massive fraction of civil bureaucrats like their military counterparts are appointed at some other profitable positions not related to their areas of expertise such as in technical institutions etc.

Civil servants are first sent to the civil services academy (situated in Lahore) just after their recruitment for general training of one year, thereafter they are posted to any among the twelve departments (according to their score in competitive exam) for the probation time period. After completing all the above mentioned procedure this fraction is appointed in BPS 17 in any district or ministry for the period of three years and from here the civil servant becomes the part of the ruling elite of the country. Ruling fraction of the country is divided into two categories. One fraction got power and prestige on the basis of inheritance and wealth i.e. feudal, industrial and religious elite of the country. The other fraction got privilege on the basis of intelligence and calibre i.e. the civilian and military bureaucracy.

When a young bureaucrat becomes a part of the ruling elite due to his calibre and personal capabilities (massive fraction of bureaucracy in Pakistan belongs to educated middle class of the country) he too wants to enjoy a life style like industrial and feudal factions of the society and from this point the destruction process starts. Here we will discuss many aspects of civil servants in Pakistan alongside the performances of their concerned departments, let's have a look.

- **Police**

Police is the constituted body of persons who are imposed by the state to enforce the law and for the provision of protection to the masses alongside with limiting the chances of civil disorder. Police has been the integral part of every civilised society from the very beginning of human modernisation. Police in Pakistan is controlled through federal ministry of interior affairs. Federal secretary of Interior (Commonly called as Home Secretary in Pakistan) is responsible for all the policing in the country and answerable to federal minister of interior. Police in Pakistan is categorised into three ranks. Superior fraction of the Police are the CSPs (called as Police servants in Pakistan- PSP'S) who are appointed by the central government, then come the junior officers recruited though provincial public service commissions and lastly the low ranked staff recruited through the internal recruitment system of the provincial police departments.

According to a report of Transparency International (2011), Police is the most corrupt public sector organisation in Pakistan, massive fraction of media and civil society also believes that not only is the Police corrupt in Pakistan but it also possesses a very harsh attitude towards the masses-the ordinary ones of the society. Being the essential part of the bureaucracy it plays its part in the bad governance as well. As massive fraction of population in the country have direct linkages with Police so most of the population are witnessing the deep-rooted corruptions, favouritism and nepotism in this organisation. One fraction of population also thinks that massive fraction of Police in Pakistan is incompetent enough and possesses no modern techniques for the reduction of crime and provision of protection to masses living in the country, according to them, "One can't rely on them for the purposes of security and protection".

Administration of Police in Pakistan has always been in the hands of CSP'S (with few exceptions in the past when officers from non-PSP cadre were appointed as Inspector General of Police-IG) and an officer who starts his career as an Assistant Superintendent of Police (ASP) can achieve destinies of IG and Home Secretary. Second category of command in Police could be extended for non-CSP's as well in some cases i.e. a junior officer who is recruited through Provincial public service commission can go up to the post of Superintendent of Police (Could be appointed as head of Tehsile or smaller district). In modern day Policing of the country all District Police Officers (DPO's), Regional Police Officers (RPO's) and Capital City Police Officers

(CCPO's appointed as a head of force in capital of a province) are chosen from Police Services of Pakistan while Station House Officers (SHO's) belong to the junior factions of the officers.

As Police play an important part for the provision of social justice or injustice so its performance matters a lot for the massive fraction of population in the country. Massive fraction of population in the country believes that corruption is widespread and deep-rooted in both factions of the organisation i.e. CSP's and non-CSP's and this is causing severe repercussions on the masses. Common view point about the corruption of Police in Pakistan is very clear that upper fraction of it (CSP's) are involved in more technical corruption i.e. loot of funds etc., while lower fraction (SHO's and other low ranked officials) are into very nude type of corruption i.e. bribes for the registration of First Information Report (FIR) etc. Above mentioned both the conditions are producing severe repercussions on the massive fraction of population in their own ways.

"Major reason for the poor performance of Police in Pakistan is the massive loot of those funds given to it for its expenditures", said Furqan Ahmed a human right activist from Lahore. "If DPO's will grab all the funds allocated for the provision of fuel to Police vehicles and other expenditures of the force in the various districts then what will be the moral and working style of organisation?", he added. "There are many DPO's even in Punjab (Punjab is considered or propagated as relatively less corrupt province by a fraction of media in the country) who are involved in the loot of the funds reserved for the provision of fuel to Police Vehicles. Many among these high ranked officers only appoint those Inspectors as SHO's who are not willing to demand funds for fuel that's why one can find very rare patrolling of police vehicles even in many districts with worst security circumstances. This practice has produced severe repercussions on both the efficiency and moral of honest Police fraction (though honest officials are very rare in Police here) officers are no more willing to work as SHO's. So massive fraction of above mentioned category in Police is involved in highest level of corruption for fulfilling their own desires as well as those of their high ranked officials".

Thana culture is a typical word used to describe the miserable circumstances of police stations and the rude and to some extent criminal attitude of Police officials with the ordinary citizens of the country. It's a matter of fact that the country stands among the worst law and order bearing nations in the world even then the attitude of Police is very humiliating with the massive fraction of the population. Monthly (bribe received through various mafias and criminal gangs by the Police on monthly bases) is a famous terminology used in Pakistan to describe the connections of Police with different mafias and factions of culprits. Massive fraction of population have a strong faith that majority among the Police officials in the country is responsible for providing protection and cover to all illegal and legal (massive fraction of population who are doing legal business like some factory owners also like to give bribes to police or are forced to do so for the continuity of their businesses) ongoing businesses. Massive fraction of brothels, gambling houses and alcohol suppliers (though above mentioned all businesses are not allowed legally in the country) are doing their business with the help and cooperation of Police in the country. Prostitution, gambling and usage of drugs is banned in Islamic Republic of Pakistan but one can sell or get all the above mentioned prohibited things by making the Police happy and everyone in the country even foreigners are well aware of this fact, let's have a look at this example.

"I visited a brothel in southern part of province (Multan) with one of my friend there and I was astonished to see a photo of a police officer (SHO) with the lady owner of the brothel", said Solemn Alfred (name disguised), a businessman from Ghana living in Lahore nowadays. "I was familiar with the fact that this country imposed Islamic rules through constitution so I felt a little afraid during my early days of stay here for contacting the people for the provision of alcohols and girls for my sexual desires but now I am fully aware of the situation that one can get anything here as well on the basis of money and influences. The lady owner of the brothel was very much confident due to her links with high officials of Police, she claimed that the SHO in the photograph was a very good friend of hers and she provided pleasures to him with newish virgin girls and she also stated that her linkages goes up to the higher ranked officials as well", Alfred added more.

Massive fraction of Police is receiving heavy bribes from brothels, escort service providers, casinos in posh areas of big cities through a typical manner. Low ranked officials (constables normally do this) of concerned police stations collect money from all above mentioned hubs of illegal activities which after deduction of self share is further transferred to the head constable (normally called Munshi of Thana). From here starts a cyclical chain, SHO of particular Police station after collecting his share passes on this amount of bribe to Deputy Superintendent of Police (DSP is a non-CSP officer who is considered as an officer-in-charge of a Tehsile). In similar fashion DSP transfers it to SP (Superintendent of Police) and hence the process continues and even the highest ranked officers also get their shares from the businesses of prostitution, gambling and drugs supplies in Pakistan.

"Though the Police bureaucracy in Pakistan is not directly involved in receiving bribes from suspected types of businesses but they are very much familiar with the practices of their subordinates and are taking their own shares through low ranked officials in a typical manner", said Hassan Bajwa, a human rights activist from Islamabad. "Officers – CSP's, are involved in big games and their repeated wrong practices have pushed this country into most miserable and severe period of its entire history. When elite fraction of the police is involved in such method based corruption, severe repercussions on low ranked officers like SHO's is inevitable. Once an SHO admitted in front of me (Bajwa) that police station of Bhai Phero (an industrial area within the premises of Lahore region) is a most profitable station in terms of income (bribe) due to massive industrialisation there. "Every factory owner gives 20,000-30,000 per month with ease and comfort to SHO appointed there and when I was appointed there I used to earn (loot) more than one million PKR per month", he added more.

Humiliation and destruction of self-respect by violation of human rights, norms and values is another dark aspect of police character in Pakistan. Massive fraction of population in the country believes that Police is a great source of insult and social injustices for masses in the country due to its unprofessional and non-ethical attitude.

Dar-ul-Aman (place of safety and peace) for nobles and Dar-ul-Hisab (place of accountability) for criminals are the words which are displayed with highlighting in almost every police station of the country but actually the police station places exude contrary ethos to the above mentioned words. Massive fraction of population is of the viewpoint that Thana or a police station is a safe haven for criminals and mafias and some sort of hell for the gentle factions of the population. I (Writer) want to induct my own experiences with the police as well, I had had to go to police station in my home town for some minute reasons (once I lost my national identity card and had to register a report for getting its duplicate copy from National registration and data base authority (NADRA) and another time I had to get a police clearance certificate for travelling abroad) twice but both the times my experiences were bad enough. Being a journalist I was not in acceptance of such a harsh attitude from the officials sitting in the local Thana, both the times they delayed the procedures and demanded bribes in a straight forward manner even though I displayed my identification. I was astonished at their behaviour and said to them, "Do you know that I am a journalist and working with a renowned media house?", the reply to this was even more astonishing, head constable (Munshi) said, "at least you should give us something, say expenses for a one time lunch", I said to them, "you look like beggars, why should you humiliate yourself in this manner, you are just fulfilling your duty and not doing me any favour", to this remark the constable was rendered mum.

Apparently corruption seems the only malaise of the police force in Pakistan but incompetency is another issue which has been neglected since a long span of time and it has also produced severe repercussions on the massive fraction of population. Commoners are wasting both money and time in police stations and courts due to non-professional attitude of the police here. Improper investigation, delaying tactics and possessing minute or nil awareness about the technical and legal aspects of the circumstances are such issues responsible for the unjust behaviour of the police. This practice has widened the gulf between commoners and police to a large extent.

"People here are frightened of the general attitude of the police, that's why massive fraction of population does not like to call police even in an emergency", said Usman Khan, a social scientist from Karachi. Majority among the commoners are not willing to lodge an FIR with the police even after suffering from a criminal activity as there is a common widespread fear against the attitude of police, a fraction of population even claims that they (Police officials) are dacoits in uniform. One among the families of my friends was looted by a gang of criminals in South Punjab. Dacoits who entered in their house were equipped with the latest arms and looted cash and jewellery of more than five million PKR by taking into hostage all family members for more than three hours. After the departure of the dacoits, one among the family members who was not present at home at the time of the loot, came from outside and untied them and then they contacted the police. Police came after almost two hours and at once through their attitude suggested that the robbery had been done with the mutual cooperation of the victims and offenders. Policemen were angry and inhuman with them and instead of carrying out any positive investigations they started to threaten the victims and frequently started to ask about the sources of income and other irrelevant questions. According to the victims they had to entertain the police and pay for their breakfast, lunch, tea, fuel of vehicles, cell phone cards etc., of more than one dozen officials daily but even then the police made no efforts in the right direction. "At last my friend and his family was fed up enough of their attitude and requested them to not proceed any further", Khan added more.

- **A Little Glimpse of Police Bureaucracy**

Pakistan: A hard country, is a famous book by British author Peter Paul Anatol Leven published in 2010. Leven spent enough time in Pakistan during 1989-2009 and observed the political and bureaucratic system of the country in substantial depth. *Army with a state* was a title of a chapter in this book, in which Leven described the supremacy and lavish life style of the armed forces officers in the country as compared to the other factions of the society. I feel little difference of opinion with Leven and as per my experiences Pakistan is a haven for the corrupt political and bureaucratic elite (including civilian bureaucracy as well) of the country.

Police bureaucracy of the country is familiar for its corruption and inhuman attitude towards masses. There is a widespread attitude of hatred for the high ranked officials (Police services group officers) of the police force among the lower ranked constables. Attitude of PSP's is very autocratic and humiliating towards lower officials and this is a major reason for the politicising of police culture. Lower ranked officials in the police are recruited through political influences so they are more loyal to their political masters including PML (N) as compared to their institute. Moreover, lower ranked officials in police need protections from cruel victimisation of bureaucracy so they feel better to attach themselves with political forces of the country which has become a great source of disharmony in the country. Police is the abbreviation of polite, obedient, loyal, intelligent, courageous and efficient, but after having a look at the police in Pakistan (both higher and lower ranked officials) one can't find any of the above mentioned qualities in the police force of the country.

"Existence of police is for the security of masses but police in Pakistan is either providing security to their own officials or are appointed for the protection of political and bureaucratic elite of the country", said Akbar Ali Khan - an advocate from Multan. "Police officers of all cadres including Capital city police officers (CCPO's) and District police officers (DPO's) lead a life style like ancient emperors. Eighty per cent of total police force is deployed for the security of high ranked police officers and other VVIP's. I was astonished to observe a motorcade containing six vehicles including a land cruiser in which an officer was sitting surrounded by five other vehicles commonly called as *dallas*. I thought might be the Inspector General of the province of Punjab is visiting the district but the officer sitting in the land cruiser was not more than a DPO". Listen, he once again got my attention, "one patrolling vehicle of Punjab police contains 10-12 officials, if 60-70 guards are protecting one District police officer of a tiny district what security this police will provide to us?", he added, "Thousands of lower ranked officials are involved in such type of protocol duties in Punjab the so called well governed province", he added more.

We had enough discussion about the role of police in Pakistan and its characteristics; it's time now to discuss another very important fraction of bureaucracy in Pakistan which is also playing a vital role in the promotion of socioeconomic injustices.

- **District Management Group**

District management group commonly called as DMG-renamed as Pakistan Administrative Services (PAS) is a very essential part of bureaucracy and playing its part in ongoing corruption, loot and destruction of the very fabric of the state, alongside with some other factions. DMG was formed in 1973 as a result of administrative reforms during the regime of ZA Bhutto. DMG or PAS officers start their careers from the portfolio of Assistant Commissioner –entrusted with the administration of state lands alongside with the management of revenue matters and provision of coordination between different government departments. This fraction of officers is also responsible for the maintenance of law and order so the versatility of administrative powers and prestige has ranked this group among the top cadres of bureaucracy in the country and this is also a big reason of massive corruption and favouritism in this fraction of officers.

DMG officers start to enjoy the massive administrative powers which results in abuse of power though at senior level (in BPS 21 or 22), massive fraction of these officers performs as a secretary i.e. Secretary information, interior or chief secretary of a province etc., which make them as a centre point of power and prestige among all the bureaucratic elite of the country and this practice has led them towards massive scams of corruptions through abuse of power. According to a report of Daily The News published on August 15, 2012, forty one CSP officers many among them belonging to DMG were facing the highest level enquiry for their alleged involvements in corruptions and frauds through various means. Now have a look on the survey of National corruption precipitation published on 28-11-2011, according to this survey land revenue department is most corrupt among all public sector departments in the country.

Land Revenue department commonly called as Revenue department in the country comes under the supervision of DMG or PAS officers who are utilising the powers of administration and tax collection at the same time. Assistant commissioners supervise the works of Tehsildars and Patwaris (though a low ranked office of land revenue department but possesses key importance in the collection of revenue for the state, Patwaris are considered as most corrupt fraction of the system as all ongoing corruptions even at highest levels are not possible without their support and coordination). Officials of In-land revenue are responsible for the collection of both agricultural and commercial taxes, so a massive fraction of population get to interact with them in this process. But the poor performance and corruptions of these officials including highest level of bureaucracy is causing severe repercussions on the fate of both i.e. masses and the very fabric of the country. With more than a thousand billon of budget deficit, the country is not able to enhance its revenues and the bureaucracy of land revenue is responsible for this to a great extent.

One former chairperson of NAB once admitted (during his regime in 2012) the fact that tax evasion in Pakistan has gone upto two thousand billion–massive fraction of this evasion belongs to land revenue. It would be very astonishing for the citizens of developed world that land record even in the year 2014 is not computerized in Pakistan. Records of state and private lands are still managed manually by the patwari's in registers which is causing massive corruptions. Above mentioned fraction of officials are involved in great manipulations of land records which is producing great repercussions on commoners and every year thousands of commoners are suffering from the massive frauds and scams. Now let's have a look at how the system of corruption works.

"There is a chain of corruption in land revenue starting from patwari and going towards the highest level of bureaucracy", said Farhan Shah a property dealing agent from Lahore. When we purchase any type of land i.e. agricultural, residential, commercial etc., we have to pay a certain percentage (two to three per cent of original amount) to Tehsildar or his deputies for transferring it to our name. Above mentioned type of corruption is very open and nude in Pakistan and highest fraction of bureaucrats i.e. Commissioners are also getting their shares from this method of bribe collection at lower levels. Officials of land revenue are so corrupt that they are looting millions of rupees every year and their life style is enhancing day by day. I am familiar with a Lady Assistant Commissioner (CSP) who was the part of a deprived family but now within three years of her first appointment in South Punjab she owns a lavish life style. CSP land officers (Assistant commissioners) generally belong to lower middle and middle factions of the society but with in initial periods of their services they adopt luxurious life styles. This fraction of officers is familiar to purchase big bungalows in posh societies of Lahore, Karachi and Islamabad and also ultra modern vehicles for their own personal uses. This fraction of population also likes to spend their holidays at recreation stations of Europe and United States. Can all the above mentioned luxuries be attained in a moderate salary without involving in any corruption?", Shah asked me.

According to a report of Daily Express Tribune published on January 30, 2014 massive fraction of farmers in Punjab have accussed land officers for manipulating land records and demanding heavy bribes for the transfer of land records. Report stated that thousands of farmers from district Faisalabad set a massive agitation against land revenue officers for their alleged corruptions and non-human attitude towards the farmers. "Bribe has gone up so much in their veins that they are not ready to listen to us without money", said Ghulam Ahmed - one of the protestors, while talking to above mentioned newspaper. "Initially I was hesitant to pay bribe but when I realised that this is the only way to get Farad (proof or certificate of ownership of land) then I paid the desired amount, astonishingly record of my land which had disappeared since last few months was presented in front of me", Ahmed added more.

As we discussed earlier that a DMG/PAS officer at Tehsil, District and Division (one division possesses six to eight districts in Pakistan) combines the powers of both a magistrate and revenue collector so this fraction of officers possess enough liberty and comfort for practising massive corruptions and spreading favouritism. Formally commissioners (commissioner is an officer of BPS 20 or 21 sometimes with lot of administrative and financial powers, responsible for the management of a division) were working under the supervision of Member Board of Revenue but now they are only answerable to the Chief Secretary of province and this practice has also provided more liberty to this fraction of officers for causing scams in developmental projects.

During the regime of former military dictator Pervaiz Musharraf (1999-2008) an ordinance for the devolution of power at local level was introduced in 2001 which led to the new system of local government and non-political (so called non-political but in reality they are political) District administrators were chosen by members of local council. Though this system was also full of shortcomings but its brighter aspect was the involvement of masses in developmental projects at lower level without the interruption of bureaucracy. Grants and funds were allocated to these District and Tehsil administrators who utilised these funds for various projects, but after 2009 once again district governments came under the full control of bureaucrats and since then no election (with the exception of province of Baluchistan) of local government has been held in the country.

5

Dilemmas of Judiciary and Media in Pakistan

Judiciary and media being the 3rd and 4th pillars of a state respectively possess key importance in any part of the civilised world of modern day but here in Pakistan these two key institutions have also failed to a great extent in delivering in the favour of commoners. Though some factions of both judiciary and media has shown some sort of character against the ongoing socioeconomic injustices and discriminations but a minute sympathy from above mentioned powerful factions of the society is no more than a peanut for the deprived, hungry, discriminated and miserable factions of the country. Both judiciary and media attained lot of powers and privileges during the last decade –In fact, these two factions emerged as new centres of power after the conventional centre points of force i.e. Civil-military bureaucracy and political super elite class (combination of feudal and industrial elite of the country). A major fraction of population from deprived classes still believes that judiciary and media will rescue the nation in future disasters imposed by the influential mafias but many others among the commoner's possess views against these two pillars of the state as well.

It's a matter of fact that superior judiciary and massive fraction of electronic media in Pakistan is showing some sort of activism since early 2000's which is responsible for the provision of multi-dimensional repercussions. Nowa-day's characters of both media and judiciary is more trustable among the educated middle class and deprived factions of the society as well as compared to ancient centres of power or in other words massive factions of the population are disappointed a lot by the old centres of power in the country so they are welcoming the relatively new and emerging centres of power. Boom of both judiciary and media since 2005 has shown some hopes to deprived factions of the society who are facing discriminations and massive injustices from the very beginning of this country and at many stages they have lost hopes for the future. Massive fraction of population still believes that nothing is going in their favour so there are widespread and deep-rooted frustrations and conflicts existing among the deprived factions of the society and their hopes with judiciary and media are also dying. Now let's have a look at the hurdles and destructive elements among both the above mentioned pillars of the state and have a detailed discussion about their each and every aspect.

- **Judicial System of Pakistan**

Judiciary possess more importance than any other pillar of state i.e. parliament, executive, media etc. in the modern era as it bears the heavy responsibility for the provision of instant and durable justice to the citizens of state. The performance of the Judiciary has always been considered as the basic yardstick to differentiate between a successful and a failed state, it's a matter of fact that countries possessing weak and politically influenced judiciaries are living with very weak social fabric. On the other hand provision of instant, low cost and durable justice from the above mentioned faction, guarantees order and peace in the country, strengthens the writ of state and enhances its control over institutions.

Judiciary in Pakistan comprising of a system of hierarchy has two factions, the superior or higher judiciary including Supreme Court of Pakistan and all high courts and the lower fraction of judiciary which includes the session and district courts. Superior fraction of the judiciary has remained in much lime light due to its hyper activism during the last decade in the country as compared to any other institution, that's why massive fraction of population still believes that this fraction will play an important part in the alleviation of miserable circumstances of the society. Superior judiciary wing of the country composed of all high courts follow the Federal Shariah (the Islamic way of justice). The Supreme Court of Pakistan has its branches (Registries) in Lahore and Karachi alongside the main bench in the Capital city. High courts are located in major cities like Lahore, Peshawar etc. and Superior judiciary as its name suggests, possesses superior powers as the constitution of the country has entrusted it with the obligation to preserve, protect and define the constitution of Islamic Republic of Pakistan. Massive practice of judicial activism during the recent history of the country is an evidence of its extended role in state affairs as compared to the past, this activism of the judiciary has produced many repercussions on the very fabric of the state.

Subordinate or lower judiciary consists of civil and criminal district courts and many specialised courts which address issues related to banking, drugs, anti-corruption and consumers (consumer courts), anti-terrorism and environment. Special Tribunals dealing with specific cases particularly those that came up during the days of Martial laws (Military courts also address civilian issues as well) are also an integral part of the subordinate judicial system of Pakistan.

Supreme Court of Pakistan (SCP) is the highest court within the hierarchy of many legal jurisdictions and the final arbiter of legal and constitutional disputes. It possesses a permanent seat in Islamabad Capital Territory (ICT) and also few registries in Karachi, Lahore etc., where cases are heard. SCP consists of seventeen judges including a chief justice; all members of this superior court are nominated by the President after consulting with the prime minister of the country. Part vii Chapter 2 of constitution deals with powers, rules and responsibilities of Supreme Court of Pakistan. Below in hierarchy to the SCP there are five high courts (one each in the four provinces and one in ICT). Territories of Gilgit, Biltistan, Azad Jammu and Kashmir and FATA possess their own systems of judiciaries apart from this primary system.

Lahore high court the most prominent among all the other high courts of Pakistan, is situated in Lahore the Capital of Punjab province, it also has branches in some other parts of the province as well like in Multan. Lahore high court comprises a bench of sixty judges appointed by the President of Pakistan through a consultation (so called) with concerned Chief Justice. Sind high court being the second largest of high court in the country comprises of twenty nine judges appointed through the same above mentioned procedures. Peshawar and Baluchistan high courts represent the superior fraction of judiciary in KPK and Baluchistan and comprise of seventeen and fourteen judges respectively. Islamabad high court, situated in the capital of the country was established in 2010 through the eighteenth amendment of the constitution, it comprises of fourteen judges including a chief justice.

- **Judiciary before and after 2007**

Judiciary in Pakistan especially its superior fraction has set a different character, norms and values after March 9, 2007. By abuse of power, the then military ruler Pervaiz Musharraff declared the then Chief Justice (CJP) of Pakistan Non Functional, this caused severe repercussions on the long held rule of the military dictator. Suspension of Iftkhar Muhammad Ch, the then CJP caused the whole judicial system to revolt against the ongoing traditions. Massive fraction of lawyers started a mass movement in favour of CJP which was halted briefly (for almost three months) when Supreme judicial council of the country reinstated the CJP back to his position on July 20, 2007. The reinstatement of the CJP was an alarming development for the military ruler Pervaiz Musharraff, as the CJP was very firm on the issue of the restoration of the constitution in its original shape for establishing the rule of the constitution in the country.

Military dictator Pervaiz Musharraff perceived a free and fair judiciary as a massive danger for his future regime, so he imposed a state of emergency in the country (as a chief of armed forces of Pakistan) on November 3, 2007 and dismissed the CJP and sixty other members of the superior judiciary. Lawyers from all corners of the country gathered once again and started a much mobilised and efficient movement for the restoration of the CJP. Lawyers gathered in Islamabad in June 2008 and conducted a long march for attaining its purpose but remained unsuccessful. Before this moment political scene of the country was very much different, the ruling party during 2002-07 PML(Q) was familiar by the name of King's party as military establishment favoured it during the general elections (so called) of 2002, PML(Q) was defeated in the elections of 2008 held on February 18. Two conventional but then deprived political factions PPP and PML (N) emerged again as mainstream political forces and they formed a coalition government in March 2008. Both PPP and PML (N) were favouring a free and fair judicial system and restoration of CJP and other judges to their positions but after coming to power, PPP started to retract from its previous decision, that's why a long March was launched against the party by lawyers and its coalition partner PML (N) at that time. It was the month of June in 2008 when lawyers alongside the factions of civil society, human rights activists and PML (N) started a long march from Karachi to Islamabad which was led by the leaders of lawyer movement, the march concluded with the decision to continue the movement until the entire dispute was fairly settled.

After the suspension of the constitution in November 2007 military ruler released a provisional constitutional order (PCO) and a fraction of judges from superior judiciary took new oaths on it. This new fraction of judges tried to isolate the CJP but the movement for the CJP's restoration started again and continued. Lawyer's movement got boom after September 2008 when PML (N) an important ally of PPP in central government decided to quit the government and join the opposition on the judge's issue. According to most media people, during this military regime, fraction of bureaucracy which also comprised of top ranked government officials started to threaten the leadership of PPP from supporting the CJP, due to this pressure PPP was also not in a position to restore the CJP and this was the major cause of division between PPP and PML(N).

Lawyer's movement now was at full swing as PML (N) provided it a massive strength by the provision of political workers and now they decided for a final attempt in Islamabad. It was 3rd March 2009 when a massive crowd led by Nawaz Sharif (now prime minister of Pakistan) alongside with lawyer leaders started to move forward towards the capital of the country from Lahore, the crowd travelled only sixty kilometre within ten hours (as a massive crowd was travelling) and the destination was achieved. The government now failed to show any more resistance as the military establishment put their weight in favour of the demand and forced the government to restore the CJP alongside the other sixty judges of the superior fraction of the judiciary. Above mentioned crusade provided a new type of dignity, respect and power to the superior fraction of the judiciary in Pakistan.

After reinstatement as a CJP, Iftkhar Muhammad Ch introduced many reforms in the judicial system of the country which provided some good and some bad repercussions as well. New norms, values and rules of business became the part of this judicial system and helped the judiciary to restructure its working. Superior judiciary in the past was very familiar for taking oaths on provisional constitutional orders during different regimes of dictators but judiciary under the supervision of above mentioned CJP decided to stop this practice forever in the future. On 31st July 2009, Supreme Court of Pakistan declared null and void all the dictates of the military ruler Pervaiz Musharraff enforced during the state of emergency (3rd November 2007 to 15 December 2007)...

Judiciary being an important pillar of state remained under heavy criticism for validating the military rule in the country in the past, all martial laws of 1958, 1969, 1977, and 1999 were given validity by the superior judiciaries of those times. A massive fraction of judges showed their loyalties with military rulers against their oaths (which prohibited them for supporting any unconstitutional action) causing severe repercussions on the entire fabric of the country.

"When judges of the superior judiciary wing take oaths on PCO's ordered by the military rulers knowing that they are supporting extra constitutional actions then how can they be honest in decision making?", said Ali Jafferi an advocate of Lahore high court and a human right activist. It's my observation that corruption increased in all factions of the judiciary during the regimes of Martial laws in the country as judges felt no fear of accountability during these periods. Judges who took oaths on PCO's in the past showed a biased attitude during decision-making, above mentioned practice not only enhanced favouritism and nepotism but increased corruption as well. Many renowned and honourable judges from the upper fraction of the judiciary including Fakher-U-din Jee Ibrahim, Wajeeh-U-Din Ahmed and more refused to take oath on PCO during military regimes. Massive fraction of the judiciary no doubt was biased and politically motivated in the past but now we are witnessing a new face particularly of its superior faction", he added more.

Judges were inducted in the superior judiciary through direct nominations from the President of Pakistan until the recent past which was (still is) a great cause of biased and politically motivated attitude of judges and decision-making, this practice has caused severe repercussions on the whole judicial system of the country as well. Though the President is still involved in appointments but role of judicial council was enhanced during the regime of former CJP Iftkhar Muhammad Ch and now the President can appoint only seniormost judges with the consultation of Chief Justice (concerned) in the superior judiciary after the 19th constitutional amendment.

Era between 1970 to mid 2000's is marked with many controversies for the judicial system of Pakistan and massive fraction of media and civil society have declared many decisions taken by the superior judiciary during that particular span of time as biased and politically motivated. Pakistan People's Party one among the most elected parties in the country also claims that the execution of its founding chairperson ZA Bhutto through a judicial trail (in a murder case) was a judicial murder, Bhutto was sentenced to death on March 18, 1978 by a larger bench of judges of the Supreme Court of Pakistan and was executed on April 4, 1979. Trial of the former prime minister of the country lasted for five months during October 1978 to January 1979 in the highest court of the country, Bhutto demanded a retrial in January 1979 declaring then chief justice Molvi Muhtaq as a biased person but the court refused his demand.

- **Corruption in Judicial System of Pakistan**

Corruption has always been a great matter of concern for massive fraction of population and is prevalent in all the public sector organisations at every level but the impact of corruption in the judiciary system on the common people is far worse than in other organisations. During the era of 1990's severe allegations of corruption were indicted on the judiciary by the many factions of the society including various political groups. PPP raised voice against the alleged judicial corruption during 1990's and 2000's as it felt that its political workers were victimised by the judiciary of the country during the particular span of time. 2005 proved to be a year of change in the judicial history of the country when CJP Iftkhar Ch started a series of Su motto actions against ongoing corruptions, favouritism and discriminations in public departments and ministries. Former CJP enhanced the role of judiciary in different state affairs (though some fraction of lawyers called this practice as judicial activism but massive fraction among them were in favour of it) and utilised Su motto action as a tool to reduce massive ongoing corruption, discrimination and injustices from the society.

It's a major concern of modern Pakistan that corruption is not only widespread and deep-rooted here but multi-dimensional as well in both public and private sector organisations of the country. Recent statistics about corruption in Pakistan published by Transparency International and some other reputed publications show that the country is amongst the list of most corrupt ones in the world. Corruption perception index (CPI) ranked Pakistan 139 among 172 countries in the list in 2013. Corrupt factions have always been an integral part of the judicial system in the country in both its lower and upper wings and they have been facing severe criticisms for their corrupt actions by the massive factions of society since a long span of time. According to different surveys and reports published in both national and international media about the judiciary in Pakistan there is slight improvement in the corruption index of the superior judiciary (massive increment in the salaries of judiciary during the last few years may be a factor for this) but lower judiciary is still passing through miserable circumstances in this regard.

According to a report of Daily The News published on January 23, 2013 the then chairman of NAB - Admiral (Retired) Faseeh Bukhari declared judiciary as the most corrupt public sector organisation of the country. The report stated that Bukhari accused the judiciary of being the most corrupt fraction of the society in a video conference with NAB staff. The conference was regarding the investigation of the murder of an NAB official in Islamabad in 2012. In the year 2002, through a report "Nature and extent of corruption in public sector" Transparency International described judiciary as the most corrupt organisation of the country. Above mentioned report stated that throughout a vast portion of Pakistan's history the people associated with the judicial system have extracted the highest amount as bribes from deprived people seeking justice. Later in 2010, Transparency produced a detailed overview of the whole judicial system and its repercussions on the majority of population. According to another research conducted by CPI, various actors of the judicial system of Pakistan (judges and lower staff) have been involved in corruption. Research stated that most respondents said that in the event of any judicial process, either they or their family members have had to face acts of corruption during interaction with any form of judiciary. Report further stated that when the respondents were asked about the role of the various actors of the judicial system in corruption it was found that 33.62 per cent of the respondents were demanded bribes by court employees, 23.7 per cent of the victims blamed public prosecutors, and 18.23 per cent indicted that the judges had directly demanded bribes from them and a minute fraction (12.43 per cent) blamed the witnesses.

"Hiring of a judge is a better option as compared to hiring an expensive lawyer," is among the very firmly held notion of most people in modern day Pakistan. Majority among the commoners in the country believe that the judicial system of the country constitutes a very weak fabric inept for the provision of justice to the deprived factions of the population. "Judges too are human beings and men in this part of the world are easily lured with money", said Tariq Khosa - a young lawyer from southern part of Punjab. "Real practice of law is very different here as compared to what we learn in universities, success in this profession is clearly associated with your company and influence on judges as in the current judicial system of the country no one can claim to establish a career solely on the basis of his/her abilities", he continued. "I still remember the lavish life style (like a prince) of one of my class fellows whose father was a civil judge. Astonishingly just after completing his law degree he started earning in millions through his practice, many among my colleagues believe that his success in a very short span was due to his father's links in the judiciary", Khosa added more.

- **Superior Fraction of Judiciary in Pakistan**

Pakistan Bar Council (an elected body of lawyers in the country) published a white paper in May 2005 about the role of superior judiciary during the first six years of dictatorial regime of military ruler Pervaiz Musharraff (ruled the country during 1999-2008). According to this white paper, Superior judiciary of the country played a very significant role in validating and strengthening the dictatorship in the country, it further stated that superior fraction of the judiciary supported the rule of military throughout its history and when the military took over in the most recent past (12th October 1999) it was welcomed again by the judiciary. The paper also stated that massive fraction of superior judiciary worked for getting attentions of military ruler Pervaiz Musharraff and attained benefits by pleasing him. Above mentioned report also claimed that superior judiciary of that time played a significant role in the sacking of the then President of Pakistan - Muhammad Rafiq Tarar by the military ruler Pervaiz Musharraff by an absolute abuse of power, here we will present a paragraph from above mentioned white paper for describing the role of judiciary in the induction of military dictator Pervaiz Musharraff at the highest constitutional portfolio of the country.

"After the judgement in Zafar Ali Shah case, military government steadily gained strength and confidence. Supreme Court from this point onward started being regarded as junior partner of military rulers. It complied with all the previous judgements and verdicts which were being rendered in this process. President Muhammad Rafiq Tarar was removed and evicted in a very indecent way by the military Chief Executive-who took over the office of the president after his removal. Chief Justice administered the oath of Pervaiz Musharraff without taking into consideration the constitutionality of this act. Such assumption of office was never envisaged in the judgement of Zafar Ali Shah case because the term of President Tarar was to outlast the periods of three years but was given to military chief executive instead under the said judgement. Upon retirement, the Chief Justice Irshad was rewarded by the position of chief election commissioner of Pakistan." .

Now we will add a paragraph about the massive ongoing corruption in the judiciary from the same white paper, have a look at this too.

"Judiciary in Pakistan has suffered from massive corruption throughout its history, however, it reached its peak during the last three years. Judicial corruption during the past three years has been unprecedented; this problem has become very critical after the assumption of office of Chief Justice of Pakistan by the Justice Sheikh Riaz Ahmed in February 2002. Corruption at the highest level of judiciary has become so rampant that it remained no more a secret for anyone in the country. Military regimes looks happy while witnessing the corruption among the superior fraction of the judiciary because it thinks that judges with compromised integrity would not dare to put up questions on the actions of the military rulers. If the position of chief justice is occupied by a corrupt judge then he can be easily manipulated by the dictatorial authorities. Supreme Judicial Council has also shown an absolute failure in reducing the widespread corruption among the superior fraction of judiciary."

Iftkhar Muhammad Ch, the former chief justice of Pakistan (held the office during June 2005-December 2013 in different intervals, possesses a unique position in the judicial history of the country, was the youngest ever CJP and was non-functional twice and retained office twice as well after his suspension) is among one of the most popular judicial officials in the world, he too faced severe criticisms by different factions of society in 2012 (then CJP) for the alleged involvement of his son in a corruption scam. Malik Riaz Hussein, a real estate tycoon in the country blamed Arslan Iftkhar Ch, (indirectly the CJP) son of chief justice Iftkhar on June 11, 2012 for receiving heavy bribes from him. Hussein claimed that he paid more than 340 million PKR to Arslan Iftkhar through a company of his son-in-law, Salman, for attaining favours in judicial affairs through his father the CJP. Hussein also claimed that he was blackmailed by the son of chief justice on behalf of his father; Hussein refers to the CJP as "Don of Judiciary" in Pakistan.

Massive fraction of commoners, who were exulted enough on the restoration of Iftkhar Muhammad Ch as CJP on 3rd March 2009, felt a lot of disappointment upon the discovery of above mentioned scam. Mr Chudhary later faced more severe criticisms by the factions of media and civil society for giving favours in this scam case. Malik Riaz Hussein appeared before the two member's apex court on June 13, 2012 for hearing after Su motto action by the CJP but later the CJP declared the commission appointed by the particular bench for as biased and refused to appear before it. According to massive fraction of media and civil society in Pakistan Arslan Iftkhar scandal is a little glimpse of the worst circumstances prevalent in the judicial system of the country and there are thousands of other stories hidden here. According to Hassan Raza - Advocate of Lahore high court, massive fraction of population which was ready to accept a radical change in the judicial system of the country after the reinstatement of Justice Ch is now more disappointed about the future of justice in the country.

- **Miserable Circumstances of Lower Fraction of Judiciary in Pakistan**

As we discussed earlier that corruption is an integral part of the whole system in Pakistan and judiciary too is much steeped in corruption and this has caused great repercussions on the very fabric of the state. It's a fact of the day that the commoners are more severely affected by corruption in the judiciary and particularly the lower judiciary than corruption in other organisations as more than ninety per cent cases of deprived factions of the society are associated with lower fraction of judiciary here. Hence corrupt judges and their staff from lower judiciary has been a great hindrance to the provision of justice in the country since a long span of time. Lower courts in the country are widely utilised for the hearings of all types of cases including very heinous types as well like murder etc., so corruption at that level in judiciary is responsible for producing conflicts, disorder and anarchy in the society and so truly speaking massive ongoing corruption, favouritism and nepotism in above mentioned fraction of judiciary is producing severe repercussions on the very fabric of the country.

It's a great dilemma of modern day Pakistan that lower fraction of judiciary has failed to a great extent to act against corrupt mafias and criminal gangs due to its own corruption, favouritism and incompetency. Corruption is very widespread and deep-rooted in the whole judicial system of the country and lower fraction of judiciary is also utilising it as a great tool for the enhancement of its life style and luxuries. According to a senior lawyer of Lahore high court, Judges here are spending heavier amounts for getting profitable posting and from these positions they are attaining too much in forms of bribes and gifts. "Corruption is massive and widespread in the whole judicial system of the country but it has produced worst impacts on the lower fraction of the judiciary", said Mehmood-Ul-Hassan - a senior member of Sind Bar Council from Karachi, while addressing a press conference at Sukkhar Press club on June 16, 2013. "Not merit, only bribes (paying money for promotions) and favouritism are the only criteria for attaining progress in this judicial system", he continued. "Recently only those civil judges were promoted to the positions of additional district and session judges who were familiar for their corrupt dealings. Tradition of appointments on the basis of clean track record and performances are no more valid in Pakistan", he added more. "Though corrupt factions in the judicial system of the country have been present from the very beginning of its history but the superior judiciary has undertaken no solid reforms", he concluded to encounter it.

Former CJP Iftkhar Muhammad Chudhary during his long tenure (2005-13, excluding times of two suspension periods, 9 March 2007 to 20 July 2007 and November 3 2007 to March 3 2009) showed a concerned attitude and introduced few reforms for the reduction of massive corruption in lower judiciary but this too could not produce very good repercussions at the end. Mr Chudhary who has been named among the world's hundred most influential personalities in 2012 by Time Magazine, was also rewarded with the prestigious International jurist award (2012). He tried a lot for the improvement in the judicial structure of the country but massive fraction of media and civil society now realise that his actions were not sufficient enough for the establishment of less corrupt judicial institutions in the country. During his regime though he took strict actions against the corrupt factions of judicial system both in superior and sub-ordinate judiciary which provided some repercussions as well. But after his retirement (December 13, 2013) corrupt mafias in both factions of the judicial system once again resumed their old businesses with liberty and ease.

While taking to Times of Pakistan on September 19, 2010 the then President of Supreme Court Bar Association of Pakistan (SCBA), Qazi Anwar said that in one form or the other corruption exists in lower judiciary of the country. He further said that Lowers alongside with civil society should launch a joint venture for the reduction of corruption, favouritism and political influence from this fraction of judiciary.

It's a fact of the day that corruption in lower fraction of the judiciary is a great hindrance for the provision of instant and economical justice to the massive fraction of population who are not able to purchase expensive justice. Corrupt judicial system of the country which has failed to deliver for the commoners has promoted the concept of self-justice in massive fraction of population as majority among the commoners particularly in rural areas prefer to resort to self-actions for their revenges. Massive fraction of commoners also prefer to contact criminal gangs and dacoits for protecting and revenging themselves against their enemies as they feel judiciary is no more able to provide them justice.

"If someone grabs your agricultural, residential and commercial land in Pakistan it's better to contact mafias and criminal gangs rather to inform Police and going through a life time judicial procedure", said Hafiz Salam (name disguised) - a renowned religious scholar from Muzaffar Garah district of South Punjab. There are thousands of such examples in which judiciary has been procrastinating such cases since dozens of years and those who got verdicts in their favour were still not able to attain their properties from these land grabbers as Police failed to deliver for them. "Judges are responsible for providing shelter to the above mentioned mafias in the form of stay orders", he added, "a gang of land grabbers had occupied my piece of land as well which I purchased for the construction of my house in my town. After two years of humiliation in courts and Police stations I decided to tackle the matter through the other way and contacted with a religious militant organisation who demanded five lakhs (0.5 million PKR) for threatening that gang and for giving the land back to me. I paid them their desired amount and that fraction of militants released my land and I got it back again, within few days of my occupancy I sold it at twenty seven lakh (2.7 million PKR), though market price was much higher than this but I wanted to get rid of the land and not again become a target of the land grabbers", Salam added more.

- **Justice Denied is Justice Delayed**

Judicial systems of Pakistan possess enough hurdles in the provision of instant, cheap and pure justice to the massive fraction of the population. Majority among the commoners feel that justice is not an attainable thing for the massive portion of population in the country and like so many other things justice too here is a purchasable good affordable by a very minute fraction of population. It's a big concern of modern day Pakistan that a majority (more than 85 per cent) among the population is not able to pay for justice. Deprived factions of the society i.e. population below the poverty line (42 per cent of total population), lower class and lower middle class as well are too far away from attaining any form of justice. Middle class is also facing severe circumstances in both courts and Police stations so massive fraction of this population also prefers to solve their disputes outsides the courts.

According to a report of Pakistan Today published on February 08, 2013, more than a million cases are pending in the courts of the country. The report stated that 19,632 (statistics of 2013) cases of every nature are pending in Supreme Court of Pakistan. Lahore high court the largest among all high courts has 1,24,587 cases in pending, Sind high court has 36,612 cases pending while Peshawar and Baluchistan have 9776 and 5619 cases pending respectively. If we discuss about the cases pending in Sub-ordinate or lower judiciary the circumstances here are too worst. Lower judiciary of Punjab contains highest number of pending cases among all factions of lower judiciary in Pakistan and it has 89,52,313 pending cases. Though Punjab is the most populated province (with more than 100 million population it is more populated than 225 countries in the world) but its ruling Sharif family claims that it has held a track record of good governance among all other provinces of the country, miserable circumstances of lower judiciary and police in the province show how false are the claims of the ruling family of Punjab which has been ruling the largest province of the country since 1985. Sind province has second highest number of pending cases in Pakistan and 1,03,889 cases are pending in its district judiciary. In the same tune, lower judiciaries of KPK and Baluchistan have 97,789 and 7461 pending cases respectively.

There are many reasons for delayed justice in Pakistan. Poor and biased investigation of Police is playing a vital role in it but corrupt factions in the judicial system are also contributing a lot towards delaying justice: Both upper and lower factions of judiciary are involved in postponing cases for a longer than usual period of time, massive fraction among the judiciary claims that there is much unbalance among the quantity of cases and staff deployed in the judicial system of the country. Judges are less in number and dealing with a massive amount of cases which is beyond their capacities. Above mentioned reason looks very valid as less number of judges are not able to deal with too many cases, and it also disturbs their efficiency as well.

Witness is a key factor for the provision of justice and for punishing the culprits in every judicial system of the world but a very weak, very fabric of the judicial system of Pakistan is inept to provide instant justice just because of witnesses. A massive fraction of witnesses who appear before the court face severe type of pressure and many among them are either killed or kidnapped by the criminal gangs and mafias or pressurized in such a way that they either refuse to face the court or bounce back from their given statements. In modern day Pakistan judicial activism is another big reason for delayed justices in the court. Superior fraction of judiciary has a massive number of pending cases but it remained indulged with Su motto actions and has been neglecting its prime duty during recent years.

Massive fraction among the legal experts in Pakistan believe that too many Su motto actions from Superior judiciary of the country during recent years on various issues has diverted the attentions of this fraction from its original duties. According to Qalib-E-Hassan - Vice President of Pakistan Bar Council, Su motto actions by the superior fraction of the judiciary has over burdened the work of this fraction of judiciary and created a massive back log, he insisted that superior fraction of judiciary should design a mechanism to deal with Su motto cases and opposed the jurisdictions of Su motto cases in apex court. Justice (Retired) Tariq Mehmod, a renowned law practitioner of the country has suggested that cases should be equally distributed among the different benches of top court to clear the back log within a certain time frame otherwise it will create more hindrances in the future towards the provision of instant justice.

It's a matter of fact that delayed justice has produced great repercussions on the very fabric of the state particularly during the last decade. According to a fraction of political commentators and analysts one major reason for the growing Talibanisation in the country is the failure of both sub-ordinate and superior judiciaries in providing instant justice. It's a matter of fact that Talibans have produced widespread and deep-rooted influence in many settled areas (not part of Tribal belt) of KPK, Punjab and Sind during the last five years. Massive factions of population in southern part of Punjab (most deprived portion of the country) and some parts of Sind (including some parts of Karachi as well) are heavily influenced by the teachings of Taliban as they feel that the Taliban has introduced an instant system for the provision of justice in Afghanistan during their five-year rule (1996-2001) there. Influence of orthodox militant groups was very minute and existed only in FATA a decade ago but it steadily has now spread to its adjacent province (KPK) as well and in the year 2014 writ of the state seemed to have vanished from KPK alongside FATA. According to some factions of media in Pakistan Taliban are familiar for the provision of instant justice in their controlled areas of FATA and KPK, that's why a massive fraction of population who possess traditional values and norms is getting inspired from the above mentioned orthodox group and this development is producing severe repercussions on the very fabric of the state.

Delayed justice is also a major cause for growing crimes particularly in rural areas of the country like South Punjab, Interior Sind etc., during the last few years. A massive fraction of population in the rural areas of the country is following their old customs and traditions and revenge holds an important position in these followed norms and values, so if someone is involved in a murder of their opponents in this rural system and the victims fail to get instant justice (as normally happens) from judiciary then victims take law in their hands and they too kill someone among their opponents. A series of killing starts from these types of actions which leads towards great anarchy and conflicts in the society. To recapitulate it can be said that judiciary an integral part of the very fabric of the state has failed to a great extent to provide instant and economical justice to the massive fraction of population throughout its history.

Media is the Fourth Pillar of State in Pakistan?

"Media is the most powerful entity on earth, they possess the power to make the innocent guilty and guilty innocent and that's power because they control the minds of the masses."

Malcolm X

Malcolm X an African-American human right activist and intellectual described the strength of media in such a way some fify years ago and it looks feasible in modern circumstances as well. Media is considered as fourth pillar of state after Parliament (Legislators), Executive (Bureaucracy) and Judiciary in the civilised world of modern day. Some factions of media and civil society have even declared it more powerful than all other ancient pillars of state. Here in Pakistan media has been an emerging power since early 2000's, yet it is still not fully recognised as the fourth pillar of the state in the real sense.

Media in Pakistan has been facing severe circumstances since a very longer span of time and it was not even able to declare the guilty as guilty as it was fully controlled by powerful state agencies, so what to talk of its declaring the innocent guilty and guilty innocent! Modern day media in Pakistan though vocal enough but it too is facing multi-dimensional challenges as well, of late it has been able to take a little sigh of relief as compared to the past but still it is facing severe circumstances imposed by both the state and non-state actors. Massive fraction of media in various parts of the country (both print and electronic forms of it) still seem conflicted, frustrated, suffocated and unprotected, but it is trying to improve and reform itself and also moving towards self-accountability as well which is a good sign for its improvement. A nation whose massive fraction is suffering from hunger, diseases, terror, injustices and discriminations has expectations from the media as well, since the last decade independent media in the country has been largely trying hard to highlight the severe circumstances of commoners. This endeavour though has played a minute part in the reduction of anger and frustration of the deprived factions of population but still there is a long way to go.

All forms of media i.e. print, electronic and social (called as informal as well) are playing an important role in nation building in this modern era as it has become an important part of human life. Men of twenty first century like to have bed tea while reading a newspaper or tablet, spend the day with interactive media (Facebook, Twitter etc.) in office and end the day with watching shows on TV with family. So media has now taken 24/7 place in the life of modern men in most parts of the world.

As per 2014 statistics, Pakistan possesses a large and fertile range of all forms of media, with more than 350 dailies including at least one dozen nationwide circulated dailies, 363 weeklies, 200 monthly published magazines, 30 news agencies (both state owned and private), 110 privately owned television channels (including news, entertainment, sports, food, regional etc.), five state-owned television channels (For news, entertainment, and sports), 29 medium wave radio stations, 131 commercial Frequency Modulation (FM) radio stations and 35 Amplitude Modulation (AM) radio stations. Alongside these, massive fraction of population particularly educated fraction of youth is also utilising social media for expressing their views since mid 2000's. In 2014, the investments (in PKR) made in the various forms of Pakistani media were more than 24 billions in satellite T.V., 13.5 billons in cable T.V., 1.8 billions in Interment protocol television (IPT) and 47 billions in other electronic media. Currently privately owned print and electronic media outlets in the country are providing employments to people. It's a fact of the day that media in Pakistan is stretching forward for enhancing its strength and power so as to maintain itself as a pressure group, and for attaining its purpose it is utilising freedom of expression as a tool which has produced many negative repercussions as well.

- **Expansion of Media in Pakistan**

In the year 2014, Pakistan had more than 140 million viewers of electronic media among the population of 200 million (near about). There has been a rapid enhancement in the viewership of electronic media in the country after 2000, according to statistics of 2000 there were only 45 million viewers of Television in 2000 as massive fraction of population in even larger citis were relying on only state-owned television transmissions but with the introduction of cable TV there occurred a rapid enhancement in viewership of Television in Pakistan during the last twelve years. The era between 2000-10 is considered as the prime time for the progress of privately-owned media houses particularly for news channels, many among the tycoons of business and industry invested in the field of media during the last decade due to which more than hundred media outlets (massive fraction of it belongs to news houses) were established in the country during that particular span of time. After the emergence of electronic media on the national scene as the most powerful form of media, print media's importance for the commoners reduced to a great extent, but even then many new newspapers have still been introduced during the last few years and this is a healthy sign for newspaper industry as well. A very vocal, active and thinking fraction of interactive media commonly called here as social media also has a great following like the other above mentioned forms of media. Massive fraction of journalists from both print and electronic media and writers have their accounts in social media for interacting with masses and gathering their opinions on various issues, currently more than 40 million Pakistani's are connected with each other through social media.

According to recent statistics 350 daily newspapers are being published in the country among which less than one dozen are being published in English, 30 in regional languages like Punjabi, Sindhi, Baluchi etc. Many among the regional language newspapers have good readerships, Sindhi language newspapers are very popular in the interior part of the Sind and some among the Sindhi papers have more readership as compared to mainstream Urdu newspapers in above mentioned areas of the Province. But it's a great dilemma of modern day Pakistan that readership of newspaper is going down with the boom of electronic media in the country, hardly two or three mainstream newspapers have been inducted during the last decade in the country and few were closed as well due to massive reduction in circulation. Majority among the mainstream dailies are going through severe circumstances and are fighting for their survival as emergence and boom of electronic media has diverted the tilt of advertisement from print to electronic media.

Pakistan Television commonly called as PTV (the state-owned media outlet dealing in news, sports and entertainment) was only source of information in the form of electronic media for massive fraction of population up till 2000. Most newspapers were not able to provide freedom of expression as state agencies controlled print media in a strict manner. But the emergence and boom of electronic media since early 2000's has given lot of courage to print media outlets as well, currently most of the print and electronic media outlets are interrelated with each other due to same ownership. Many among the conventional print media outlets have invested in electronic media as well with the emergence of electronic media. According to massive fraction of senior journalists there is a vast difference in working of orthodox media houses (who invested in electronic media as well) and newly emerged electronic media houses. Conventional media groups like Jang group of publications (the largest independent media corporation in the country which owns most circulated Urdu newspaper daily Jang and most rated news channel Geo news), Dawn group (which owns most credited English newspaper of the country) and Naway Waqat group are following the traditional norms, values and ethics of journalism very strictly and are paying heavy prices of their stance since a very long span of time. Contrary to this, massive fraction of newly emerged electronic media houses in the country (which are owned by industrial and business tycoons) are following specific agendas and policies and have promoted yellow journalism to a great extent during the recent past.

Pakistan Television Corporation Limited was founded on November 26, 1964 during the military regime of Ayub Khan, for too many years despite of its very limited transmissions (restricted for few years due to lack of resources and technology) PTV was the only source of information for the massive fraction of population in the country. Initially PTV was all in one channel which telecasted news, entertainment, sports etc., but later (during 1980s) it started a special channel for current affairs talk shows as well. During the second half of 1990's state-owned organisation started hourly news bulletins and morning show as well. Syed Tallat Hussein was the first anchor to start a morning show in Pakistan from PTV that included comments on news and discussions on current affairs. During the early 1990's under an agreement with Network Television Marketing (NTM), Shalimar Television (STN) became Pakistan's first ever private channel. STN got much viewership (though its transmission was restricted within few urban areas) due to its bold approach in its dramas and shows. Music shows and other entertainment programmes of STN got much popularity in those days as it showed some sort of innovation and creativity to masses as compared to the orthodox shows of PTV.

Emergence of STN started a process of change in electronic media of the country but as it was restricted for entertainment only so the masses could not feel the socio-political repercussions of this change, but with the emergence of privately-owned electronic media news outlets a new milestone was created. Geo News currently the most viewed news channel of the country founded on August 14, 2002 was a big milestone in this regard as it has provided the news telecasting a new style and look. Before the emergence of Geo News a leading businessman of the country (Late) Abdul-Razak Yaqoob started a news channel by the name of ARY ONE WORLD in the year 2001 and in the same year another electronic media outlet started its transmission by the name of AAJ but emergence of GEO was a stunning addition to the electronic media system of the country. Jang group of publication started a multiple purpose Television channel on the Independence Day of the country in 2002 which included news and entertainment. Above mentioned group had a lot of experience in print media as Jang is the largest circulated newspaper of the country (Having more than one million circulation it has the massive fraction of readership in the country) so it provided many innovations and attracted massive fraction of viewership within a very short span of time. Three years later in the year 2005 Geo News was started separately only for telecasting news and current affairs programmes, while Geo became an entertainment channel. Currently both Geo News and Entertainment has the highest numbers of viewership. In the year 2014, with two mainstream national newspapers (one in English and one in Urdu), three smaller newspapers, one most circulated magazine (Akhbar-E-Jhaan) and with five electronic media outlets (two belongs to news, two to entertainment and one to sports), Geo group presently holds more than 70 per cent of viewership in both print and electronic forms of media in Pakistan.

After the emergence of Jang group in electronic media there came a flood of electronic media outlets in the country, other print media outlets like Dawn group, Naway-Waqat etc. also invested in electronic media. Some among the business tycoons of the country who were observing the growth and enhanced influence of media in Pakistan also invested in electronic media. Some among these tycoons later started their print media outlets for attaining success in electronic media by utilising their specific agendas. During a short span of a decade (2001-11) more than 100 news and entertainment electronic media outlets were established in the country so in the year 2014 total number of electronic media outlets including news, entertainment, sports, food etc. was more than 130. Currently Geo news, Dunya News, Express, Dawn, ARY and Samma are considered among the mainstream electronic media outlets of the country. Regional news channels like KTN in interior part of Sind, Rohi in Southern part of Punjab, City 42 in Lahore, Metro one in Karachi and Khyber in Peshawar have reasonable numbers of viewers as well.

KTN (Kashish Television Network) was the first regional language news channel of Pakistan founded in October 2002 with its operational headquarters in Karachi. KTN owns massive viewership in interior parts of Sind (Sindhi speaking areas) and in some factions of Karachi as well. Similarly, Khyber is a Pushtoo language news outlet telecasting its transmissions in various parts of KPK. City 42 and Metro One are Lahore and Karachi based news channels and have a focused segment of viewers interested in the affairs of the two above mentioned metropolitans of the country. Many cable TV channels are also operating in various cities of the country and have a minute viewership as well, so a journey which started in 1964 has come a long way since then yet it will take more time for the provision of a fully mature and responsible electronic media in Pakistan.

Limitations for Media in Pakistan

Media in Pakistan has faced severe control of state-owned agencies for a very longer period of time. After going through a continuous struggle, media in Pakistan has attained little liberty and ease in the recent past (after 2005) but the destination of fully free and unbiased media is still too far away. Apparently mass media in the country looks free and fearless but actually its going through the most critical period of its history as its challenges are multidimensional and deep-rooted. Throughout its history massive fraction of independent media faced severe repercussion and paid a heavy price for the freedom of expression, both military and civilian governments utilised various tools like blockage of news print, threatening and kidnapping of massive fraction of journalists etc., since a very long span of time. Many among the journalist class have faced severe circumstances due to different extremist groups as well and governments have failed to protect media houses and journalists, this has caused severe repercussions on massive fraction of media in the country.

It's a fact of the day that military regimes in Pakistan proved worst for the majority among the independent media houses in the country, military dictators in every period of their intervention in democratic system of the country used extensive power to sabotage the freedom of expression. Editorial contents and headlines were approved by Inter services pubic relation (ISPR –Information department of military in Pakistan) for massive fraction of print media during the regimes of military dictators Ayub Khan, Yahiya Khan and Zia-ul-Haq. Though role of electronic media during the periods of above mentioned dictators was very minute (only state-owned Television and radio were operating) and that too was fully controlled by state agencies. A strict censorship was imposed in all forms of media and any violations of limits had severe repercussions.

Massive fraction of independent journalists faced severe circumstances during the military regime of Zia-ul-Haq (July 9, 1977-August 17, 1988). His rule proved cruel enough for the majority of the independent journalists, his era seems like a horror dream to a massive fraction of media in the country. Victimisation of media started with a ban on Daily Maswat a left wing Urdu language news-paper which was familiar for its socialist point of view (also called as representative of Pakistan People's Party). Many among the journalists who attempted a hunger strike against this cruel action of military dictator in December 1977 were arrested and put into rigorous imprisonment of one year. Later period of Zia's regime proved to be even more darker and many among the key journalists of the country faced severe circumstances, law enforcing and secret agencies tortured and kidnapped journalists and threatened them for using freedom of expression against the military ruler.

Pervaiz Musharraff the most recent military ruler (1999-2008) in Pakistan tried to prove himself relatively different from his predecessors but in reality he too failed to give liberty and ease to massive fraction of media in the country. Musharraff kept the dual attitude by claiming himself as a champion of human rights and freedom of expression but in reality treated massive fraction of media in a very inhuman manner as he too resorted to keep the media under torque like his predecessors. Pervaiz Musharraff imposed a state of emergency on 3rd November 2007 as a chief of army staff and put a ban on all privately-owned news channels of the country that were telecasted through the cable operators. Ban lasted for more than forty five days and during that particular span of time none among the seventy news channels of the country from private sector were allowed to telecast through the cable operators, only state-owned Television was source of information for the country in those days. Secret agencies strictly monitored the news and editorial contents of both print and electronic media outlets throughout the regime of General Musharraff.

It's a great dilemma of media in Pakistan that it not only faced severe circumstances during the regimes of dictators but it also faced difficulties during the democratic periods as well. Democratically elected Prime Ministers including ZA Bhutto, Benazir Bhutto and Nawaz Sharif also adopted dictatorial attitude towards media during their regimes. Above mentioned all prime ministers were involved in bad practices against the media houses and journalists of the country. They used to threaten journalists by utilising state powers and tried to purchase their loyalties as well.

Jang group the largest independent media house in the country has faced severe circumstances during both the dictatorial and democratic regimes, its newsprint and telecast have been stopped several times throughout its history by various rulers. Njam Aziz Sethi a very renowned journalist and political commentator (currently associated with Geo News, then was also part of Jang group as a columnist) was taken in custody by a secret agency on 8th May 1999 without any charge during the democratic regime of Mr Sharif. It was 1st June 1999 when Sethi was charged for condemning the creation of state and advocating abolition of the sovereignty of the state of Pakistan and also for promoting enmity between different groups, but on 2nd June the Supreme Court of Pakistan ruled that due to the government's failure to provide sufficient evidences the charges against Sethi cannot be justified and hence government had no choice accept releasing him.

Sacred Cows or Non-Touchables for Media in Pakistan

Certain factions of the society are like sacred cows or non-touchables and the Media in Pakistan is not allowed freedom of expression against them. The media in Pakistan is unfortunate enough as there are many such sacred cows in the Pakistani society and anything published or telecasted against them can produce severe repercussions. Violations of certain boundaries imposed by various such non-touchables (comprising of both state and non-state actors) can make difficult the social or economic circumstances of a journalist and can even be life threatening for him/her or his/her family members. Among the many sacred cows two of them possess key importance, the military and its allied agencies are the prime one and second comes the judiciary. Military and its allied organisations (ISI etc) are considered among the top non-touchables for media in Pakistan, here I will quote an example (there are hundreds of examples but one is presented here to provide a little glimpse of the picture).

Hamood-ur-Rehman commission report (prepared after the incident of fall of Dhaka and separation of East Pakistan into a new country named as Bangladesh) assessed the involvement of officials of Pakistan army in killings, tortures and abuse of Bengali (then East Pakistanis) men and women during a military operation in 1970-71. Findings of the commissions also declared involvements of Pakistani armed forces officers in sexual abuses, burning and looting of banks and killing of civilian Bengali officers, industrialists and intellectuals during the mentioned period. Commission report declared that General Yahiya Khan (then commander-in-chief of Pakistan army, 1969-71), General Abdul-Hameed Khan, Lieutenant General SGMM Peerzadah, Lieutenant General Gul Hassan, Lieutenant General Amir Abdullah Khan Niazi (then commander of eastern command of Pakistan army in Dhaka), Major Generals Umar and Mitha and few other officers of high ranks were involved in that crises and report recommended the trial of all the above mentioned officers. None among the above mentioned officers faced any trial, contrary to this they received full prestige and protocol till their deaths and the report was put in cold box. Media in Pakistan was not allowed to discuss its absence even during the civilian regimes of Benazir Bhutto and Mr Sharif (1988-99) as military establishment of the country was not in favour of an open debate on the issue. Hamood-U-Rehman commission report was leaked and published in an Indian magazine India Today in August 2000 and from there Daily Dawn picked this report and published it in Pakistan.

Military elite in Pakistan is very conscious about the debate of its accountability as an institution as it has always remained too notable for its unaccountability to the media regarding this issue. Officers of Pakistan army were involved in serious crimes against Bengalis during 1970-71 but not only were they saved from any kind of trial but were also promoted by the civilian Prime Minister Z.A Bhutto and from there on a sense of extra superiority emerged among the military bureaucracy of the country. Era of 1990 emerged with corruption scandals in Pakistan and leading politicians of the country including two prime ministers, Benazir Bhutto and Nawaz Sharif, faced severe allegations of corruption. Among the others were the top level leaders including Asif Ali Zaradari (later president of Pakistan 2008-13), Yousaf Raza Gillani (later prime minister of Pakistan 2008-12) and more...Massive fraction of politicians including Asif Ali Zardari faced severe trials and rigorous imprisonments.

Most journalists believe in Pakistan that politics and politicians were defamed during the era of 1990's by their own colleagues through secret agencies, a fraction of politician admit that they were used by military establishment against their counterparts. Massive fraction of media too played an integral part in this process and many among the renowned journalists of modern day were working (still working) for the attainment of the goals described by the establishment of the country. Role of military, its direct and indirect interventions in politics and alleged corruptions have remained non-touchable matters even during the period of scandals for media in Pakistan. It's a harsh reality of the land of pure that massive fraction of media who conducted massive trial of politicians on the allegations of corruptions remained very silent when this sort of situation occurred for the fraction of military bureaucracy. General Pervaiz Musharraff dismissed the elected government (which possessed two-third majority as well) of PML(N) through an extra constitutional action but massive fraction of media in Pakistan remained very silent as many among the media houses and journalists lacked the courage for raising voice in these sort of situations. Many among the columnists and anchors who claim to be among the champions of democracy and rule of law in the country wrote columns in favour of the dictator upon his arrival.

As we discussed in previous chapters that corruption is not only widespread but is also deeply-rooted in both public and private sector organisations of the country, like many other officials of public sector organisations massive fraction of military elite is also involved in various types of corruptions. Examples of Admiral (Retired) Mansoor-Ul-Haq, Lieutenant General (R) Javeed Ashraf Qazi, Lieutenant General (R) Saeed-U-Zafar, Major General (R) Hassan are few among those top military bureaucrats who faced (and were convicted too) severe allegations of corruptions but the massive fraction of media in Pakistan showed enough biased attitude and failed to highlight the scams in the case of military bureaucracy, although in the case of corruption in political fraction the media has come out as comparatively more vocal and strong. Admiral Mansoor-Ul-Haq (Served Pakistan Navy during 1958-97) was involved in a massive corruption as a chief of Pakistan Navy through a submarine deal (Agasta class submarine) and was arrested by the NAB officials. He later did a plea bargain (a method of recovery applied in Pakistan through which some portion of looted amount is handed to authorities and remaining is legalised) with National accountability bureau (NAB) and was released. Massive fraction of media who made lot of noise on the alleged scams of political elite during 1990's remained almost silent on this issue. Similarly, Javeed Ashraf Qazi (former Director General of ISI who served the organisation during 1993-95), a retired Lieutenant General alongside with two other Generals were allegedly involved in a mega scam named as "Royal Palm country club".

Mr Qazi too faced no media trial as massive fraction of the journalist elite of the country was afraid of discussing about a former chief of ISI. It's a great dilemma of modern day Pakistan that institutes like ISI who hold key importance in defence strategy and security are directly or indirectly involved in mainstream politics of the country as well, this diverts its focus from its real job and has produced severe repercussions on the very fabric of the country. Whosoever has tried to question this issue has faced severe reactions.

- **Incident of Hamid Mir and its Repercussions on Media**

A life threatening attack was made on Hamid Mir, a veteran Journalist/ column writer and a very popular talk show host (rated as a top anchor of the country) on April 19, 2014 in Karachi. Though Mir survived from this rigorous attempt of killing but was wounded badly and faced severe health issues for almost three months thereafter (still not recovered fully but rejoined his duties as an executive editor of Geo News) after receiving six bullets on his body on that particular day. At least one dozen bullets were fired on Mir's car by the offenders while he was on his way to the office of Geo News in Karachi. Mir was immediately taken to a private hospital where a major surgery was done on him for removing the bullets, after being under treatment for one month in Karachi he was later shifted to London for more treatments by the organisation for whom he is working.

Mir, aged forty eight, has had a very strained relationship with the military establishment of the country during the recent past (although some factions among the journalist elite of the country claims that he attained the highest positions in different media houses through his connections with the military bureaucracy during the early and middle phases of his career). Being a very bold journalist he raised many questions about the character of the country's premier intelligence agency (ISI) in his talk shows and columns, he also considered ISI responsible for the alleged killing and kidnapping of political workers in Baluchistan during and after the regime of General Pervaiz Musharraff in Pakistan. Mir repeatedly raised the question of missing persons from Baluchistan and interviewed "Mama Qadeer" a 73 year old Bloch nationalist who marched from Quetta to Islamabad alongside with his many fellows and covered a distance of two thousand kilometres in around one month. It was the month of February in the year 2014 when massive fraction among the media remained silent on the long march carried out by Mama, only Mir was the person to raise this issue with an extensive approach.

Mir also frequently criticised the political role of ISI during the recent past, he repeatedly blamed top officials of the organisation including Lieutenant General Ahmed Shuja Pasha (served as the Director General during 2008-12) for their alleged involvements in the politics during above mentioned span of time. It was the 25th of November 2012 when a planted bomb was found in the lower part of Mir's car which was parked outside his home in Islamabad. The bomb was defused by the bomb disposal squad of the capital territory. According to a senior journalist from Lahore this was the last warning for Mir by the most powerful fraction of the society.

After the murder attempt on Mir on April 19, 2014, Geo News at once claimed that the particular attack was carried out by the premier intelligence agency of the country, sources say that Mir had already informed the top management of his organisation about the threats to his life and also provided the instructions about the offenders as well and that's why Geo News at once blamed ISI for the incident. Hamid Mir who has been working for Geo News since 2002 is considered as a very renowned face not only in Pakistan but in international media as well and the organisation for whom (Geo News) he is working has a viewership of 76 per cent among the total viewers of News Channels in Pakistan. The attack on him was considered as attack on Geo and since Geo represents the massive fraction of electronic media viewership in Pakistan, so attack on Geo was attack on the whole media and it produced severe impacts on the other factions of media as well.

- **Repercussions on Geo Group**

Attack on Hamid Mir produced severe repercussions on his organisation as well and Geo News/Jang group of publications is still bearing the intensity of circumstances imposed by the particular factions on it after the above mentioned incident. Government (Military bureaucracy actually) utilised the cable operators for closing the transmissions of Geo News and the most viewed news channel of the country vanished at once from the scene of mainstream media. Not only the transmissions of Geo news were completely closed down but its allied organisations (Daily The Jang -most circulated newspaper of the country and entertainment and sports outlets of electronic media) also faced (In fact still facing) severe repercussions as well. Jang/Geo group has borne economic losses of more than seven billons PKR since then. These circumstances have shaken the very fabric of the organisation badly and raised a big question mark on the future of freedom of expression in the country as well as its more than 10,000 employees.

Later Pakistan media regularity authority (PEMRA) imposed a fifteen day ban on Geo news and also fined the organisation ten million PKR for discussing, blaming and correlating the character of country's premier intelligence agency with the incident of Hamid Mir. Federal minister for defence, Khawaja Asif later stated that punishment of fifteen days ban and fine of ten million was not enough for Geo news and government is thinking of imposing a longer ban on Geo and its allied organisation. This statement drew the attentions of international agencies and most of them criticised not only the statement of the federal minister but also the punishment given to Geo news. Reporters without borders, International Federation of Journalists and many other media organisations of the world strongly condemned the ban and fine imposed on Geo News.

Victimisation of Geo News and its allied organisations was not stopped then but it continued (still going on) for a longer period of time. Geo Entertainment an allied organisation of Geo news was also banned for fifteen days and fined with ten million PKR for exploiting the religious views of a particular sect which seems very ridiculous as massive fraction among the religious intellectuals of the country stated that above mentioned organisation was not involved in any sort of intentional humiliation of any sect but authorities once again showed quite a cruel attitude and Geo group faced another loss once again. Recently, a lower court from Gilgit (Gilgit Baltistan though an administrated part of Pakistan but its area is not included in the country like Azad Kashmir it is not constituently part of the country as well, as per Pakistan issue of Jammu and Kashmir should be resolved according to United Nations resolutions) sentenced Mir Shakeel-U-Rehman - Editor-in-chief of Jang group, for twenty six years in absentia for the exploitation of religious views through the transmissions of Geo Entertainment. Astonishingly Mir Shakeel had absolutely no connection with that particular telecast as he was heading the print outlets of the group, moreover PEMRA had already given a massive punishment to Geo Entertainment for the above mentioned mistake. Massive fraction of media still believes that severe repercussions on Geo group are continuing because it raised a voice against the non-touchables.

- **More Threats for Media**

Now we will move forward and briefly discuss about some more threats faced by the media in Pakistan. There are many other sacred cows and pressure groups that scare the media here and majority among the journalists are facing repercussions imposed by the mafias and criminal gangs as well. It's a matter of fact that different factions of religious militant organisations also behave like mafias with the massive portion of media in modern day Pakistan. Though a minute fraction of media have sympathies for the orthodox type of religious militant organisations but most journalists hold a very firm opinion against the above mentioned groups yet they refrain from expressing anything against religious terrorist groups due to fear of brutal repercussions, many among the renowned journalists of the country have been targeted by these terrorist organisations in the recent past.

Njam Sethi, a veteran journalist associated with Jang/Geo group spent the whole year of 2011 in United States due to threats to life from some orthodox militant organisations operating in the country since 2004. Similarly, Raza Roomi a progressive column writer, editor and anchor (previously associated with Express media group) was attacked on March 27, 2014 by a religious militant organisation. Mustafa, the driver of Raza Ahmed (familiar by his pen name Raza Roomi) died on the spot but Roomi narrowly escaped and within few days of that incident left Pakistan and settled in London. Both Roomi and Sethi are familiar for their liberal views and supporting United States policies against the ongoing war against terrorism, so massive factions of orthodox militant groups have been in search of them since a long span of time. Not only the two above mentioned journalists but many others like them have also been targeted by the different groups of religious (Seatrain) terrorist organisations during the recent past.

Influence of Heredity in Pakistani Media

As we discussed in previous chapters that influence of heredity is a great dilemma of modern day Pakistan and it has produced worst repercussions on both public and privately owned organisations of the country. It's a fact of the day that in modern day Pakistan elites of every type here whether political, industrial, religious, journalistic etc., are promoting only their families and relatives for the high positions. Above mentioned formula is working in media as well, though massive fraction of media in Pakistan belongs to private sector even then the influence of heredity is widespread and deep-rooted in it not only at management level (key positions like editor-in-chief, managing editor etc., always belongs to owners even if they are illiterate as they are the investors) but also at middle and lower level portfolios.

Before going in to more details lets a have a brief look on the structure of media in Pakistan. Among at least 130 electronic media outlets in the country majority belongs to the fraction of News and current affairs and major share among these outlets belongs to private sector and state-owned Pakistan Television corporation owns only six among them. Similarly, among 30 operating news agencies in the country only two (News National International, NNI and Associated Press of Pakistan, APP) belong to the government sector, remaining are owned by the private sector. Almost all mainstream newspapers among the 360 dailies are owned by private sector of the country.

Pakistan Television Corporation like many other state-owned organisations of the country possesses a great culture of heredity, kinship and political and bureaucratic influence. Majority among the anchors, news readers, reporters and even artists working with PTV have attained their positions by utilising their influences, that's why standards of news bulletins, talk shows and other programmes of PTV has gone to such low extent during the last few years that massive fraction of journalists are not any more rating it among the top level News outlets of the country. It's a great dilemma of media industry that its state-owned media organisations are not able to fully utilise the tool of freedom of expression while on the other hand privately-owned media is using it in a manner such as to suggest a massive abuse of power. A very large fraction of privately owned media in Pakistan is involved in yellow journalism for meeting its commercial agendas, this aspect of journalism is also causing severe repercussions.

Appointment of non-professionals or poorly trained ones at key positions through influence of heredity, kinship and other influences is a great matter of concern for massive fraction of media industry in Pakistan. Almost all editors from leading media outlets including both print and electronic media are holding their positions due to influences of heredity. Most owners are greatly involved in directing editorial and news policies despite their scarce knowledge about journalism. Above mentioned practice is greatly responsible for biased and politically motivated journalism in the country. As we discussed before that after the success and influences of conventional media groups (who are mainly attached with journalism) a fraction of business and industrial tycoons decided to invest in media in early 2000's era. This fraction of investors were only interested in protecting their commercial and political interests rather than journalism and they sought to only utilise the media as a tool for threatening governments and protecting and enhancing their real business, so their emergence in the media industry also produced severe repercussions on traditional norms and values of journalism in Pakistan.

It's a matter of fact that those business and industrial tycoons who invested in the field of media during the last fifteen years have grown their businesses in a very astonishing manner. A very important industrial group of the country was facing severe circumstances during the early days of military regime of Pervaiz Musharraff due to its tax evasions and bank frauds. NAB arrested the chief executive officer of the group in 2000 but later released him after settling a deal through plea bargain. After facing such humiliation, the owners of the group decided to invest in media and the particular industrial group launched a nationwide Urdu newspaper in 2002. Later the group invested more in media and launched a news channel and English language newspaper as well, currently the group is considered among the leading media outlets of the country. As per its rivals, the above mentioned group received massive commercial interests during the PPP led government of 2008-13. This particular media group provided a massive support to the PPP led coalition government throughout its regime, an act which was heavily criticised by the massive fraction of other media. Similarly, a businessman-cum-politician (Nazim-e-Ala) who served as Lord Mayor of Lahore district for two consecutive terms of 2001-05 and 2005-09 respectively also entered in the arena of media in 2008, before the end of his second term. This media group is now considered among the most influential media outlets of the country.

Jang/Geo group is the largest independent media corporation in Pakistan and considered most vocal and active in the fight for the basic rights of freedom of expression in the country. Editor-in-chief of Jang media group Mir Shakeel-U-Rehman is groomed and equipped enough and has high journalistic values due to extensive trainings provided by his legendary father (Late) Mir Khaili-U-Rehman, commonly known as MKR. MKR is considered as the founding father of Journalism of modern day Pakistan who he spent a massive portion of his life for the cause of fearless and unbiased Journalism in the country. Jang/Geo group has paid heavy prices for its stance against ongoing injustices and discriminations in the country. Administrations of some other media groups alongside with Jang/Geo group are in the hands of what one can call as 'the real Journalists'. Dawn and Nway-Waqat groups also familiar for their traditional editorial and news policies are headed by Hameed Harron and Ramiza Majeed Nizaimi respectively. Similarly, Mujeeb-ur-Rehman Shami another very renowned veteran journalist heading Daily Pakistan is also among those who are following the norms, values and principles of journalism. Massive fraction of Editors other than above mentioned media groups are associated with industrial and business tycoons and they have very limited knowledge about the media.

Editors of non-journalistic backgrounds have been involved in massive exploitation of the journalistic community generation after generation. Recently, an editor of mainstream news-paper from Lahore was involved in an incident of massive violence with one of his staff members. The crime of this miserable staffer was that he had enquired about his remaining salaries of the past six months from the so called editor. This particular Editor holds his post as his father is performing as chief editor in a similar organisation. Above mentioned incident is just a little glimpse of the picture, there are many others like this so called editor who are involved in severe crimes and massive exploitations of their staff members. It's a great dilemma of media industry in Pakistan that massive fraction of ignorant, cruel and low calibre editors are ruling over a very well educated and skilled fraction of journalists in Pakistan due to their influence of heredity.

Majority among the young editors who are holding their offices due to hereditary influences are of low calibre and very unfamiliar with journalistic norms and values yet they are the integral part of the ruling elite of the country as they were born with silver spoons. It's a matter of fact that like many other dynasties such as political, religious, industrial etc., there exist media dynasties as well in Pakistan. Massive fraction of media workers believe that the attitude of young editors who got their positions through hereditary influences is autocratic enough and very similar to their political counterparts, so here too influence of heredity and kinship is playing a vital role for an individual's progress and achievements.

Now we will discuss another aspect of influence of heredity in Pakistani media and this dilemma belongs to senior editors or the journalistic elite who are not part of owner's community. Journalistic elite of the country (both in print and electronic media) are familiar for promoting their next generations in their organisations and for discouraging talented youth not belonging to their family and kinship. It looks astonishing but it's a very harsh reality that massive fraction among the media elite are always seeking to fit in their family members at key positions in the renowned media outlets of the country. Massive fraction of senior editors in both the public and privately owned media organisations of the country treat their juniors very inhumanly and discourage them so as to make space for their own relatives, let's have a look at few examples.

Nazir Naji a senior journalist and Editor of Daily Dunya faced severe criticism by the massive fraction of Junior Journalists in the country for promoting his son Aneeq Naji in electronic media, currently Aneeq is hosting a show by the name of Talash (Search) on Dunya News which is a sister organisation of Daily Dunya and among the top rated electronic media outlets of the country. Previously Mr Naji was attached with Daily Jang as a senior columnist and there too his son Aneeq was hosting a show by the name of Band File (Closed file). Similarly Yasir Peerzadah columnist of Daily Jang and analyst of Geo news/former co-host of the show Chauraha is the son of Atta-Ul-Haq Qasmi, a senior columnist of Daily Jang and a public office holder in Punjab government. Another senior anchor and producer of Geo News, Abdul-Rauf, faced severe criticism by the massive fraction of junior journalists for introducing his teenage son Hamza in talk show Hamza Nama telecasted few years ago by Geo News. Ummar Chudhray and Bilal-U- Rasheed are sons of senior journalists Asad-Ullah Gahlib and Haroon-U-Rasheed, (holding key positions in mainstream newspapers of the country) hence there are many among the young journalists who have been able to acquire their positions only due to their family influences in the media industry.

TV Anchors a New Form of Elite in Pakistan

Expansion of electronic media after 2000 in Pakistan has produced a new form of elite in the country which are called as talk show hosts or anchors. Before the emergence of electronic media print version of media was not a much profitable source of earning and with the exception of a few most journalists were very deprived economically. But in modern day Pakistan the presenters of news in electronic media (particularly Television form of it) are among the very influential factions of the society. Salaries up to millions, and widespread popularity has created almost a stardom for them and has given such a boom to this class that it has now become an integral part of the ruling elite in Pakistan.

Boom of electronic version of news outlets has produced severe repercussions on the newspaper industry and its circulation is now restricted within specific circles only. Massive fraction of commoners who possess no interests in columns, editorials and features are now heavily dependent on Television for watching news. Most people are now very much familiar with Television anchors and are following their debates and talk shows as majority among the commoners like to discuss politics in streets and drawing rooms.

Contrary to this, the reporters, news editors and column writers have lost their grandeur to a great extent during the last few years and due to this massive fraction of print media outlets are going through very difficult circumstances.

Emergence of electronic media outlets during last fifteen years in Pakistan has produced different kind of impacts on media industry in the country. Investments by the fraction of industrial and business tycoons in electronic media has forced the conventional tycoons of print media to invest in electronic media as well and this has produced both good and bad repercussions on massive factions of journalists in Pakistan. Majority among the journalists were earning minutely before the emergence of electronic media in the country but with its emergence and stability many among the journalists are now fetching more as electronic media outlets have generated more opportunities for the massive fraction of senior journalists. Column writers and editors who got positions in electronic media alongside their conventional positions in the print form of media attained boom and glory within a short span of time. Earnings of above mentioned fraction of journalists increased in a rapid manner and they inducted themselves among the upper factions of society. But the other side of the picture is not so bright, as with the emergence and stability of electronic media, print media has been shifted to the back seat and even the media houses that have both print and electronic presence are now more focussed on the latter. Hence revenue of most print media outlets have gone down and massive fraction of employees in these organisations started to feel the deprivation shortly after the boom in electronic media. Faction of owners are giving more preference to electronic media as many among the Senior Journalists now prefer to work only for the electronic media. Print media outlets are carrying on with relatively junior teams and induction of new and enthusiastic talent in print media has stopped as many among the young journalists now seek to attain positions only in electronic media, due to this trend standard of print media has gone down to a great extent during the last few years.

Profession of journalism had no attraction for the educated fraction of upper income groups in Pakistan up till the late 1990's and only a minute fraction of educated lower middle class was willing to be the part of the media industry in that particular era. Journalists of lower middle class were involved to a great extent in highlighting the issues of ordinary people like hunger, disease, injustice and discriminations, but the emergence of Television Journalism attracted the educated youth of upper income groups as well, many among the young goons of the elite and upper middle factions of the society are now part of Television Journalism due to its widespread influences and boom. Many among the sons and daughters of civilian and military bureaucrats and youth from the fraction of business elite have also became the part of this class during the last few years. These Mummy-Daddy (a terminology used in

Pakistan for describing the youth from upper factions of the society) guys and girls got solo flights for attaining highest positions in electronic media and superseded most of the already working journalists of humble backgrounds, that's why many among the new generation journalists are not familiar with journalistic norms and values.

Unlike massive fraction of journalists from humble backgrounds, the new age journalists from wealthy families are not well known to the socioeconomic issues of the commoners so they have failed to a great extent in discussing the severe circumstances of the ordinary people in their talk shows. It's a matter of fact that journalists from lower fraction of population who have worked in print media have been able to contribute much more to television journalism also due to their understanding of socioeconomic problems faced by the commoners of the country. Senior anchors including Hamid Mir and Javeed Ch who have emerged from lower middle class fraction of the society are more focused on socioeconomic issues as compared to their young counterparts from upper income groups. Young talk show hosts hailing from upper income groups including Shahzeb Khanzadah, Sana Buccha, Usama Ghazi and Mehar Bukhari have faced severe criticism by many senior journalists for their non-professional attitudes and misconduct with guests during their shows.

To recapitulate all we summarise that boom of electronic media on the positive side has provided more chances to commoners for raising their voices against the ongoing discriminations and injustices and have increased employment opportunities, but on the negative side it has also enhanced conflicts and frustrations among the deprived factions of the society as the newly emerged elite of anchors have still not been able to highlight the core issues of the country in its correct perspective.

Part III

6

Religion as a Tool of Terror and Discrimination in Pakistan

Islam is considered as the most modern religion by its followers among all divine faiths due to its latest time span. It possesses enough flexibility and encourages inter religion harmony and peace and prophesizes mutual cooperation and understanding among masses. Muhammad (PBUH) the apostle of God and the first ruler of Islamic state Medina showed a character of diplomacy and cooperation towards non-Muslim inhabitants. Muhammad (PBUH) played a role of a mediator and diplomat to enhance socioeconomic cooperation among the Muslims and non-believers (Jews) and designed first ever written constitutional document for human beings on earth. Political, civic, and religious clauses of charter of Medina are the reflector of prophetic wisdom, vigilance and flexible attitude of Muhammad (PBUH) towards humanity. This charter protected the rights of both Muslims and Jews and constituted one political Ummah (mutual national cooperation) and formed a society based upon the mutual respect, dignity and economic-political cooperation.

Islam being a religion, always promoted order, peace and harmony among masses and discouraged hate ridden attitude. Quran, the divine book, through its teachings promotes provision of order and stoppage of disorder and injustice among Muslims and the whole mankind. Let's have a look at some Quranic verses that teaches mankind about peace and order.

"When it is said to them, create no disorder in land, they revolt; we only seek to promote peace. Take note most certainly it is they who create disorder but they realise it not.

(Al –Baqrah verses 12-13)

Above mentioned verses of Holy Quran describes the behaviour of unlawful people involved in breaching the orders of the Almighty and creating disharmony and conflicts among the masses, the holy book has given a strict verdict against such people. Islam not only promotes inter religion peace but it also advises its followers to stop conflicts among Muslims as well for the formation of a Umma. Let's have a look on another verse of Quran advising Muslims for unity.

"And hold firmly the rope of Allah altogether and do not involve in division, Remember you were enemies but by his favour now brothers, you were on the edge of a pit of fire and he saved you from it. This the Almighty makes clear through his verses so that you may be guided.

(Al-Imran 103)

But religion of peace, harmony, justice and mutual human cooperation is widely used for disharmony, conflicts, injustice and discrimination among both Muslims and non-believers and among Muslims as well in the so called land of pure. Modern day Pakistan has become a great hub of socioeconomic, political and religious injustices through various means. Religion too is widely utilised for spreading injustice, discrimination and terror with too many other tools.

It's a matter of great concern that religious militant organisations are involved in killings of their opponents. Almost every sect among the Muslims in Pakistan possess its militant wings. Injustice and discrimination is very deep-rooted and widespread in the name of religion in Pakistan. Citizens of the state are facing harsh attitude in public and private sector organisations, residential areas and in other social institutions just because of their religious views and practicing sects. Religious organisations possess monopolies in social, educational and public institutions where they promote or discriminate people on the bases of religion and sect.

- **Discrimination in Social Institutions**

Social institutions like colleges, universities, parks, cinemas and other public and private sector organisations hold a key importance in growth and development of nations and societies. Religion is kept apart from social institutions in civilised and globalised world of modern day. But here in Pakistan lobbies and monopolies on the bases of religion and sect (in fact, sect is the cause of division among major fraction of society as more than 95 per cent of total population is Muslim) are involved in the destruction of social institutions. This has weakened the very fabric of social institutions and majority among the masses are getting involved in massive conflicts and adopting a hate ridden attitude for each other.

Religious organisations in the country representing different sects are influential enough and they are utilising their power and influence to promote their dear and near ones to important portfolios. Islamic orthodox groups possess massive influences in educational and other social institutions where they manipulate merit with the help of their fellows and promote people of specific thoughts and views. Religious biasness is producing severe impacts on social institutions of the country; let's have a look with some examples.

With more than 30,000 students, University of Punjab is the largest and oldest top level public sector educational institute in Pakistan. University of Punjab commonly called as PU has been under constant influence of orthodox Islamic student union, Islami -Jamiet-e-Talba (part of orthodox Islamic political clerics Jamat-e-Islami) since a long span of time. IJT is under heavy criticism since early 1960's from different factions of the society due to its manner of involvement in admissions and appointments of staff in the university. Due to its massive influence, IJT imposed Islamic clerics in the guise of teachers who promoted its ideology and specific views through discriminated attitude towards its non-followers. IJT formed a state within state during 1960 to 2000 for promoting a specific agenda and its own type of Islam through its influence and power. Many among the former students of PU confirmed that they were forced to join IJT during their stay in the university. IJT influence was at its peak during 1970-2000 but after 2000 it started losing its grip but even in 2014 it still possesses substantial influence and is involved in student politics in the name of religion.

Students and teachers of IJT adopted a hostile attitude towards their opponents during 1960 to early 2000's. Opponents of IJT claim that office holders of student organisations were given full privilege by the teachers and awarded with good grades and this procedure continued generation after generation. As to how this system of discrimination on the basis of religion and sect works, let's have a look.

"It was a boring interview and it seemed that the panel had already pre-selected the candidates for the posts advertised and interview was just a formality", said Ali Naqvi a chemical engineer graduate from University of Punjab. "Head of panel was a former Nazim (former leader of IJT) of Islami Jameat Talba. He treated me and some others in a very rude manner though I had very good academic records, but those who were part of IJT were given much preference. It was very astonishing for me that among the selected candidates more than 90 per cent were the part of a specific student organisation and majority among the rejected ones including me were not a part of that student organisation", Naqvi added more.

It's not only the matter of Punjab University, Jamat-e-Islam and its allied organisations possess influence in other different public and semi-government organisations and its members promote IJT workers in those organisations. Labour organisations of Jamat are also functional in different public sector organisations "Preem" is the name of labour union of Jamat in Pakistan railways. Preem too faced severe allegations for promoting people on behalf of specific views. President of Preem, Hafiz Salman Butt (former member of National Assembly) came under heavy criticism for not only corruption but for spreading religious violence.

Images of Violence and Burning in a Chirstain Colony of Lahore

Many other religious groups also possess influence in public, semi-government and in some private institutes (also few industrial groups) where they promote or discriminate people on the basis of religion and sects. Tabeeghi-Jamat, a group of Sunni orthodox Muslims also possesses enough influence in many public sector organisations of the country. Members of this religious group are known to promote only their sect fellows. According to a former Professor of Faisalabad University of Agriculture, one former dean (Professor Dr Shoiab Akhtar) of faculty of veterinary and animal sciences of UAF only promoted the members of Tableeghi-Jamat during his tenure from 2003-08. Faculty members and students belonging to other sects heavily criticized Dr Shoiab Akhtar for giving undue favours to members of TJ in faculty matters. According to another Professor majority among the faculty appointed during the regime of above mentioned Dean belongs to TJ, now those members of faculty are also involved in similar discriminations.

Pakistan is a country of Sunni majority as most of the population (88-90 per cent) in the country belongs to this fraction of Islam. Shiites (called Shia's in Urdu) are in minority. According to Pew research centre, Washington, Shiites are 10-15 per cent of total population in the country. Some other sources claim that the population of Shiites has increased during last twenty years in Pakistan and now it is between 18-20 per cent. Shiites are generally very well educated, skilled and qualified as compared to the majority masses, so they hold most of the high profile positions in civil and military bureaucracy. Some Sunni journalists and intellectuals believe that Shiite bureaucrats and other high ranked officials in public sector organisations are utilising their influences to sabotage merit and promote their own community.

"I was sitting in front of a section officer of ministry of commerce and trade in Islamabad", said Ahmed Hassan a trader from Bahawalpur. "My file was pending for several months and concerned officials were not responding to me properly. I got the reference of above mentioned officer from a friend and went to meet him. After listening to me he too denied to help me out. I was disappointed enough but was asking him for some solution when suddenly a peon of the section officer came inside the room and informed that a person named Almadar Husain (famous Shiite name in Pakistan) wanted to meet him. Then a man came inside the office (who was unfamiliar to him but was from his religious community) and greeted him with a Shiite slogan. The officer responded to him in a very warm manner and neglected me at once. That man described his issue which was very much similar to mine, to this the officer at once conceded to think about the issue and said that hopefully a solution will also be found, whereas upon realising that I was still in his office he dismissed me by saying that he had to go somewhere and would discuss the issue later."

- **Role of Religious Institutions in Violence and Terror**

Religious institutes of all sects like Masjids (Mosques) and Madarsas (Religious schools of different sects) are widely utilised for spreading violence, terror, conflicts and hate in Pakistan. Islamic clerics from all school of thoughts are responsible for spreading violence and terror in the society and for this purpose they utilise their institutes as a means. Freedom of expression is widely used to expand sectarian differences among different sects. It's a reality that office holders of different sectarian organisations are responsible to a great extent for widespread and deep-rooted sectarian violence in the country. Most among the office holders of religious institutes (more than 99 per cent religious institutes in Pakistan belongs to private sector, unlike the developed Islamic countries like Turkey and Malaysia state-owned religious institutes are very rare in Pakistan) show hatred for the opposite sects with ease and comfort though their speeches and writings and feel no accountability for such behaviour.

It is very strange that there is no regular pattern for the appointments in religious institutes in both private and public sector. Most among the Immams (prayer leaders) in both rural and urban areas are not very well literate in either religious or formal matters. Very few among prayer leaders in urban areas are well educated. While addressing the Friday prayer on some special occasions like Eid Festival etc., majority among the religious speakers criticise opposite sects and through their stance promote violence and terror. It has been witnessed that rural Immams and speakers are more involved in sectarian violence as compared to their counterparts in cities. Religious schools in larger cities possess relatively educated and moderated members of staff. Many among the religious schools situated in larger cities of country like Karachi, Lahore, Rawalpindi etc., possess international donors (Pakistani settled in USA, Europe and Middle East with religious back-grounds like to donate for these religious schools). Some among these donors are willing to make changes in traditional system of religious schools so they ask the religious leaders for reforms and modifications in typical system of religious education. Some among the religious schools working in larger cities are offering both religious and scientific education to their students, which is a good sign for the society. But majority of religious schools in Pakistan are in rural areas like South Punjab, FATA and Interior Sind and these areas are a great hub of militancy, terror and extremism.

- **Influence of Heredity in Religious Institutions**

Like many other public and private sector organisations influence of heredity is widespread and deep-rooted in religious institutions in Pakistan as well. Selection of heads/office holders in majority of religious schools in Pakistan is not democratic or merit based. Religious institutes too follow the principal of influence of heredity like political dynasties in Pakistan. In other words, we can say that like political dynasties there are religious dynasties as well in the form of Madarsas. Religious schools of almost every school of thought like Sunni, Shiite, and others (Deobandi, Braelvi etc.) support the influence of heredity during major appointments. A deceased chairperson is replaced by his closest next generation kin at the same portfolio. Successors who get the position due to their ancestral superiority perpetuate the same traditional policies (mainly based upon hate ridden attitude for other sects) for the survival and enhancement of their business. This attitude is the main source of ongoing conflicts among different sects generation after generation.

Influence of heredity is followed in all types of religious institutes in Pakistan including religious schools and shrines as well. Shrines possess great importance among religious institutes in Pakistan. There are hundreds of shrines of Sufis and saints widespread in every corner of the country. Guardians of most of the shrines in Pakistan belong to Sunni Berelvi sect though many shrines belong to the Shiites as well. A deep-rooted system of heredity is associated with these shrines in Pakistan. The office of Sajadah Nasheen (spiritual leader, custodian of shrine) of a religious institute is equivalent to the office of a chairperson and is allocated on the basis of heredity and kinship. This system of heredity and kinship was not common in the ancient and medieval periods of Islam. Saints and Sufis of pious and noble characters preferred to nominate their successors on the basis of Islamic education and character, but with the passage of time those traditions have degraded and now religious heads are also chosen on the basis of heredity and kinship in Pakistan.

A spiritual leader holds key importance in Pakistani society; his influence is widespread and deep-rooted. Spiritual leaders commonly called as Peer Sahabs, Maulanas and Sajadah Nashhens by the different sects show harsh attitude towards the opposite sects so as to establish their own superiority among their followers. Almost all type of religious schools, shrines and mosques are involved in public charities and donations, very few among them receive government grants but a fraction of religious schools in Pakistan receive foreign aids. Spiritual and religious leaders who are running shrines and religious schools adopt different tactics for fund generation. Easiest way to generate fund is to produce hostile attitude towards opposite sects. Majority among the spiritual leaders exploit the emotions of their followers and utilise this for their own interests. Repercussion of this is enhancement in sectarian violence which has reached an extreme level during the last few years. When a religious leader of any sect claims that his is the religion that is true, divine and gifted among all other faiths, he also demands more funds from his followers for the enhancement of that particular type of faith across the world.

- **Sectarian Violence in Pakistan**

Sectarian violence is very common in modern day Pakistan. Clerics of every type (belonging to different sects) are involved in motivating the masses against each other on the basis of religion and sect and the repercussion of this practice is massive bloodshed in every corner of the country. Sectarian violence started in the country during early 1980's during the regime of military ruler Zia-Ul-Haq. Pakistan played an integral part in the Soviet cold war in

Afghanistan (started December 24, 1979 and ended February 15, 1989) and faced its severe repercussions.

It's a matter of fact that Sunni militants belonging to different factions like Al Qaeda, Jamat-e-Islami, Itehad Islam and other orthodox groups participated in this cold war in Afghanistan against the USSR with the cooperation of ISI and CIA. Collapse of USSR and victory of USA in proxy war in Afghanistan with the help of its allies including Pakistan, Saudi Arabia, Sunni militant groups etc., produced severe repercussions on Pakistan after the end of the war. Pakistan though was a major participant (provided manpower and techniques) but it faced severe repercussions of its favours to USA during the war against Soviet Union. Sectarian violence, smuggling and increased crime rate were the major side effects for Pakistan after the end of Soviet invasion in Afghanistan.

Sunni orthodox groups from Afghanistan, Pakistan, Saudi Arabia, and from other Gulf countries gathered in Afghanistan for challenging USSR under the supervision of two major intelligence agencies (CIA and ISI) of the world. Above mentioned agencies played a vital role for the utilisation of Sunni extremist groups against USSR in the name of jihad. End of war and dissolution of USSR was a great success for both USA and Pakistan but the residue warriors were left without any rehabilitation.

Some among these militant groups who were the integral part of war against USSR got involved in civil war in Afghanistan very soon after the war and the remaining diverted their intentions towards Pakistan. These militants (who migrated to Pakistan) intermingled with different local militant groups and started different crimes in the country. These clerics who were left alone after the end of Soviet war became a very solid threat for the writ of government in Pakistan. They were paid in the last days of cold war by USA but now they had no livelihood choices other than committing robberies, smuggling drugs, kidnapping for ransoms and target killings, and these they did with ease and comfort.

Pakistan was not very familiar with sectarian violence until early 1980's but since then it has been a great hub of violence in the name of religion and sect. According to a report of Daily Dawn published on January 6, 2014, sectarian violence has increased in the country during the last few years particularly during the last year. Report stated that suicide attacks were used frequently during the last five years in this war between different sects. According to Pakistan security report published by Pakistan Institute of Peace Studies in 2013, there has been a constant increment in sectarian violence in the country since 2011. The report stated that the number of suicide attacks related with sectarian violence increased upto 39 per cent during 2013 in comparison with its previous year. It stated that there had been 208 incidents of sectarian violence in the country during the previous year. These incidents caused 658 deaths and 1195 were seriously injured. The report also claimed that most among the suicide attacks during 2013 in Pakistan were associated with sectarian violence.

It's a harsh reality of day that dozens of religious militant groups in Pakistan are involved in sectarian violence with full ease and comfort and they feel no accountability for their activities. These religious militant organisations were formed during mid 1980's and early 90's. In the year 2002, military ruler General Pervaiz Musharraff banned almost all sectarian organisations but after 2008 with the end of military regime of General Musharraff these religious militant groups regained their influence and started operations with changed names and slogans across the country. Here we will discuss some among the religious militant groups in the country. Sipah-E-Shaba Pakistan commonly called as SSP is a banned militant turned political organisation which started its operations in mid 1980's. Being a Sunni orthodox group it started its operations against Shiites minority and got influence among a fraction belonging to Deo Bandi School of Thought of Sunni population. SSP was banned in 2002 by military ruler Pervaiz Musharraff due to its massive involvement in violence against Shiites, SSP faced severe criticism from different factions of society due to its alleged involvement in target killing of Shiites in the country during 1985 to early 2000's. In 2002, military administration in the country declared it as a terrorist group and froze its accounts and assets.

End of another military regime (August 18, 2008) in the country was a sigh of relief for SSP and other religious terrorist organisations in Pakistan, SSP was dissolved into different smaller factions with the same ideology before the end of General Musharraff's rule and these small factions felt liberated after his resignation as a president. Now-a-day's Ahmed Ludhyanawi, a cleric from the city of Jhang is carrying the political and religious legacy of Azam Tariq (Late) the founding chairman of SSP. Ahmed renamed SSP as 'Jamat-e-Ahla Sunat' and is presently participating in parliamentary politics as well. Ahmed Ludhyanvi according to some analysts tried to portray himself as a moderate religious leader for the sake of his political career but majority among the political analysts of the country still believe that he is still following the former agenda of SSP. Ahmed got 40,000 plus votes for the seat of national assembly and remained second against the PML (N) candidate Sheikh Muhammad Akram from NA-89 Jhang.

Repercussion of sectarian violence is a great human loss during the last twenty five years in the country, thousands of ordinary and even VIP's lost their lives and thousands of others got serious injuries due to this terror and injustice in the name of religion and sect. Innocent citizens from all sects were victimised by religious militant organisations operating under the banner of particular sects. Both Sunni and Shiite militant groups are involved in massacre of their opponents and this is leading towards massive conflicts and anarchy among the masses as well and this has been going on since the last twenty five years.

Lashkar-e-Jangvi commonly called as L.J a spilt group of the former SSP has also been accused for several incidents of violence against Shiites in Pakistan during the last fifteen years. L.J was formed in 1996 when SSP activist Riaz Basra (later killed in police encounter) broke away from SSP due to his differences with senior leaders of SSP and formed his own organisation. L.J is declared as a terrorist organisation in Pakistan and United States due to its involvement in attacks on Shiite Muslims since a long span of time. L.J started its operations in mid 1990's with a widespread and deep-rooted mechanism against the Shiites in Pakistan. Riaz Basra co-founder of L.J alongside with Akram Lahori (founder of L.J with Basra) gained notoriety when he orchestrated the assassination of Iranian diplomat Sadiq Ganji in Lahore. Basra was involved in killing of Iranian air force cadets who visited Pakistan in early 90's. Basra's organisation L.J was very much responsible for producing strain in diplomatic relationship between Pakistan and Iran. Some sources claimed that L.J was also involved in the murder of Benazir Bhutto (twice prime minister of the country 1988-1990 and 1993-1996, killed on December 27, 2007).

Benazir Bhutto commonly called as BB being the chairperson of Pakistan people's party (one of the progressive political party in the country) was very popular among the liberal factions of society in Pakistan. She was not only a seasoned politician but possessed a worldwide recognition as a scholar on politics and international affairs but orthodox fraction of society in Pakistan was not happy with her politics and policies. Being a part of moderate Shiite family she was in focus of Sunni militant groups from a long span of time. Militants who were in search of her were not able to cause her any damage as she was in exile and living in London and Dubai during the regime of military rule of Pervaiz Musharraff. She came back to Pakistan in October 2007 under an agreement (National reconciliation order was signed among military ruler Pervaiz Musharraff and BB, according to this agreement military government conceded to close the corruption cases against BB which were filed in the 1990's by the then PML (N) governments in return for her acceptance of Musharraff as a president) with the establishment for the provision of safe passage for her future politics. She was attacked with suicide bombers on 18th October 2007 when she landed in Karachi airport. More than 150 workers of PPP lost their lives and more than 500 were seriously injured but BB escaped narrowly. But fortune was not with her on 27th December 2007 when she was again attacked after a political address in an election campaign for the elections to be held in January 2008 (later elections were postponed for one month and held in February 18, 2008). A bullet was fired which damaged her skull and she lost her life on the way to hospital. Death of BB was a great loss of Pakistani politics as her political was a great asset for the country.

L.J took the responsibility for the killings of 26 Shiite pilgrims who were travelling towards Iran by a bus on 20th September 2011 in the Maustung area of Baluchistan. L.J is also involved in some other incidents of such killings, it took the responsibility of February 2013 incident of Quetta in which 81 men and women were killed and 178 were seriously injured in a terrorist attack on religious public gathering of Shiites.

As we discussed earlier religious militancy in Pakistan comprises of both Sunni and Shiite militant groups. Both sects accuse their opponents for spreading terror and discrimination in the name of religion but Sunni's are in majority as more than 88 per cent among the Muslims in Pakistan belongs to Sunni sects (Sunni's too possess different sub-sects and they too have rivalries with each other but it is not too severe). Shiites are at least 12 per cent of total Muslim population in the country and they too are divided into different sub- sects as well. Shiites are generally very well educated, skilled and moderate in attitude as compared to majority of the Sunni population of the country. But even then Shiites too possess some militant elements among them. Spiah-e-Muhammad Pakistan is a Shiite militant group in Pakistan which emerged in 1994 in reaction to violence against Shiites by the Sunni orthodox groups. Some other Shiite militant groups are also involved in activities against the Sunni's. According to some analysts there is a widespread and deep-rooted belief in the masses that both the Sunni and Shiite militant groups are being supported by foreign aids. It is always being said that Sunni militant groups are getting finance from Saudi Arabia and some other countries in gulf region for working against the Shiite minority. Similarly, Sunni factions of population accuse Iran for supporting Shiite militant groups. Both Sunnis and Shiites accuse each other for the target killings of their spiritual leaders. The Shiites accuse SSP and L.J for the target killings of Shiite leaders in the recent past and the Sunnis accuse SMP for their involvement in the killings of various Sunni leaders.

- **Killing of Hazara Community in Pakistan**

Hazara is a very peaceful, very well educated and moderate community in Pakistan which belongs to Shiite Islam. Most among the Hazaras are living in the province of Baluchistan since hundreds of years, so this community is native of Baluchistan though is spread in Afghanistan and Iran as well. At least 3000 men, women and Hazara children were killed and 5000 were seriously injured as a result of attacks on the Hazaras during the last few years in Pakistan. According to a documentary 'I am Hazara' telecasted by one of the top news channels in Pakistan-Dawn News, the documentary stated that 10,000 Hazras have been killed in target killings in Quetta the capital of Baluchistan. Such a massacre has forced this shrinking community in Pakistan to search for escape routes and leave their homeland which is much precious to them as compared to anything in the world.

Demonstartion aginst Shia Killing in Lahore

It was the era of early 2000s when the persecution of the Hazaras in Pakistan started in Quetta. On 9th of February 2001 six passengers were shot dead and five were seriously injured in a public van travelling on the route of Hazara town to Alamdar road, Quetta. This was the first of the heinous attacks against this community in the capital of the province, responsibility of the attack was taken by a Sunni militant group very soon after the attack. Since then the Hazaras are facing severe repercussions of their unknown crimes. This community has been targeted in a merciless manner by the orthodox militants and these killings have led to severe repercussions. In the year 2007 there were 5,50,000 Hazaras in the country but according to statistics of 2013 more than 1,00,000 members of the community left Pakistan and currently only 4,00,000 have remained here and majority among them are also trying to migration to Australia, Canada and Iran.

The 2003 Quetta mosque bombing incident was the first of its type of terrorist attack in Pakistan as it was the very first time in the history of the country that suicide bombers were used to target a place of worship. It is considered among the deadliest attack on the Hazaras in Pakistan. At least 50 men died and 70 were seriously injured as a result of this attack which occurred when the victims were offering Friday prayer. According to sources Lasker-e-Jhangvi was involved in this massacre. In the year 2004, 48 more people from Hazara lost their lives as a result of different attacks carried by Sunni militant groups. It looks heart breaking that more than 1000 Hazaras lost their lives in the various targeted operations of the orthodox militants during 2004-10, in the capital of Baluchistan.

September 2010 bombing in Quetta, Hazara town Quetta shooting in 2011, January 2013 bombing, February 2013 Quetta bombing, and Mustung killings in 2014 are such incidents in recent days which has produced great loss to the Hazaras in Pakistan. At least 73 people were killed in September 2010 Quetta bombing and 160 were seriously injured on the occasion of Qudas day when the Hazaras were carrying processions to express their solidity for the Palestinians.

2011 Hazara town shooting refers to massacre of Hazaras on May 6, 2011 in Quetta. The shooting took place early in the morning around 6:30 am in a public park, three rockets were fired which were followed by heavy gun fires as well. At least one dozen people were killed at the spot and 15 were seriously injured. L.J took the responsibility of the incident within few hours. Sources say that atleast 55 innocent people from Hazara community were killed in different incidents of target killings, bombings and suicide attacks in 2012. Month of January 2013 proved to be very unfortunate for the Hazaras of Baluchistan when more than 130 members of this community lost their lives in two brutal incidents of Quetta and Sawat, 270 were injured seriously as well. It was 10th of January 2013 when several bombing incidents took place against the Hazaras both in Quetta and in Sawat Valley located in the northern part of the country." "It was such a heinous incident which shook the very fabric of the state in the country. Responding to this the then Prime Minister Raja Pervaiz Ashraf terminated the chief minister of Baluchistan Aslam Raisani from his office and imposed governor rule after a continuous agitation from the Hazara community and civil society of Pakistan. Measures taken by the PPP led coalition government to prevent such type of incidents in future were not sufficient enough for the provision of security to the Hazaras as the massacres continued. After the above mentioned incident Hazaras refused to perform the funeral of the dead ones until the arrest of culprits, they put the dead bodies on the roads of Quetta and started agitation which caused great defame to the PPP led government in the centre . The then federal minister for information and broadcasting conducted various meetings with the leaders of the community and ensured them about their protection in future and requested them to perform the funerals of those who had died in the above mentioned incident. At last the Hazaras agreed to carry out the funerals of the dead people upon the commitment of future protection.

The Hazaras were unfortunate enough that all their protests went in vain and security arrangement provided to the community once again collapsed within one month of the previous incident. Another heinous attack once again crushed the Hazaras, 16th of February was another dark day in the recent past of the country when at least 120 Hazaras were killed and more than 200 were injured in an explosion at the market of Hazara town, Quetta. Chief police officer of Quetta (then) Mr Zubiar Mehmood told the journalists that 70-80 kilogram explosive material was installed on a vehicle standing in the market place. Police sources claimed that Al-Qaeda affiliated Sunni orthodox group was suspected for the incident. According to some other sources L.J took the responsibility of the incident.

Protest Against Killings in Pakistan in London 2012

At least 30 Hazara's were killed in the incident of 30th June 2013 and 75 were seriously injured when a Sunni militant group carried out a suicide attack and exploded an improvised explosive device in a crowded area of Ali Abad in Quetta. Most recent incident against Hazaras in Quetta happened on 21st of January when a blast targeted the convoy of two Hazara pilgrim buses and four security vehicles near Dirnagar area of Mastung district Baluchistan. At least 32 people including women and children were killed in the particular incidents and 40 were seriously injured. Sunni extremist group took the responsibility of the incidents.

Above mentioned incidents are little glimpses of terror and discriminations on the basis of religion and sects in modern day Pakistan, thousands of other relatively smaller incidents are not even reported by the media as media too is under threats from orthodox groups, especially from some Sunni militant groups who are associated with Al Qaeda and Taliban.

Collective Funeral of Hazara's in Quetta

It's the fact of the day that sectarian violence is responsible for great conflicts and anarchy in the society. It is a great cause of migration and brain drain in modern day Pakistan. Thousands of qualified professionals including Shiites (Hazara, Ismailia), and some others belonging to non-Muslim minorities like Ahmedi's were compelled to leave Pakistan due to the worst circumstances and are now settled in UK, USA, and Australia. Many among these NRP's (Non Residential Pakistani's) are willing to serve the country but are not able to came back due to immense fear of the different militant groups.

Shia Massacred in Quetta 2013

- **Persecution of Non-Muslims in Pakistan**

Islamic republic of Pakistan possesses an absolute majority of Muslims, among 192 million of population 96.1 per cent comprises of Muslims.

Remaining 3.9 per cent are religious minorities including Christians, Hindus, Sikhs and Ahmedi's. Christians, Hindus and Ahmedi's are considered among three main factions of minorities among the non-Muslims in Pakistan. It's a harsh reality that religious minorities alongside with some other discriminated factions of the society are facing severe repercussions of injustice and terror. Constitution of Islamic Republic of Pakistan is based upon the orthodox principles of Islam and reduces the character of a non-Muslim in the society of Pakistan. According to Article 62 of the constitution of Islamic Republic of Pakistan a person who is willing to contest general elections in Pakistan for upper and lower houses of parliament (National Assembly and Senate) and for provincial assemblies as well should abide by Islamic teachings. Firstly, the person should possess adequate knowledge of Islamic teachings and should practice obligatory duties prescribed by Islam as well as abstain from major sins. Secondly, the person should be righteous, non-profligate, honest and pious.

Above mentioned article of constitution indicates that non-Muslims are not able to participate in general elections in the country as a non-Muslim can't be familiar with Islamic teachings and principles. It is a basic discrimination among Muslims and Non-Muslims in Pakistan, however non-Muslims possess a special quota in parliament (both in provincial assemblies and in National Assembly as well). After the most recent constitutional amendment, minorities can fetch four seats in upper house of parliament (Senate of Pakistan) as well. Non-Muslims are not able to hold the prestigious offices of prime miniter, president, chief miniters and governors due to

Pakistani Talbian Giving Interviwes to Diifrent Media Houses with Ease and Comfort

constitutional limitations. Similarly, minorities are not eligible for other important public offices such as chairperson of a public department, though there is no constitutional hurdle in it but biased attitude from Muslim majority does not provide opportunities to the religious minorities for achieving important portfolios.

Among 192 million, population of the country, religious minorities (Non-Muslims) are between 8.5-10 millions. Christians are between 3.5-4.5 millions and are considered as major fraction of minority in Pakistan. Hindus are between 3-4 millions and also considered among the sizeable fraction of minority, remaining 1.5-2.5 millions are minute factions among including Ahmedi's, Sikhs and Zorastrians etc. Ahmedi's or follower of Mirza Ghulam Ahmed of Qadiyan (a city of East Punjab) were declared non-Muslims in September 1974 by the 2nd constitutional amendment. The then spiritual leader of Ahmedi's, Mirza Nasir Ahmed (Fourth caliph of Ahmediya according to Ahmedi sources) was called in national assembly of Pakistan and had discussion with orthodox Muslim parliamentarians. After that long discussion between him and religious Muslim scholars, national assembly of Pakistan declared the Ahmedis as religious minority of Pakistan. Ahmedis in Pakistan have names, norms and values much like the Muslims, so it is difficult to estimate actual population of Ahmedis in Pakistan. Ahmedis claim that their count is between 4-5 millions in Pakistan, and most among them are settled in Punjab.

- **Socioeconomic Injustice with Non-Muslims in Pakistan**

Religious minorities in Pakistan are facing extremist attitude from orthodox pressure groups in the country. Christians, Hindus and Ahmedis are treated inhumanly most of the times by the militant religious organisations and by the orthodox groups of the country which is defaming the image of Pakistan in front of the whole world. Majority among the religious minorities in Pakistan is restricted within boundaries of their own social structure and not allowed to intermingle with Muslim population socially, economically and politically. Unlike most of the civilised and developed world, social interaction between the factions of majority (Muslims) and the minority (Non-Muslims) is very rare. Pakistani Muslim Diaspora in United Kingdom (More than 2.5 million people of Indian and Pakistani descent are settled in United Kingdom who got residencies after the partition of India) is very much intermingled with the majority English population. Unlike religious minorities in Pakistan, Muslims in UK and USA are enjoying full facilities and liberties like their majority population. Even in India, Muslim minority (though ratio of Muslims in India is much higher than the Hindus in Pakistan, Muslims are 15 per cent of total population in India while Hindus in Pakistan are not more than 1.5-2 per cent of total population) possess more socioeconomic and political involvements in the society as compared to minorities in Pakistan.

Muslim actors, singers, writers, directors and technicians have major participations in Bollywood. Fan following of Muslim actors including Shah Rukh Khan (called as King of Bollywood), Amir Khan (titled as Mr Perfect) and Salman Khan is much higher than the Hindu actors working in Indian film industry. Massive fan following of Muslim actors, directors and writers in Hindu majority indicates the fact that Muslims and other religious minorities in India are more prosperous as compared to Pakistan. It also describes the fact that Indian majority is more generous as compared to Pakistan as Muslims of India are more active in all fields of life. Among 13 Presidents of India 3 Muslims (Zakir Husain, Fukhar–U-Din Ali Ahmed and APJ Abdul Kalam) and one Sikh (Giani Zail Singh) took this prestigious office and, Manmohan Singh the renowned Indian economist who served as the prime minister of India during 2004-14 is also a Sikh. Singh is the only prime minister after Jawaharlal Nehru to be reelected for the next successive term.

Muslim community in India is also involved in various types of businesses in different parts of the country. Muslim traders of Hyderabad, Uttar Pradesh (Lucknow) and Gujarat (Ahmedabad) are contributing enough for the Indian economy. Azeem Hashim Preemji, a Muslim businessman from Bangalore is the third richest man in India. Preemji the chairmen of Wipro Limited possesses the net worth of 15.3 billons, the sixty eight year old tycoon was declared among the twenty powerful men in the world in 2000 by Time Magazine. He was listed among 100 most influential people in the world by the same organisation in 2004 and 2011 as well. He is the only businessman in the world to hold the title twice.

The content of official text books in Pakistan has been criticised since a very long span of time by the liberals and civil society of the country. Text books taught in Public schools and colleges (even majority among the private sector educational institutes have adopted the same books and course work) comprises enough material against the religious minorities of the country. During the regime of military dictator Zia-ul-Haq a programme for the Islamisation was started which included induction of Islamic chapters into text books. According to sustainable development policy institute, since the 1970's Pakistani text books started inducting hatred material against all religious minorities, especially Hindus, in a systematic pattern.

Daily Dawn reported about the hate content in Pakistani schools published on September 03, 2012 in this way "The primary and secondary schools curricula (being taught to children in public and private schools in Punjab and Sind) is replete with content that can fan hatred, prejudice, torture, extremism and religious intolerance in the society". "It is a matter of great concern that curricular content is targeting all religious minorities including Hindus, Christians, Sikhs and other minute factions of society but governments are adopting the policy of silence and not taking any action, a stance which has produced severe repercussions on the very fabric of society. Human rights organisations and civil society have been making lot of efforts to stop this brainwash through the medium of text books of the country since a very long span of time but their struggle has not been able to achieve results yet."

Sustainable development policy institute (SDPI) and International centre for religion and diplomacy presented a detailed report about ongoing widespread hatred instilled through text books in Pakistan and also discussed its repercussions. Above mentioned organisations used the methodology based upon following guidelines: (a) Analysis of all text books (b) Interview of students and teachers (c) Case study of incidents of discrimination (d) Inclusive coverage, education system of religious schools alongside with public schools were looked into.

Now we will have a look at some findings of SDPI through the material collected against Hindus, Christians and Sikhs in the text books of public schools. Let's have a little glimpse of the picture. Grade V text books of social study taught in KPK province stated as, "But Hindus never cooperated with Muslims, they were not ready to accept existence of Muslims in the Sub-content", Punjab text book board of grade VI contains such remarks about Hindus "Before the Arab conquest people were fed up with the teachings of Buddhism and Hinduism. The foundation of Hindu set up was based upon injustice and cruelty. The system of Islam which was based on justice, equality and brotherhood as descried earlier improved the Hindu culture and values."

It's a matter of great concern that text books in the country not only contain severe criticism about Hindus but it has not spared other religions as well. Few lines from grade VII social study text book of Punjab board describe Christians as thus, "Under Muslim region in Jerusalem, Muslim rulers treated non-Muslims including Christians and Jews in a very fair and just manner. They provided Christians all rights which they deserved but Christians never appreciated this, they never liked Muslim rule in Jerusalem and provoked their clan to fight against Muslims". Extract from a social study text book of Sind board thus describes the Sikhs, "The British and Sikh soldiers insulted the Muslims and killed their children. Great numbers of Muslims were forced to vacate Delhi and only one-fourth of total Muslim population remained in the city". An extract from a text book of social studies of Baluchistan board, thus implicates regarding Hindus and Sikhs, "Hindus and Sikhs started a massacre in Bharat (traditional name of India), in order to protect their lives, property, and honour 12.5 million Muslims started to migrate towards Pakistan."

National commission for justice and peace (NCJP) a peace and human rights organisation also indicated that the hatred instigating material in the text books of the country towards the religious minorities is a great reason behind the discrimination of minorities living in Pakistan. While talking to British Broadcasting Corporation (BBC) a senior journalist from Lahore said that the current circumstances of terrorism and extremism in the country are very much related with official academia of the country which is responsible for enhancing attitude of hatred among the masses. He claimed that extremist attitude of majority towards the minorities is the repercussion of syllabus taught in schools and colleges.

SDPI also described the rare interaction among Muslims and minority students in schools, colleges and Universities. The organisation conducted a survey among the students of different public and private educational institutes about the interaction among majority and minority factions of students. More than 70 per cent among Muslim students denied any interaction with non-Muslim students. Here are some remarks of Muslim students about their interactions with their counterparts belonging to the minority factions, "I do not want any friend from a non-Muslim fraction of society as their religion differs from us", said a male student from Punjab. Some other male students expressed the same sort of views like the above mentioned one. Female students looked more conscious while expressing their views on interaction with non-Muslim class fellows. "I do not have any non-Muslim friend in class as my parents do not allow me to do this", said a female student from Sind.

It's a true reality that religious minorities in Pakistan are facing severe socioeconomic injustice since a long span of time. Military dictator Zia-Ul-Haq started process of inducting orthodox Islamic rules in the society by the dint of the powers of martial law in 1979. This produced severe repercussions on the very fabric of the society. Masses in the country were liberal enough during its early history (1947 to late 70's), both ordinary citizens and upper fraction of society were intermingled with the minorities to a great extent-Karachi the largest city and first capital of the country had respect for religious diversity up till early 70's. Hindus, Christians, Buddhist, Zoroastrians (Parsis) and Jews were also the integral part of the society alongside with Muslims. Enough population of Hindus and Sikhs were residents of Lahore before and even after the partition of the Sub- until late 1960's.

Sikhs and Hindus who were the residents of Lahore and some other cities of Punjab after the partition slowly and gradually migrated either to India or settled in interior part of Sind. Majority among the Hindu population in Pakistan is settled in interior part of Sind very few have remained in Punjab now. According to Pakistan Hindu Council only 4821 Hindus are still living in Lahore among 10.5 million population of the city. Growing influence of Talibans on Pakistani society has produced very severe impacts on the overall social structure during the last few years. It has enhanced the ideology of forced Islamisation which was introduced during the regime of military dictator Zia during 1977-88. As we discussed earlier that there are three major factions of religious minorities in Pakistan including Hindus, Christians and Ahmedis, we will discuss all these one by one. Let's have a look.

- **Hindus in Pakistan**

The population of both Hindus and Christians are almost same in the country with a minute difference, statistics available about the population of religious minorities in Pakistan describe Hindus as the largest fraction among religious minorities in the country but some Christian organisations claim that Christians are more in number as compared to Hindus, so it seems a complicated and disputed issue some times. Population of Hindus in Pakistan is between 3.5-4.5 million (Wikipedia statistics of 2012) but Pakistan Hindu Council claims that Hindu population in the country is 7.2 million. Last census in Pakistan was held in 1998 so we can just estimate and have to depend on sources like Wikipedia.

Over whelming majority among the Hindus living in Pakistan is concentrated in Sind province, according to Pakistan Hindu Council Hyderabad and Tharprker districts comprise the bulk of Hindu population with a count of 10,47,501 and 11,09,994 respectively. Districts of Badin, Sanghar, Mirpur Khas, Umer kot and Ghotki also have a reasonable Hindu population between 1.6 to 2 million.

Hindus in Sind province of the country are facing harsh attitude of the feudal elite since a long span of time. Hindus in interior part of the Sind alongside with some other districts in Baluchistan has faced too much difficult circumstances in the recent past imposed by the local feudal class and gangs of criminals. In 1951, Hindus were 12.5 per cent of total population (this included East Pakistan as well, today's Bangladesh). Today number of Hindus has gone down to 1.7 per cent in Pakistan and 9.5 per cent in Bangladesh. The Hindu population in Pakistan was between 3.8-4 per cent at the arrival of 1970's which has now gone down to a great extent. At least 2.5 -3 million Hindus migrated to India during 1970-2014 from Pakistan.

Hindu girls are kidnapped and raped frequently in interior part of Sind and Baluchistan, traders too have been kidnapped for heavy ransom during the last three decades in rural areas of Sind and Baluchistan. Most among the offenders belong to feudal elite of both the provinces. Alliance of local criminals with feudal elite has caused more severe repercussions on the Hindus of Sind and Baluchistan; Daily Dawn reported a story on May 6, 2014 about recent violence against minorities in Pakistan in Larkana district of Sind where a mob caused a massive damage in a temple of Hindu community. According to the report an armed mob of dozens of people arrived at midnight, looted the gold and other precious ornaments from the temple and flew away with ease and comfort.

According to media reports, March 2013 proved as the worst month for the Hindu community of Sind in the last 20 years as more than six incidents of looting and burning the temples occurred in that particular month. According to a statement by 'Life for all' (A human rights organisation), at least five temples among nine in district Larkana were targeted in the month of March 2013. Syed Ali Shah reported in Daily Dawn that five Hindu children were abducted in Baluchistan during May 2014, according to the report the incident was reported in district Jafferabad an adjacent district to Sind province. While talking to media persons Syed Zafar Ali Shah the deputy commissioner of district Jafferabad told that children were going to school and armed men abducted them near Deara Allahyar. According to Ishfaq Ahmed, the district police officer, ages of children were between 5-10 years.

Kidnapping of members of Hindu community of Sind and Baluchistan is very common as they are among the easiest targets for the criminal gangs due to their widespread businesses and less influences in bureaucracy and government services. Hindus commonly called as 'Dewans' in Sind and Baluchistan are involved in different type of businesses so they are a great source of revenue generation for criminal gangs operating in interior Sind and Baluchistan. Due to this massive injustice with Hindus in Pakistan many among the top businessmen from the community have either shifted to India or to Dubai, Singapore and Malaysia during the last few years. Ram Singh Sodhi, a former member of Sind provincial assembly was shifted to India alongside with his twenty family members in 2011 due to security threats to his life and family. Sodhi was a Member of Parliament and among the upper fraction of society if he too was not secure imagine about the worst circumstances of lower income group of Hindus in Pakistan. Example of Sodhi is a little glimpse of picture predicting the growing extremism and terror against the religious minorities in Pakistan.

It's a great dilemma of modern day Pakistan that Hindu professionals including Doctors, Engineers and IT (Information technology) experts are not able to serve in the country due to massive security threats to their lives. Pakistani Hindus are very well educated and younger generation of community possess enough passion for education in Sind and Baluchistan. Hundreds of Hindu youngsters do graduations from Mehran University of Engineering and Technology, Sind Agriculture University, Liquate Medical University and Chandka Medical College Larkna and from other renowned Universities of the world. But these Doctors, Engineers and other professionals very rarely remain within the boundaries of Sind and Pakistan. Many among the young Hindu professionals have settled in India, UK, USA, Australia, Canada and gulf countries during the last few years. This has caused not only a massive brain drain from Pakistan but also a great defame for the country as well.

Forced conversion to Islam is another great matter of concern for the Hindus living in modern day Pakistan. Feudal elite alongside with other influential elements in rural areas of Sind and Baluchistan are involved in this shameful action. These influential factions of society are involved in kidnapping of young Hindu girls for the fulfilment of their sexual desires and forcefully convert them for keeping them in their harems. Above mentioned fraction in Pakistan practice polygamy, so they use these girls as a tool of their sexual satisfactions and treat them as sex slaves. According to a report of Pakistan Today more than 1000 Hindu and Christian girls are converted to Islam every year after being kidnapped.

Alex Rodregez reported for Loss Angeles Times on April 22, 2012 that majority among the Hindus in Pakistan accuse Muslims for kidnapping their teen aged girls who are exploited sexually later. According to this report different militant groups from interior Sind and Baluchistan have been involved in these types of activities since a long span of time. Have a look at this incident. Reena Kumari, a 16 year old girl from Jacobabad district was shopping for dresses in the main bazaar of the city before being kidnapped in May 2012. According to her family the man who abducted her was not a street wanderer but a police officer. The little poor girl faced massive barbarism from that police officer and her parents were not able to release her from the prison of that man as they possessed very less influence as compared to him.

Shaiza Hassan's (reporter at Daily Dawn) article for Daily Dawn published on February 17, 2014 states that the Hindu community in Pakistan is very much fed up by the forceful conversions of their children. As per an excerpt from the article, at a seminar titled Hindus in Pakistan–issues and challenges held at Karachi Press Club, Raj Kumar, Uncle of a Rinkle Kumari had asked, "Can you accept the forcible marriage of your daughter to a Muslim man?" asked. Raj Kumar then called a sixteen years old girl Juma on stage and said in front of the media that Juma alongside with her ten years old sister Pooja was also being forced to change her religion. Raj Kumar asked the children of the age group of Juma and Pooja that do they possess knowledge about different religions. "Children of age ten barely know anything about their own religion, then what can Pooja and Juma know about Islam? This is height of Injustice", Kumar added more. According to parents of Pooja and Juma they were the residents of Akhtar colony in the district of Mirpur Khas. It was the 4th of February when their girls went for selling toys as they were forced to send their children for work due to immense poverty. "The two girls were missing even after a long time and it was alarming for us", said their mother. "Through several reports of media and higher bureaucracy we were confirmed that our girls are living with a man named as Rajab Pathan. The police of our area later produced them as Muslim children after which the court sent them to

Dar-ul-Aman (Public shelter home) over suspicions of child abuse at home", said the mother of the children with weeping eyes.

- **Christianity in Pakistan**

Christianity is the second largest religious minority in Pakistan after Hinduism, population of Christians is estimated between 2.8-3.5 million (2012) in the country. Unlike the Hindus Christian population is distributed very uniformly across the country and not restricted with in a specific territory, however, Punjab contains more population of Christians as compared to other provinces. Christian population in Punjab is between 1.8-2 million. Lahore, Faisalabad, Gujranwala and Sahiwal consist of most of the Christian population of Punjab. Federally administrated tribal areas (FATA) possess minimum numbers of Christians in Pakistan. Only 0.07 million of the total Christian population of the country are living in FATA. Both the major factions of Christianity namely, Roman Catholics and Protestants constitute almost equal numbers out of the total Christian population of 2.8-3.5 million. Christians in Pakistan are descendents of the people who converted to the religion during the British rule in the Sub-continent.

Pakistani Christians particularly who are living in Islamabad capital territory, Punjab and Karachi seems to be more intermingled with Muslim majority as compared to Hindus living in Sind and Baluchistan. But Christians living in KPK and FATA are not feeling well and secure. Killing of Shabaz Bhatti in 2011 the then federal minister of minorities in Islamabad has produced severe repercussions on Christians in Pakistan. Bhatti was an out spoken critic against blasphemy laws in Pakistan. Tehrek Taliban Pakistan (TTP) claimed the responsibility of his killing.

Majority among the Christians in Pakistan are facing both social and economic challenges, unlike Hindus an overwhelming majority of Christians are not very well educated here. Religious minorities in Pakistan though possess the quota in government services but due to low literacy rate, massive population among the Christians are employed in very ordinary jobs. Majority among the public servants from Christian community in Pakistan are employed as sanitary workers. A massive fraction of Christian population is not able to utilise its quota in Superior services like, civil service of Pakistan due to their less qualification. Quota reserved for Christians in Punjab (As Christians are more populated in Punjab as compared to other provinces) in the superior jobs of the government have remained unfilled many times during the recent past due to lack of qualified candidates.

A massive fraction of Christian population in South Punjab, Faisalabad and even in Lahore is living under miserable circumstances due to scarce economic resources. Christian community in South Punjab are living in very severe circumstances as compared to their fellow residents of Karachi, Lahore and Quetta as many among the members of the community from these cities are now settled in USA, UK and other countries of Europe and are supporting their families in Pakistan from abroad. Unlike Hindus, Pakistani Christians are not too familiar with businesses so a large fraction of this community from urban areas including Lahore, Faisalabad and Gujranwala are either working as sanitary workers or doing other ordinary jobs.

Above mentioned circumstances describe the misery of Christians in Pakistan but there exists an elite Christian fraction as well. Ordinary members of community (majority in fact) accuse these elite groups alongside with government for their problems and living standards. Yamin Maseeh, a fifty five years old Christian sanitary worker feels that there is enough loot and corruption and fraud in the name of poor Christians in Pakistan. According to him these are the factions of elite including Christian members of parliament and the Chairpersons of NGO's who are involved in making money in the name of Christian welfare in Pakistan. "They (accused elite) are running NGO's in the name of social welfare of Christians in Pakistan and are receiving plenty of funds and grants from the western world but all is going to their kitty and nothing is reaching us", Yamin added more.

According to another prominent Christian from Lahore all members of parliament from religious minorities (though these members are not elected through general elections and possess memberships on the basis of reserved seats) are allocated the same quantity of funds like the Muslim members of Parliament but these minority members of parliament have been accused of swindling with these funds very similar like their Muslim fellows. As member of minorities of parliament are not elected through the vote of public so they feel free of any public accountability, and this too is a major cause of less interaction between members of parliament and masses of the country.

- **Blasphemy Laws and Christians in Pakistan**

It's a fact of the day that both Islam and Christianity are divine religions and both the above mentioned (also every religion in the world) faiths intend to propagate peace, tolerance and humanity. Both Christianity and Islam are focused on inter religion cooperation and coordination among the followers of different religions. Muhammad (PBUH) and Jesus Christ both were very kind on humanity. Massive factions of both (Muslims and Christians) religions are willing to live in a peaceful manner for the rest of the world. It's a genuine fact that Islam verified the Prophethood of all prophets including Jesus Christ, according to Islamic teachings Insult or humility of any prophet including Muhammad (PBUH) is a sinful act which will be punished. Similarly, Islam forbids its followers and others who are non-Muslims as well from defaming or destroying a place of worship of any religion. Respect and dignity for the Muhammad (PBUH) holds a key importance in Islam for its followers so defaming or insulting Muhammad (PBUH) is a very heinous action and punishment for this is death according to Pakistan penal code.

Several sections of Pakistan's criminal code is regarding the blasphemy laws in Pakistan, it contains Articles 295, 295A, 295B, and 295C defining blasphemy laws in Pakistan alongside with their consequences. Massive factions of Christians in Pakistan have always shown a concern about the severe repercussions of blasphemy laws on them. Let's have a look at the various sections of Pakistan penal code. According to it 295A forbids outraging religious feelings, 295B deals with the respect of holy book "The Quran", 295C forbids defaming Muhammad (PBUH). If a charge is placed under section 295-C trial for the same takes place in session court headed by a Muslim Judge. Similarly, 298, 298A, 298B deals with the issue of hurting religious feelings .The provisions of these sections are meant for the protection of all religions from any offense, but a massive fraction of Christians believes that these laws are widely utilised by Muslim extremist groups to target Christians only.

Shahbaz Bhatti a Christian Politican was Killed by a Poiceman in Janurary 2011 on the Name of Blashpmey

"When allegation of blasphemy is raised against any Christian or Hindu it produces severe repercussions on others as well, thousands others from the community faces its repercussions", said Kamran Samuel a Christian human rights activist from Multan. "You just recall the recent incident of Joseph colony in Lahore where a mob of 3000 extremist Muslims burnt the whole colony after coming to know that a Christian by the name of Sawan Maseeh had been alleged of blasphemy. It's a great dilemma here that such a sensitive issue is widely utilised for attaining personal motives and victimising people from the minute factions of society. If any Muslim happens to get into a dispute with a non-Muslim, the former tries to put a blame of blasphemy on the latter. The poor non-Muslim will have to face severe repercussions in any case, either orthodox Muslim factions will kill him or he would face severe repercussions from law enforcement agencies and judiciary who will try to punish him whether he is involved or not due to the massive social pressure. There is too much injustice with the Christians /non-Muslims in this country and we are not able to do anything to prevent it", Samuel added more.

According to National Commission for Justice and Peace (NCJP) only seven cases of blasphemy were registered before the partition of India (in united India until 1947). Astonishingly after the creation of Pakistan no case of blasphemy was registered during 1947 to 1986 (during a long span of 39 years) but during the last 28 years (from 1986-2004) 1064 cases of blasphemy were registered. Among these massive number of registered cases for blasphemy, 456 and 132 cases were launched against the Ahmedis and Christians respectively.

Severe practice of targeting Christians in Punjab by the extremist fraction of the society started from the incident of 'Shanti Nagar', (a place of peace) a village in the district of Khanewal, part of South Punjab. It was the month of February in the year 1997 when some torn pages of Holy Quran were found from an old Mosque of a particular village with some writings against Muslims. There was enough abhorent material in these writings against Muslims and they were challenged to take revenge of that particular incident of humiliating the Quran pages. This news spread like a fire and Muslim elite of that town registered a first information report (FIR) against seven members of Christian community whose name were found written on the torn pages of Quran. These seven people were the residents of Shanti Nagar. At the same time some 20,000-30,000 people from surrounding areas (adjacent villages and cities including cities of Khanewal and Jahanian) gathered in Shanti Nagar, the mob ordered the villagers to vacate their houses. Sensing threat and conflict in the air Christian population vacated their houses and were looted by the mob very soon. After having amassed enough loot the mob burnt all the houses in the village mercilessly. The victimised Christian population had to stay in relief camps for several days, provided by government and NGOs. Above mentioned incident was the starting of a cruel series of violence against Christians in Pakistan which led to many other horrible incidents against the minority.

2009 Gojra (small town near industrial city Faisalabad) riots were a series of attacks targeting Christians in Punjab. These riots resulted in the deaths of several Christians including a women and a child. Attacks were triggered on the reports of desecration of Holy Quran. It was reported that three Christians insulted the Quran during a marriage ceremony. A case was registered against the three Christians whose names were Mukhtar, Imran and Jalal Masseh according to district police officer under Section 295-B of Pakistan panel code. Police started proceedings against the named ones but Pakistani Christians are unfortunate enough that before any serious action could be taken by the police, the extremist fraction among the Muslims started its violent actions. Forty houses were set afire and a Christian man was burnt alive by the orthodox Muslims on August 1, 2009. According to residents a mob comprising of hundreds of people started destructions in the Christian residential area of the city, police was informed and it arrived but it remained silent even after watching the offenders committing the offense. A banned Islamic group was suspected for the incident.

"Growing extremism in the country especially violence against minorities is creating a gulf between majority and minority", said Martin Sidique a human rights activist from Islamabad. "We are peace lovers and promote peace. You can't blame whole community against wrong actions of some individuals. There are a few black sheep in every community and would be some among the Pakistani Christians as well, but this does not mean that all the Christians living here are involved in wrong actions. I respect all religions including Islam but Muslims living in Pakistan should play their part as well for the reduction of conflicts and for the enhancement of friendly atmosphere among the Muslims and the minorities living here". "Victimisation of hundreds among the minorities every year through extremist groups is not a good sign for the future of the country", he added more.

- **Ahmedis in Pakistan**

Ahmedis – followers of Mirza Ghulam Ahmed of Qadyan, (a town in district Amritsar, India) commonly called as Qadyanis, are among the major factions of minorities in Pakistan. Ahmedis were declared non-Muslims on September 17, 1974 in the country through second constitutional amendment during the first regime (1971-77) of the so called secular political fraction of Pakistan people's party. Since then Ahmedis are facing severe repercussions of above mentioned action in the form of massive socioeconomic and political discrimination in the country through different extremist groups. Population of this fraction in the country is between 2.5-3 million (some sources claim that it's upto five million). Majority among Ahmedis in Pakistan are settled in Punjab, town of Chenab Nagger (district Chiniot) still called as Rabwah (its old name, renamed as Chenab Nagger in 2000 on the pressure of orthodox Muslims) by major fraction of Ahmedi population due to their religious attachment with that name, massive fraction of community population is settled in that particular town. Majority among the remaining Ahmedis are settled in other parts of the country but Lahore, Faisalabad and Sargodha also possess reasonable numbers among the Ahmedis in Pakistan. As Ahmedis are following the Muslim names, norms and traditions so it's difficult to estimate about their real population in the country. Like other religious factions Ahmedis too comprise of two sects including the Orthodox and Lahori (a split group from the Orthodox formed in 1914 after the demise of Second Caliph) but constitution of Pakistan has declared both these sects as non-Muslim.

Ordinance XX was imposed in 1984 by the then President (Military dictator) Zia-Ul-Haq for the reduction of role of this fraction of population in Muslim society of Islamic Republic of Pakistan. This ordinance put massive restrictions on the socioeconomic, political and religious role of Ahmedis in Pakistan. Ahmedis were barred from utilising Muslim names, norms and traditions through this ordinance.

Sunni (particularly Dev Bandi School of Thought) fraction of population utilised this ordinance as a tool for the discrimination and harassment of Ahmedis in Pakistan. On December 3, 2012 in Model Town (a posh area of the city) Lahore an Ahmedi graveyard was desecrated by some extremists from a banned militant organisation. The militant group specifically targeted the graves for utilising 'Kalma' and 'Quranic' verses. Many among the orthodox Islamic groups in the country believe that no one other than Muslims should be allowed to use Muslims names, norms and traditions. According to them Ahmedis are declared non-Muslims by the constitution of Pakistan so they possess no rights for using Islamic norms and traditions and doing so will cause severe repercussions. Contrary to this, despite the fact that the Ahmedis were declared non-Muslim through constitutional amendment they (Ahmedis) still claim to be part of the Muslim world and so they use Muslim norms, names and traditions.

It is a harsh reality that many among Sunni orthodox groups in Pakistan are involved in spreading hate ridden attitude against this minute fraction of population. On 28th May 2010 two Ahmedi Worship places were attacked in Lahore by orthodox militant groups, results of these attacks were very severe in which 94 people died and 144 were seriously injured. Incidents occurred in two worship places (where proceedings for the Friday prayers were going on) of Lahore in Model Town and Garhi Shaho. Both incidents were very well-planned, militants used bombing and massive shooting for mass destruction. Punjabi Taliban an allied group of TTP was suspected for the incident. Lahore police stated that the incident was carried out by six militants who had links with Pakistani Taliban and were trained in North Waziristan part of FATA. Soon after this incident another attack was made on a hospital, where the injured of the previous attacks were being treated.

Some factions of orthodox Muslims are also promoting the economic boycott of Ahmedis in Pakistan. Religious schools of particular sects are utilised as a tool for this purpose. Some religious schools are used for advertising and promoting social and economic boycott of Ahmedis. These advertisements propagate about the commercial assets including shops, factories and other businesses related to Ahmedis and Muslims are advised not to purchase any product manufactured or traded by this particular minute fraction of population.

As we discussed earlier that Ahmedi fraction of population is educated enough so they are settling abroad at a rapid pace due to threats on their security and economic activities, this is enhancing brain drain. Recent incident of Murder (May 2014 in Chenab Nagger) of a Doctor named Mehdi Ali Qmar, once again activated the silent threats against the community. The fifty years old Doctor had settled in America and used to visit Pakistan every year for providing free services to the poor population of his home town and in one such of his visits he could not return as he was killed mercilessly by some militant organisation.

Repercussions of Doctor Mehdi's death are severe enough on the Ahmedis in Pakistan. Some prominent member of this minute fraction including diplomats, politicians, writers and journalists are now hiding their religious identifications after that particular incident. I contacted many among the top religious leaders of the Ahmedis for attaining their point of view on their reservations with the government and society but except one respondent no one else wanted their real names to appear alongside their published views.

7

Socioeconomic Injustice with Women and Children in Pakistan

Women the essence of the Universe are not valued by almost all the social classes of the country. Religion, social norms and values and traditions are widely utilised for the socioeconomic and sexual exploitation of women in Pakistan. Pakistan stands at 127th position among 148 (Though total number of countries are around 240 in the world but surveys are normally conducted for significantly populated countries only) countries with respect to gender inequality in the world.

All social factions including elite and the class below the poverty line (more than 40 per cent population belongs to this fraction of population in Pakistan) possess an astonishing sameness in the matter of humiliation and discrimination of women in the country. Though the parliament consists of a significant percentage of women members (21.1 per cent in 2012) including National and all provincial assemblies, yet the women of the country are going

An Acid Victim Lady Demanding Jutice aLongside her Son

through worst human circumstances. According to Human Rights Watch report of 2009, more than 70 per cent of women in Pakistan have suffered from some sort of abuse.

Pakistani women are no doubt unfortunate enough to be subjected to every type of abuse and discrimination generation after generation and even after so many years of the country's independence their plight remains the same and they have not been able to get justice of any kind as of yet. Domestic violence, rape, harassment at work place and public places like busses, trains, parks, cinemas etc. and other forms of injustices has been going on with women in Pakistan with comfort and ease. Growing Talibanisation in the country during the last decade has also produced severe repercussions on women rights, not only has the crime against women increased but now it is also supported by the orthodox elements which are utilising religion as a tool for committing crime against this sensitive fraction of society.

Deprived Women from the Flood Affected Areas in South Punjab Protesting for thier Demands

According to a report of Daily Dawn published on August 4, 2012 around 2236 cases of kidnap and rape of women were registered during 2010. Report also stated that thousands of incidents of violence, sexual abuse and harassments of women go unreported so the registered cases of violence and rape are not actually presenting the true picture which definitely is much darker.

Crime against women in Pakistan is not only widespread and deep-rooted but it's very organised as well. Let us now have a detailed look at all aspects of crime against women in Pakistan.

- **Religion as a Tool for Crime Against Women in Pakistan**

Religion is widely used as a tool for social, economical and political injustice against women in Pakistan. Crime against women is supported by orthodox religious groups of the country and has caused severe repercussions.

Islam being a religion and as a conduct of life has defined many rights of women in all aspects like social, economical and political. Share in ancestral property, right to learning and education, right of choosing a partner and right to better life style are considered by Islam as among the basic rights of women. But some factions among the rigid followers of Islam (Orthodox groups) are widely utilising religion for the harassment and discrimination of women. Fundamentalist fraction of society particularly in rural areas including FATA, KPK and Baluchistan are involved in attacking girl's schools and making their circumstances extremely severe. Hundreds of educational institutes for women have been destroyed during the last few years in dozens of cities, towns and villages of the country.

Islamic clerics among almost all sects are determined enough to sabotage girls educational system in the country. Malala Yousafzai, now seventeen is a girl from Mengora of district Sawat, she has come into worldwide fame for her educational and social activism and has made Pakistan proud by winning the noble prize for peace in 2014. During her struggle she had to face severe repercussions for adopting a vocal attitude against the orthodox groups involved in the destruction of women's educational institutes in the northern part of the country. She started to raise her voice against this fraction from a very young age when many girls' schools were being targeted by the extremist groups in Sawat valley during 2009-10. On October 9, 2012, she was shot by Taliban gunmen on her way to home from her school situated in Sawat. The fired bullet went through her neck and head and she was brought to CMH (Combined military hospital) Rawalpindi in a critical condition after receiving initial treatment in Sawat. She remained in coma for almost one week, after coming to senses (On 17th of October 2012) and going through a head surgery in CMH she was admitted later in Queen Elizabeth hospital of London.

Ms Yousafzai was discharged from Queen Elizabeth after few months of treatment in February 2013. She is now studying in London with her two other class mates who were also injured in the same incident. The three girls received repeated threats from the militants and had to be sent to London for their safety.

Incident of Malala Yousafzai is an eye opener of the worst circumstances imposed on women by the orthodox factions of the society in the country. After above mentioned incident of cruelty against innocent girls a flood gate of heinous incidents against women opened in every corner of the country.

Hundreds of girl's schools and colleges were destroyed during the last few years by the orthodox factions of the society with ease and comfort and state writ was not strong enough to protect women from this heinous crime. Islamic clerics who challenged the writ of state and claimed responsibility for these types of incidents feel proud of their actions and have openly described this as a pious act in front of the media, in spite of such brazen behaviour this fraction feels safe enough and is not much accountable for its activities. It's a matter of fact that major factions of Islamic clerics operating in Pakistan have close ties with Taliban in Afghanistan who are familiar for their inhuman attitude with women, so crime against women is growing with the enhancement of Talibanisation in the country. TTP started its operations in Pakistan in 2004, since then women in this part of the world are under great stress and conflict.

As per a UNESCO (United Nations Education, Scientific and Cultural Organisation) report published on November 12, 2012 about the countries which violate human rights, Pakistan has been placed among the last 10 countries with respect to women education. Report stated that 62 per cent girls between 7-15 years never spent a time in a class room of any school. This ratio is too much higher as compared to India (30 per cent) and Bangladesh (9 per cent). Report also stated that girls between the ages of 17-22 spend on an average one year in educational institutes in Pakistan and as per this parameter too, India and Bangladesh are far ahead. Indian girls of similar age group spend 1.29 years while Bangladeshi girls spend 4.4 years on an average in educational institutes.

Above mentioned figures sufficiently describe the worst circumstances of women education in Pakistan and this is due to many reasons. Wrong interpretation of religion by some orthodox groups is also playing a vital role in enhancing injustice and discrimination with women in Pakistan. The majority among the population is living in rural and under developed areas under miserable circumstances with very rare connections with modern and globalised world and this fraction of population is a victim and is under heavy influence of orthodox clerics who are spreading widespread misconceptions about the status of women in Islamic religion, as per the instructions of these clerics women are considered as a tool for sex and labour.

Growing Talibanisation in rural Sind, South Punjab and FATA has produced severe repercussions on the ordinary masses during the last few years. Majority population belonging to deprived factions are (more than half population in above mentioned areas belongs to lower income groups) against the notion of women education. They feel that only religious education from an orthodox village school is enough for a girl. Majority among this fraction of population are of the view that modern school education is very harmful for girls as it leads them towards liberty and shameful ways of Sin.

Islamic clerics in rural areas of the country during their lectures to their followers describe women as third grade citizens as compared to men. Both clerics and followers belong to illiterate class of the community, followers of these clerics have been brain washed by their leaders and are subject their women to immense domestic violence as they are taught to think that women is inferior to man and man is a Master of woman. Let's have a look at some aspects of injustice with women in the name of religion.

- **Marriage with Holy Quran**

Marriage of a girl with Holy Quran is a widely spread practice in several areas of Sind (Interior Sind), South Punjab and Baluchistan and in some parts of KPK and Azad Kashmir as well. A large fraction of women from interior part of Sind and South Punjab are forced for this shameful and sinful act every year by their parents, guardians or other relatives. Girls married with the Holy book are restricted with in a room (where the Quran is placed) for their whole life. Marriage with Quran is very popular among the feudal class of the country. Some factions of land owning families who are not part of feudal elite (belong to upper middle and middle classes) have also adopted this practice as a tradition of their forefathers for passing the inheritance of land only to the male members of the family. Girls who are married with Holy Quran possess no rights to their ancestral properties. After this so called marriage, a girl is prohibited from cherishing any desires of conjugality or companionship and is forced to spend her entire life as a dead person with no social and human contacts.

According to a report of Daily Dawn published on April 19, 2012, a twenty year old girl from district Layyah of South Punjab rebelled against the decision of her family of marrying her with Holy Quran and now she is living in a public shelter for avoiding consequences of her bold action. Report also stated that the particular girl also filed a petition in district court against the harassment and threats that she faced from her brothers and parents.

Above mentioned girl was lucky enough to escape from her house and get shelter in a public home and due to her publicity in media she was protected by law enforcing agencies, otherwise every year hundreds of girls in same circumstances like her are forced to marry the holy book and they have no option other than committing suicide or destroying their lives by complying with these so called religious norms. Astonishingly the practice which is so widespread in the name of religion has no connections with Islam in reality. Let's have a view of a religious scholar on it.

"Marriage of women with Holy Quran is totally Haram (illegal according to Islamic principles) and possesses no status in Shariah (Islamic jurisprudence)", said Molana Abdul Majeed a renowned Islamic scholar from

Multan. "Actually influential elite is utilising religion for its own benefits and their paid religious scholars are involved to validate this moulded form of religion", he added. "Some land owning families in the rural areas of the country are not in favour of giving property rights to their daughters, this practice is going on from hundreds of years. Most girls from the feudal elite of the country voluntarily prefer to donate their share of property to their male siblings as they are familiar with their social influences. Those who are rebellious (a very minute faction) are treated very inhumanly by their parents and male siblings. This action of limiting the ancestral property within male members of the family with the help of so called religious norms is an absolute injustice. But when whole society is based upon the principles of injustice what can one do?"

- **Domestic Violence and Women in Pakistan**

Domestic violence is an integral part of Pakistani society widely used as a tool to abuse and discriminate women in all social classes of the country. According to latest report of human right watch an estimated 5000 women are killed every year due to domestic violence in Pakistan, thousands of other women are injured and disabled for life. Majority among the law enforcement agencies in the country do not consider domestic violence as a heinous crime and usually show a very hesitant attitude for the registration of these types of cases.

Domestic violence against women in Pakistan is deep-rooted and widespread in all social classes (from below the poverty line to super elite class) and is being inflicted with ease and comfort without the fear of any accountability. Sometimes it looks very astonishing but it's a reality that the educated upper middle class is also involved alongside feudal fraction of the society in crime against women. It is always said in Pakistan that feudal elite of the country is very much heinous towards their women but so called educated fraction is no way far behind and more so the cruel attitude of this fraction of population towards women has increased with the passage of time.

As more than 40 per cent of the population in the country is living below the poverty line and this massive fraction of population have very rare sources of entertainment. Evil genius fraction of population among this miserable section of society has adopted domestic violence as their prime entertainment for taking out their own frustration and anger. Men belonging from the lower income fraction of the population are utilising women for both sexual satisfraction and anger reduction. When a man from lower income group is frustrated enough from both social and economic injustices he uses his wife as a tool for the reduction of his own frustration towards life. Beating women (traditionally wife) is a trend in lower income group of Pakistan and used as a social norm to establish the superiority of men (so called) in the society.

Man is forced to kill women for his family pride and so called honour in most of the rural (even in some fraction of urban class as well) classes of the country. A twenty five years old girl from Lahore (second largest Urban city which is a headquarters of dozens of human organisations) was stoned to death on 26 May -2014 as an 'Honor killing' for marrying the man she loved. Daily Dawn reported on 27 May 2014 that the victimised girl named Farzana Iqbal had been engaged to her cousin by her parents but she married another man. This action was considered as a great sin from her and she faced its consequences in the result of death. At least one dozen members of her family were present at that moment when she was killed by her father and brothers within the premises of Lahore high court. Her family initially launched an FIR against her husband for kidnapping her, but later when they came to know that their daughter was not willing to come back home, they killed her. According to the police, all suspected ones with the exception of her father escaped. The father was arrested and he accepted the sin and explained in front of the media that killing was necessary because her daughter had committed a sin.

Above mentioned example is just a little glimpse of a much bigger picture, there are thousands of other such examples that can be found in the villages and cities of the country. According to 'Aurat foundation' (a non-government organisation working for the betterment of women in Pakistan), more than 1000 women are killed every year in Pakistan in the name of Honour. Honour killing now a days is a famous way of eliminating women in Pakistan in most of the rural and urban areas as well. Rural areas including South Punjab, Interior part of Sind and major portion of the province of Baluchistan are worst affected by honour killing. Above mentioned areas are considered among the most backward portion of the country and possess very less civic and social infrastructure, this part of the country is going through worst economic circumstances and massive fraction of population is living below the poverty line in these areas. This deprived and miserable fraction of population is greatly involved in domestic violence for the reduction of their anger towards life.

Faction of educated men belonging to feudal and upper middle class land owning families proudly beat their wives, sisters, cousins and other female members of their families. As polygamy (having more than one wife) is widely practiced among land owners of the country so many men use violence as a tool for settling issues and problems between their wives. A massive fraction of population other than the feudal elite practising polygamy are experiencing tight economic circumstances, this fraction of population is widely involved in violence against women. Managing two, three and four wives is much difficult financially (sometimes physically as well) for all factions of population other than the elite, so when these men are not able to fulfil the requirements of many wives they subject their wives to violence and this practice is prevalent on a very large scale in the country.

- **Honour Killing in Pakistan**

Honour killing is also gender-based violence in Pakistan in which women are victimised on the basis of social norms and values and so called family pride. As the majority (62-65 per cent) population in the country is living in rural areas so this massive fraction of population follows pride-based social norms and culture. These pride-based norms and values considers men as a superior gender and degrades the status of women. Women are always considered as a second class citizen vis-a-vis men as per these so called norms and values.

Women Protest Against the Killing on the Name of Honour

"I use to beat my wife every second or third day", said Shabbier Mughal a thirty eight years old labourer from Sargodha. "I am earning 10000-12000 PKR on an average, Sir, and my family comprises of eight members (six children, wife and myself), initial period of my marriage life was good enough as I was living in a joint family with my brothers and parents. But as my family enlarged (with the birth of children) it became more and more difficult to survive in a joint family. So I separated from my parents, since then life is at sixes and seven. Now with growing children and their demands, I am fed up of my life. Whenever my wife demands more I beat her with slaps and kicks. I was not in favour of a big family but at every pregnancy she used to say that children are a gift of God and they bring their fate with them. Now when she demands more I say to her that she has her fate with her in the form of children and forbid her to make any further demands from me. With so much inflation living on such a minute amount is so difficult in this period of life, so whenever I am frustrated from the cruelty of life I beat my wife and she has no option other than tolerating me", Mughal added more.

Express Tribune, among one of the leading English news-paper in the country reported on March 2, 2011 that every four among five women in

Pakistan are facing some form of domestic abuse. According to Strategy Papers, 80 per cent of Pakistani women experience domestic violence while one in every three women face some sort of violence like rape, honour killing, immolation, acid attacks and other types of abuses.

As we described earlier that domestic violence is a symbol of pride in almost all social classes in the country, very similar to this Honour killing is also a very popular practice widely prevalent among the rural elite of the country. Karo-Kari is a typical process of killing women in rural areas of Sind. This practice is an integral part of killing women for honour and has been going on from hundreds of years. Thousands of girls and women have lost their lives due to this cruel practice. People culpable of this inhuman practice are fortunate enough in the country as more than 95 per cent of these criminals faced no repercussions from law enforcement agencies. Police either were not able to access the culprits due to their influences or they also supported them for the cause of these so called social norms and values leading to severe repercussions on the society.

Karo-Kari is a black custom of murder of women who are suspected of having sexual relationships without marriage or approved marriage. An alleged woman is killed alongside with the man with whom she had a relationship. Hundreds of women are killed every year by their fathers, brothers and cousins for their alleged relationships with the opposite sex. The offenders feel liberty and comfort as this heinous crime is largely done for the cause of social norms and values. When a man kills his wife, sister, cousin and sometimes mother as well for entering into an illicit relationship with a man, he kills that man too so that none of the allegers remain alive to challenge his action.

Several rural social institutions like Jirga, Panchayat, etc. which are based upon social norms and values often validate the killing of women folk by declaring it as honour killing, this has happened so many times that people now feel very much at liberty for killing a women on such grounds. Media reports have suggested that majority among the girls killed were innocent and even if they had possessed an illicit relationship with a man they can't be sentenced to death. It's a matter of great concern that killers are widely utilising honour killing as a tool for fulfilling their own purposes including financial interests, revenge etc. Sometimes brothers kill their sisters for grabbing the whole ancestral property under the false allegation of an illicit relationship. Revenge is another important motive for killing women in the name of Honour. Many among the offenders of women who have committed honour killing have been involved in clan disputes and they killed their family women as a means to go against their enemies.

Express Tribune reported on August 30, 2013 that the police has not been able to take any action against the offenders in more than 95 per cent of the reported incidents of Karo-Kari (a practice in which a man kills his women due to her suspicious character). United Nations, Amnesty International and other human rights organisations in the world (even in the country as well) have shown a great concern about the massive human rights violations in Pakistan, but law enforcement agencies have not much succeeded in producing the desired results up till now.

United Nations Development Programme and UK's department for international rights started a project to reduce Karo-Kari in Sind with the coordination of Sind Police in 2010. This project has still not been able to produce the desired results as the Sind police did not participate in the project as a professional organisation. Sind is the province which has been most affected by the heinous practice of Karo-Kari. Cases like Tasleem Solangi from Khirpur, Abida and Tehmina Bhutto are the prominent examples of barbarism and inhuman attitude against women.

Daily Dawn reported on March 20, 2014 about the Chief Justice's Suo motto notice taken after a Karo-kari incident in district Shikarpur of Sind. CJP (Chief Justice of Pakistan) noticed an incident in which two girls were killed for marrying the guys of their own choice. Later a 'jirga' was held under the supervision of a member of parliament from same district which imposed a tribute of 2.4 million on each boy for committing this act. CJP noticed this and ordered Inspector General of Sind Police to appear before the court on March 22, 2014. According to Human Rights Commission of Pakistan there occurs hundreds of incidents of honour killing in Pakistan related to Karo-Kari but suo moto action is taken in very few cases, this inaction by the government and judiciary is further promoting the state of lawlessness in the country.

It's a matter of fact that social norms and values for the woman in Pakistan are extremely strict and since these are associated with religious fervour and morality issues, the majority are not ready to raise a voice against this injustice and discrimination.

- **Dowry Deaths in Pakistan**

Dowry has become a great curse and a cause of violence and death for women in Pakistan. Common name of dowry in Pakistan is Jehez which means the material and goods given to a bride by her parents at the time of her marriage. Dowry related deaths are more than 3000 every year in the country. According to Wikipedia, Pakistan has the highest reported dowry deaths per 10,000 women in the world.

As we described in earlier chapters that more than 40 per cent population of the country is living below the poverty line here, 35 per cent of total population between lower class and lower middle class so 75 per cent of total population in the country is living below the actual middle class. Ironically, this massive fraction of population is continuously adding to the population with much ease and comfort as compared to the economically well off factions of the country. With four to six daughters per family on an average, the lower income group of the country is facing severe repercussions of the custom of dowry. With very limited resources this deprived fraction of population is not able to provide their daughters with heavy dowry and this has become a great shortcoming for the family with daughters of modern day Pakistan.

Girls belonging to lower income groups in Pakistan who fetch low dowries are treated very inhumanly by their in-laws. Married life of these girls becomes a hell when their husbands demean them continuously. Massive factions of these girls become a psychological patient their lives becomes disastrous. Many among them attempt suicide at least once in their lifetimes. Low dowry is considered such a failing for women in Pakistan that its repercussions follow them until their deaths. Severe violence is inflicted on them through various means, beating with rods, burning with acid and other cruelties are very common forms of dowry-related tortures in Pakistan.

Burning of newlywed brides is a familiar type of murder nowadays in Pakistan. According to progressive women association 300-500 women are burned to death every year in Pakistan by their husbands and in laws due to low dowry. There occurs thousands (even hundreds of thousands) incidents of women abuse every year in the country by their husbands, in laws and other relatives but majority among these remain unreported due to strict social norms and values. Such biased and strict social norms and values for women rooted in blind faith have in turn given a free rein to the uncompassionate and perverse men of the society for inflicting violence upon the sensitive sex of the society.

According to Amnesty International report of 1999 "there were 1600 bride burning cases registered in Pakistan during the time span of 1995-98, but only 60 offenders were prosecuted and finally only two were convicted." Women news reported that 4000 women were attacked for fetching low dowries by their husbands and in-laws during the last eight years in Rawalpindi region of Punjab. Report stated that average age of victims was between 18-35 years and around 30 per cent of the affected were pregnant.

With the growing inflation and the increasing gulf between rich and poor, crime against women in Pakistan is also growing at a rapid rate. According to Progressive Women Association, crime against women in Pakistan especially violence for fetching low dowry has increased too much during the last five years. "Life style of lower middle and middle class has gone down to a great extent during the last decade due to price hike and too much inflation in Pakistan", said Fatimah Baig, an advocate and human right activist from Lahore. "But on the other hand society has become more materialistic, a large fraction of population not only from lower income groups but also from educated middle and upper middle class is demanding more in the name of dowry as compared to the past. When marriages are settled on the basis of material gain they lack precious values of love, care and emotions between the husband and wife. This practice is playing a major part in both the delay and failure of marriages. Massive fraction of young male population from upper middle class seek wealthy families so that they can get much in the name of dowry. Educated fraction of young males who are serving on important positions in civil and military bureaucracy has promoted this trend too much. Young Bureaucrats, Doctors, Engineers and other educated professionals are demanding too much in the form of dowry. This fraction of males wants to get each and every luxury of life from the girl who is going to be their life partner. This practice has produced severe repercussions and will be a great danger for the future of women in the country if it continues with the same pace", Fatimah added more.

- **Sexual Abuse and Harassment**

Like many other injustices and discriminations women in Pakistan is very familiar with rape and sexual harassment. During the last decade Pakistan has progressed in all types of crimes. With the destruction of social institutions and widespread frustration and conflicts, rate of sexual abuse and rape of women has also gone up during the last few years. According to a study of Human rights watch there is a rape of a woman in every two hours in Pakistan. According to Asma Jahangir, former President of Supreme Court Bar Association of Pakistan (Chairperson of Human Rights Commission of Pakistan as well) more than 70 per cent of women in the country are abused physically or mentally.

Men who sexually abuse women in Pakistan can hail from any social class. Even men from influential classes of the society including feudal and industrial elite, business tycoons, spiritual leaders and many others are known to be involved in this heinous crime with an absolute ease and comfort. Feudalists in Pakistan possess harems of several wives but even then they seek more and more. Women belonging to feudatories are playing the part of sex slaves for the feudal fraction of society in Pakistan. Wives, daughters, sisters and other female members from the families of feudatories in Pakistan are utilised for the sexual satisfactions of land owners to a great extent; but victims always remain silent due to severe circumstances of their lives.

Above mentioned type of sexual abuse is very common not only among feudatories but also in other factions of deprived class of the country. Thousands of girls from lower income groups in Pakistan are losing their virginity before marriage (or any willing sexual relationship) due to worst economic circumstances.

"Price for the sexual abuse in the rural areas of the country is very minute", said Tariq Ch (name disguised) a renowned Professor and land owner as well from Faisalabad. "Once I visited the drea (farm house) of my feudal friend in district Chiniot. I was astonished to see a very charming girl of not more than 22 years there who charmed me as well on the orders of my friend but I was reluctant so I made an excuse to decline her offer. My friend claimed that he was having illicit relation not only with that girl but also with her sister and cousin as well. I was astonished and exclaimed that the girl who does not look more than twenty must be mad to have such a type of relationship with him who is so old (near sixty) and asked him whether the girl was happy to have such type of relationship with him. The feudal replied that she was not so happy but her husband was under his debt and was familiar with the situation that ladies of his family possess relationship with the feudal. The feudal further said to me that he was doing nothing new as this type of satiation of the feudal through their feudatories is not very new for massive fraction of his class in Pakistan and such practices have been prevalent since centuries. But to me it looked like a silent rape.", the Professor added more.

- **Women Harassment and Abuse at Work Place......**

Harassment and sexual abuse at work place is a great matter of concern for women in Pakistan. Women working in all sectors such as Banking, Non-government organisations (NGO's), Hospitals and even in more recognised government institutions harbour the feelings of fear and insecurity of the opposite sex. According to Munir Mosa (a renowned research scholar) more than 80 per cent of working women in Pakistan are familiar with harassment at work place both in public and private sectors. But sexual abuse and harassment is more commonly practiced in private and corporate sectors of the country. Many among the NGOs private hospitals and other organisations of corporate sector possess notorious reputation concerning women in Pakistan. Massive fraction of women working in these organisations feel pressures from their bosses and colleagues for the fulfilment of sexual desires. But these women as discussed earlier belong to a very deprived fraction of society and do not feel empowered enough to register any report, so majority cases related to harassment or sexual abuse of women at work places remain unreported. They adopt this type of attitude for the sake of their employments. According to Munir Mosa, 96 per cent of respondents (women with whom he conducted the survey) agreed that either they or their colleagues had faced harassment at work place.

Twenty three years Saima Masood (name disguised for a specific reason) is a lady secretary of a news-paper editor. After doing her graduation from a public degree college she joined a news-paper as a lady reporter for the remuneration of only 7000 PKR, few years ago (2011) in Lahore. Soon she realised that with a very notorious reputation and with limited circulation above mentioned news-paper is not able to pay salaries to its employees every month. But her circumstances were severe enough so she stuck with the firm due to financial pressures. Admiring her abilities the Editor offered her the position of his lady secretary. Despite her passion for reporting she accepted the offer as she had little option, since then she has been at sixes and seven and going through the worst period of her life. What she says about her life let's have a look.

"I am working as a prostitute nowadays, every third or fourth day I have to perform like a professional sex worker in front of him. This fifty five year old man possesses illicit relationship not only with me but also with many other girls working in his organisation. Sexual assault is very common type of practice in these types of organisations in Pakistan. We are forced into these types of shameful activities for few thousand rupees, as with too much unemployment very less options are left for us".

Women working on daily wages or at lower salaries in smaller factories and farmhouses (as housemaids) are facing severe types of sexual assaults by their owners and officers. Women working as labour on roads /construction projects are widely utilised as a tool for sexual satisfraction by the contractors, similarly massive fraction of nurses in hospitals are facing barbarism of doctors in Pakistan. Many bonded women working at brick stations are also exploited sexually in the country as well. It's a great dilemma that not only the feudal elite of the country but educated middle class also is involved in the sexual abuse of women in Pakistan. Let's have a look at such an example.

According to Dr Sarmad Ali a young physician from the city of Sargodha, a massive fraction of senior doctors (reasonable number of juniors too) in Pakistan are involved in sexual abuse of junior women (particularly nurses) in the medical field. Nurses are greatly abused by senior surgeons even in reputed government hospitals. Dr Ali claimed that a medical superintendent of a district head-quarter hospital in southern part of Punjab has a notorious reputation for his illicit relationships with younger women staff.

Media of Pakistan also has a notorious reputation concerning the women professionals. Massive increase in the number of female anchors in the electronic media is thought to be due to the interests of the owners of media houses in exploiting them or having illicit relationships with them. According to a senior journalist from Lahore more than 90 per cent among the female television anchors in Pakistan are the blue eyed staff of media tycoons. But women working in smaller media outlets are going through worst circumstances. Owners of these media outlets alongside with senior staff members (massive faction) are involved in exploiting them with great liberty and ease. According to a senior journalist from Multan many among the female reporters, news anchors and junior editors in smaller media outlets are facing severe sexual abuse by the senior leadership of these media houses.

"As glamour and sensation has become an essential part of electronic media in Pakistan so young ladies are widely utilised by big and smaller news

Bonded Women Laborer from Interior Sindh

outlets in the country to attain viewership", said a former resident editor of a national news-paper from Multan. It has produced a great impact on the minds of young girls studying media courses in colleges or universities. Most of these girls are willing to become part of the gorgeous electronic media which has put a great question mark on the future of print journalism in Pakistan. Local media outlets based in smaller cities like Multan not only exploit women economically but abuse them sexually", he added more.

- **Economic Circumstances of Women in Pakistan**

Economic circumstances of women in Pakistan are generally deprived and destructive. Women in lower income groups (below the poverty line, lower class and lower middle class) are working more than the males of this fraction but are getting very minute wages for such hard work. Norms and values or middle income group (Including middle class and upper middle class) are not much in favour of working women despite the too much hard work which women of this fraction have to put in for mere survival. Upper income groups (including elite and super elite classes) of the society includes people who possess both liberal and orthodox attitudes towards women, some people who hail from non-feudal backgrounds are moderate enough while others mainly who have been brought up under orthodox norms are too much strict towards their women.

According to Mehvish Imtiaz and Anum Faisal, two young girls who are the graduates of King Edward Medical University Lahore, only few women work in the medical field after doing MBBS. Associated press report published

Very Deprived Women from Sahiwal Cooking Polutray waste for her Children

earlier in 2013 stated that 80-85 per cent medical students are girls in Pakistan. The report mentions about the percentages of girls and guys studying in different medical colleges of the country, according to this report, Dow medical university of Karachi had female to male ratio of 70:30 in 2013, some other medical institutes including King Edward medical university of Lahore had more female students as compare to Dow university in the same year.

Majority among the female doctors are not allowed to work after their marriage due to strict norms and values of the middle income group. Women of this fraction of population also feel ease after getting the title of housewife as she too thinks that in a maledominated society only male is responsible for earning money. But women of this middle income fraction wanting to work have to face severe resistance from the fraction to which they belong like their counterparts from lower fraction of the society.

Women belonging to lower income groups in Pakistan are more willing to work as compared to those hailing from middle and upper fraction of population as for them their job makes them fit for survival in this harsh world governed by the rule of survival of the fittest. Male population of lower income group in Pakistan is lazy enough and heavily dependent on the income of their females. Women of above mentioned fraction of population are facing severe circumstances at their work places. Women working in smaller factories, farms, houses and many other places are getting very minute remuneration for their services as compared to male labour. If a man labourer gets 400 PKR a woman labourer is paid only 200 for working on a farm. Both rural land owners and industrial tycoons are involved in fully exploiting women economically.

"This influential fraction of society is paying low wages to women workers as they think that women are weak and sensitive enough and not able to work as hard as the male labours", said Jamila a women labourer from Bahawalpur. "Women working both in urban and rural areas are exploited badly by their Masters", she added. "The owners think that we are not harder and tougher like our male counterparts but I must say that women workers in Pakistan are more efficient and composed in their jobs as compared to male workers. Government has failed to protect the rights of women workers in the country and we have no option except to bear all this", Jamila added more.

A woman from lower fraction of population who is willing to do her independent work or business is also facing severe repercussions. Those who are running smaller business like little beauty parlours, dress shops and fashion saloons in the middle class areas of the country (in urban population) are facing sever circumstances in guise of social norms and values. "I am running a small beauty shop in a bazaar of a lower middle class colony but doing this type of work in this part of the world is difficult enough", said Christiana Jacob from Lahore. "I face severe criticism every day and sometimes harassment as well by male shop owners and other factions of the society living in that particular area. When they tease me it seems very difficult for me to continue my work, some among these feel that I am running a brothel not a beauty saloon. It is very difficult for me to concentrate some times on work but I belong to a deprived fraction of the society so I can't do much except bearing all this with an open heart", she added more.

Miserable Circumstances for Children in Pakistan

Like other miserable factions of the society Pakistani children also possess severe miserable circumstances. A Pakistani child of modern day is facing multidimensional and deep-rooted problems. With too many fears and conflicts (terrorism, growing orthodox attitude, lack of tolerance etc.) generation next of the society is going through the most difficult phase of its life.

Hunger, diseases, education are still great challenges concerning the children of Pakistan. They are facing violence, abuse, discrimination and too many other problems alongside with the other deprived factions of the society. With more than 192 million population Pakistan possess annual population growth rate of 1.49 per cent which implies the addition of 28,63,780 new but miserable faces every year (very few among the new born babies belong to the blessed fraction of the society as rapid growth of the population is majorly due to the lower fraction of the population) in this already over populated country.

Basic human facilities are very rare for massive fraction of newly born children every year as more than half of them belongs to the class below the poverty line. A massive fraction of remaining 50 per cent (almost 25-30%)

belongs to lower and lower middle classes so very minute fraction of newly born babies belong to the upper income group including middle, upper middle and elite factions of the society.

Pakistan is considered among the most unfriendly countries while welcoming a new face in the world. According to Express Tribune published on February 25, 2014. Pakistan has the highest ratio of first day death of children in the world. The News paper also mentioned the report of a British-

A Liitle Girl from Karchi Gathering Garbage

A Liitle Guy from City of Okara Doing Labor for the Provsion of Livelihood

based organisation which described Pakistan among the most dangerous countries in the world for newly born children as according to this report death rate of new born babies on their first day in Pakistan is 40.7 per cent per 1000. Some other under developed countries posses better circumstances than Pakistan. Let's have a look at these figures regarding first day deaths of new borns; in Nigeria it is 32.7 per cent per 1000 children, in Sierra Leone it is 30.8 per cent, in Guinea Bissau it is 29.4 per cent and in Afghanistan it is 29 per cent. Above mentioned are countries possessing most worst economic circumstances in the world yet they have a better survival rate of new born children, a fact which is definitely very shameful for the health officials of Pakistan.

- **Children out of Schools**

As we discussed earlier that more than half of the population of the country is living below the poverty line so children belonging to this fraction of population are definitely out of schools while major fraction among the remaining is also not able to afford school education for their children as well. According to latest report of UNESCO, 6.5-7 million children are still out of school in the country. Pakistan stands second for possessing highest number of children out of schools after Nigeria. Report also stated that Pakistan is among the twenty one countries of the world facing crises of expensive education.

With the so called literacy rate of 54 per cent (officially described as but the worst circumstances for education in the country tells another story) Pakistan stands at 113th position among the ranked 120 countries for education in the world. Society for the protection of children declared Pakistan among the countries possessing worst circumstances in its report of 2011. According to recent statistics available, overall enrolment in pre-primary education is 43-45 per cent for male children while 40 per cent for female children. Punjab province possesses highest number of children with 61 per cent enrolment, followed by Sind, KPK and Baluchistan with 53 per cent, 51 per cent and 47 per cent respectively. According to statistics of 2009 the primary school attendance of the country for both sexes is between 64-66 per cent, a figure much lower than the world's estimated average of 90 per cent.

In the year 2014 when massive fraction of the world is focused on standardized education, Pakistan is still not able to spend more than 2 per cent (2 per cent is officially described, sources tells us that only 1.7 per cent of GNP is spent on education) of Gross national product on education. In addition to this, allocation of government funds is skewed towards higher education so the benefits of public subsidy on education are going out of the range of the lower factions of the population. Currently Punjab, the largest populated province of the country has claimed to provide free education upto school level but this claim is not fully true. No tuition fee is charged in the public schools of Punjab but still students have to pay registration and examination fees which too is unbearable for the lower fraction of population. Public schools are largely hubs of lower income groups of the country due to no tuition fee but still massive portion of children from a very deprived class is out of schools as this fraction of population is not able to pay for uniforms and books for children which are not free in public schools even.

"Though Punjab government is claiming to charge no tuition fee in public schools but this is not true exactly", said Faqeer Muhammad a forty seven years old vendor from Multan. I am earning hardly 500-600 PKR per day and in this much minute income the education of my children is only a dream for me. Government claims that it's not charging any tuition fee but education is not all about tuition fee. With a family of six members I am not able to provide books, uniforms, and registration and examination fee for all my children so I do not send them to school. Among my four children only my son works with me while daughters remain at home for providing assistance to my wife in house work", Faqeer added more.

- **Child Labour in Pakistan**

As we discussed earlier that poverty and hunger are major causes for the massive fraction of children out of schools in Pakistan so these children are greatly involved in child labour. These little angels are forced to work in severe circumstances by their parents and relatives who are not able to fulfil their requirements. It's a great concern of modern day Pakistan that more than 4 million children below the age of 14 are involved in very tough jobs leading to severe repercussions on their lives. According to Pakistan labour laws, no child below the age of 18 is allowed to work seven hours a day and 42 hours in a week. Moreover, children between the age 14-17 are allowed to work but not as hard as the adults do. According to Pakistan employment of children act 1991, labour before the age of 14 is strictly prohibited. As per the definition of ECA children are included in the age group below 14 and adolescent are included between the age group of 14-18 years.

Children working as house servants and maids in Pakistan are facing more severe and miserable circumstances as compared to their counterparts in factories. These children are forced to work like bonded labour in the houses of business and bureaucratic elite of the country. This miserable fraction of children is bonded for the provision of 24/7 services to their owners but get peanut amounts in the name of salaries.

Tabinda, a nine years old girl from town of Murred Kay (adjacent of Lahore) is working as a child maid in the house of a civil servant in Lahore. Her responsibilities are tough enough. She has been given the responsibility of taking care of three children aged between 5-12 years and provide assistance to the chef in kitchen. House lady is proud enough being the wife of a bureaucrat, she dislikes doing any work with her sensitive hands so she uses the little girl as her attendant. But the wages Tabinda attains in return of this extensive service is shameful enough to describe even. The little girl is paid only 1500 PKR for her 24/7 services for the above mentioned family.

It's great dilemma of the country that servants, maids, drivers and other members from the lower factions of the population are treated very inhumanly by the superiors of the society here. But child servants and maids are treated even more inhumanly as they are forced to work in early ages due to worst economic circumstances and upper fraction of the society is involved in their full exploitation through various means.

- **Child Abuse in Pakistan**

Children of a massive fraction of population in Pakistan are facing severe types of abuses in Pakistan including physical, mental and sexual. Child abuse is an integral part of violent Pakistani society or in other words violence without beating or sexually exploiting children is not completed in Pakistani society.

A Liitle Boned Laborer from Southeren part of Punjab

Salman a 10 year old Bearing Serveral Times than his Age

Umar Farooq Khan reported for Times of India on September 02, 2010 about child abuse in these words. "Reportedly one out of every three children in Pakistan is victim of some or the other kind of abuse. Most among these children are abused by their relatives and care takers but during recent days there have been many such cases as well where people unfamiliar to the children were declared guilty for abusing them".

Now let's have a look at the different types of child abuses under practice in Pakistan. Generally, children are physically punished at homes by their parents and other elders in a massive fraction of population. Trend of corporal punishment is very common in lower income group of country which treats their children in a rude manner most of the time. Above mentioned fraction of population is the deprived, frustrated and conflicted portion of the society so they like to beat their women and children for reducing their anger towards life. Children belonging to social classes below the poverty line, lower class and lower middle class are facing severe circumstances imposed by their parents and society on them. These miserable creatures are helpless against their fate and law enforcing agencies are not able to help them come out from these circumstances. Child protection department in Pakistan is also not doing anything much for the reduction of child labour and provision of a better life to this fraction of society.

Violence with child maids and servants is also a very familiar type of abuse in practice inflicted by house owners and land ladies here. According to a child protection NGO more than 200,000 children are working as house servants and maids in posh and middle class residential areas of the country. These children take violence as food given by their Masters, torture and curse is the integral part of life of this fraction of population now. According to another NGO working for the children rights in the country there were 1560 cases of physical abuse and 926 of sexual abuse of children registered in 2012 in Pakistan.

"There has been a massive increment in child abuse in Pakistan during the last few years", said Shumila Bukhari a human rights activist from Islamabad. Lower fraction of population is frustrated and conflicted enough so they are using child abuse as a tool for the reduction of their anger but what to say about the educated upper middle and elite factions of the society who are also involved in child abuse (not of their own children but of their servants and maids) as a symbol of status. Massive fraction among the wives and children of feudal lords, business tycoons and bureaucratic elite of the country is familiar to treat children of their servants (Who are also working as servants as well) very inhumanly. Sometimes so called educated professionals have been also found to be involved in the ongoing barbarism against the children of Pakistan. In recent days, story of ten-year old girl from Lahore was focused enough in the media, this particular girl was working as a child maid in the house of a lawyer in Lahore. Lawyer proved as a wild beast for this little angel who used to beat her buttocks with iron rod in an extensive manner. Is this called a human attitude?" Bukhari asked me.

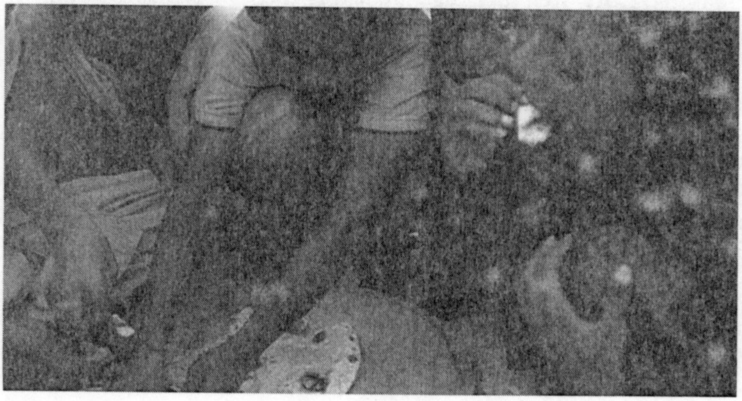

Faction of Christian Chidren from Lahore

Corporal punishment is used for the massive fraction of children studying in public and private schools very frequently. Teachers mostly in public schools like to control students with massive corporal punishments. As more than half of total population in the country is going through very severe economic

Hollywood Actress Anjeelna Joile visted Pakistan in 2012, with Dprived Chidren of Khyber Puktunhkwa

circumstances so most among the children of deprived classes are admitted in public schools which has produced great burden on the teachers of public schools in the country. Public schools almost in every corner of the country are having more students than their capacity which is causing great repercussions on teachers as well. Massive fraction among the public school teachers is not able to properly teach this vast number of student and they utilise physical punishment as a tool to control students in class rooms. On an average larger schools of the cities possess 5000-6000 students, and not more than 80-100 teachers, this practice has produced worst impacts on teachers as well so they like to reduce their anger towards government (who is not paying them accordingly but have overloaded them with work) policies through the corporal punishment of their students.

Physical punishment is an integral part of life of the working children in Pakistan. Children belonging to massive deprived factions of the society are forced to work from a very young age, this fraction of children is facing worst circumstances in the form of physical and sexual abuses by their Masters and elder colleagues. Massive fraction of children working in general shops, motor workshops, and smaller industrial units have to face severe repercussions. Majority among these children are working at very low wages (so called wages, in fact they are getting shameful salaries for their extensive work) and are also facing corporal punishment as a bonus.

Motor mechanics are considered among the very cruel persons in the society by the massive fraction of children working in different motor workshops and garages. Many among the motor mechanics in Pakistan treat their young pupils very inhumanly. Massive fraction of population from lower income groups like to send their little children at motor workshops as they feel it's a good source of earning and to work as a motor mechanic is more rewarding as compared to other skilled work options. This is true to a great extent that motor mechanics (if skilled enough) are earning well here, but a child who is seeking to become a motor mechanic has to face a lot of adversities here.

- **Sexual Abuse of Children in Pakistan**

Pakistani children are unfortunate enough that massive majority among them is living below the poverty line and are not able to attain even the basic human necessities like education, health and pure drinking water. A vast majority among the Pakistani children is forced to work as child labour. The negligence of the state has produced severe repercussions on children living in this miserable part of the world. The state organisations entrusted with the duty of protection of children have failed miserably so much so that sexual abuse of children rampant under its very nose. Sexual abuse of a child is considered as the most heinous crime in most of the civilised world and offenders are dealt with iron hands in all civilised parts of the world, but here

Chidren Collecting the Waste of Poultry in a Slum Area of Lahore

Little Cobbler from Peshawr

in so called land of pure it's a very commonly treated crime by law enforcement agencies of the country. Thousands of children are sexually abused every year in this part of the world but offenders feel liberty and ease here as accountability of the culprit is very rare.

Express Tribune reported on April 8, 2011 that 2252 children were sexually abused in Pakistan in 2010. 'Sahil' a non-government organisation working for human rights in Pakistan collected the details of 2252 victims, according to statistics of this organisation among 73 per cent of the sexually abused children were girls.

Massive fraction of children sexually abused in Pakistan belong to lower classes, majority of children belonging to this class become victim during work. Children working at barbers shops, motor workshops, furniture factories and at several other places are sexually abused by their bosses and elder colleagues very frequently. 'BOL', a block buster Pakistani film described the story of a teen transgender who was sexually abused by his senior colleagues and was later killed by his father in the name of honour.

Sexual abuse of children is a great matter of concern for the society in Pakistan since too many years but media highlighted this issue only in recent past. Both religious schools (Madarsa's) and public schools are considered among the major places where cases of abusing children have come up. Teachers and elder students of both type of above mentioned schools were found guilty in many cases of sexual abuse in these organisations. One of my friends, a former student of a religious school (now faculty member of a renowned University in Pakistan) told me (Writer) about the ongoing massive sexual abuses with children in Pakistan. Let's pay some attention to his words.

"It was a strange time in my life when I was studying in a religious school situated in Southern part of the Punjab. Apparently everything looked fine in the atmosphere of the school but sometimes I felt that there are many secret activities going on within the premises of that sacred place. One day one among our teachers (Molana) had a dispute with the administrator of the school who later sacked him. After the departure of above mentioned teacher many stories of his illicit behaviours with many young became known to us. It looked astonishing to me that a person who possessed such a respectable position was involved in these types of crimes. Few days later a watch man of the Madarsa found two guys aged 15 and 11 respectively engaged with each other in an indecent position, the elder guy was abusing the little one. Inhabitants of the village (where the religious school was situated) pressurised the administration for making an enquiry into the incident. Many amazing facts came out when the incident was put under scrutiny, not only the two above mentioned guys but dozens of others also were found to be involved in such perversities", my friend added more.

It's a matter of great concern that large factions of educated professionals alongside with the so called literate teachers of religious schools are involved in barbaric behaviour with children. Little girls working as house maids in posh and middle class areas of different cities are also facing severe circumstances inflicted upon them by their educated owners. This fraction of population is getting inspiration from feudal and industrial elite of the country. A 2009 case of physical and sexual abuse of a twelve years old girl Amina by her employer received worldwide attention. The beast like owner of the house used to lock the little angel in the kitchen with her little feet shackled to a chair and hands chained to a table. The girl was found in a horrific state by her neighbours who came to release her, blood paved her wounds and her skin was damaged. Amina is a little glimpse of a larger heinous picture, there are thousands of other Amina's who are being raped and murdered every year in Pakistan.

It's a matter of great concern that boys who were sexually abused in their early childhoods are acting as child pimps in many cities of the country. This issue was highlighted in both electronic and print media of the country in the recent past. Daily Dawn published a report by the title of 'Children sexually abused on Pakistani street' on August 26, 2011. The report stated the story of Nadeem a seventeen years old guy who had become a child pimp in Karachi. Above mentioned boy was only twelve years old when he was sexually abused for the first time by a policeman, this incident occurred in 2005. Later this guy was found to operate a little child brothel in Sadar area of Karachi where he puts up ten to twelve young guys at a time.

According to statistics of an NGO working for the rights of children in Pakistan about 90 per cent sexually abused children possess various psychological disorders. Sixty per cent children who have been victims of sexual abuses in the country claim that the police officials patrolling on the roads and streets at nights were involved in inflicting such heinous cruelty on them. There are more than 0.25 million (250,000) children in Pakistan who are sleeping on roads and streets due to their miserable circumstances. Above mentioned fraction of children is forced to do so for having no house and shelter, so massive fraction of children sleeping on roads are unsafe to a great extent. According to another NGO working for children more than 75 per cent children sleeping on the streets have been sexually abused by someone at least once in their life span.

- **Child Marriages**

Child marriage is a familiar type of imposed sexual abuse based on social and religious norms which is responsible for causing severe repercussions on the society. According to Pakistan demographic and health survey 2006-07 around one-third women in the country are married before the age of 18 and two out of ten girls in the country become pregnant between the ages of 14-18.

It's a great dilemma of modern day Pakistan that massive factions of population living below the poverty line including lower class and lower middle class consider child marriage as the solution of all their socioeconomic problems. Above mentioned factions of the society are utilising their little children as a tool to reduce their severe economic problems. Little girls between 10-17 years old are married with elder men as their parents are not able to afford their livelihood expenditures, for similar reasons little guys are also married in early years of teenage as their marriages fetch dowries for their parents.

Another major reason for child marriage in Pakistan is massive work load, social classes who are economically deprived possess enough work load in their houses due to having many family members. Due to very limited financial resources above mentioned factions of the population are not familiar with home appliances so they have to do all work manually. With too much work, frequent birth of children and other socioeconomic problems at large, housewives of above mentioned factions of the society grow old before their ages (mostly by early forties). That's why above mentioned fraction of the ladies in Pakistan is always willing to marry their teenaged sons as they look forward for a girl who can work with them and reduce their household burden.

Marriage in childhood negatively affects the health of the wedded children. Due to involving in sexual activities from early ages, these children succumb to severe complications in later stages of their lives. This custom is also responsible for causing psychological disorders and massive portion from this fraction of population adopt intolerance and violence as an integral part of their lives.

- **Kidnapping and Children Trafficking in Pakistan**

Pakistan is one of the world's great hub of kidnapping and trafficking of men, women and children. Every year thousands of men, women and children are kidnapped from various parts of the country and smuggled to different parts of the world. Business of human trafficking specially trafficking of children is very widespread and deep-rooted in the country and is growing with ease and comfort as many mafias involved in such activities possess links in law enforcement agencies of the country.

Massive factions of kidnapped children are utilised for begging, domestic services, bonded labour and for prostitution as well. Hundreds of children kidnapped from remote areas of the country like South Punjab, Interior part of Sind and Baluchistan are utilised in camel jockeying in gulf countries. According to an article of Express Tribune published on September 8, 2012 more than 7000 children were abducted during 2011 in Pakistan. Among these, large fraction of 3090 children was from the largest metropolitan of the country.

According to 'State of Pakistan', an NGO working for the rights of children in the country, there has been a constant rise in the cases of abduction of children in the country. A vast majority among the kidnapped children is smuggled to Afghanistan and United Arab Emirates every year. These children belong to lower income groups and their parents are not able to pay heavy ransoms to kidnappers.

There are different categories of child abductors in Pakistan. Local kidnappers operating in Karachi and various other parts of the country including South Punjab and interior Sind usually kidnap children for ransom and release the abducted ones after extracting ransom from the parents according to their social status. This fraction of kidnappers is running its shady business with the help of local feudal elite who provide them protection. Kidnappers of the second category are involved in kidnapping the children from upper income groups of the business and educated professional class. Children abducted by this fraction of kidnappers are usually transferred in tribal areas of the country. This area is known to be a safe haven of many mafias and criminal gangs including kidnappers since a very long span of time.

Business community from Karachi and educated professionals of Punjab has faced severe repercussions through these gangs of kidnappers. Kidnapping of Sahil Saeed, a British born child of Pakistani descent got the world's attention in March 2010. Saeed then a six years old child (born in 2004) was kidnapped by four armed men alongside with cash and jewellery from his ancestral house in Jehlem. Kidnappers demanded a ransom of 20,000,000 (20 million PKR) from his parents. Law enforcement agencies as usual failed to get back the abducted one, the child was released after the kidnappers were paid the desired ransom.

A specific fraction of abductors is operating in backward areas of the country. Children abducted through this gang are utilised for various purposes. This fraction of kidnappers abduct children from specific areas of South Punjab and interior Sind and Baluchistan, the victims belong to lower income fraction of the population. These children are either used for begging and bonded labour in the farms of feudal elite or smuggled to Afghanistan, Iran and gulf region where these children are used as slaves and for camel jockeying purposes. Many among the kidnapped children from South Punjab and Interior part of the Sind were the part of recent camel races held in United Arab Emirates. The children used as camel jockeys belong to most deprived factions of the society and are not too familiar with such animals. On being forced to ride on camels these miserable children cry out of fear making the animals run faster and this give a sadistic pleasure to the cruel wealthy Arab event organisers.

In the year 2012, United States department of foreign affairs (normally called as States Department of USA) placed Pakistan on tier 2 of human rights (countries whose governments do not comply with the minimum standards set by US government as per trafficked victims protection act 2000) which indicates the severe circumstances related to human life especially child kidnapping and trafficking in the country. According to a human rights activist (working with an NGO for the protection of children rights in Pakistan), "Government has failed to show any significant progress in controlling child trafficking in the country. No legal initiatives have been taken during the recent past to control child trafficking so this heinous crime is growing day by day", he added more.

8

Fraud as an Agent of Socioeconomic Injustice in Pakistan

Fraud is considered as an integral part of modern Pakistani society and is widely utilised for inflicting socioeconomic injustices by the massive factions of population in every field and corner of the country. Being a major vehicle of socioeconomic injustice it is of various kinds and its victims belong to all social classes of the country. It's so widespread and deep-rooted that hundreds of thousands among ordinary masses and special ones are facing its repercussions. Massive fraction of the population has now adopted fraudulent practices as an integral part of their life.

Its look astonishing sometimes that culture of fraud has changed the psyche of a whole nation but it's a reality. Massive fraction of population in the country does not feel any regret or guilt while committing fraud with their fellows as this has become an integrated part of their life now. In fact, it's not only a matter of pleasure for offenders but victims too consider it as a routine matter. Truly speaking, Pakistanis are among the most hypocritic natives of the world as many among the both elite and masses posses dual faces in real life. Every one apparently is something different from his/her portrayed face here. Disguising others with dual characters is considered among the most vital achievements of a personality in the land of pure. In this part of the book we will discuss some very familiar types of frauds commonly practiced in this part of the world.

Pakistanis are basically comfort and ease loving people and do not possess any passion for hard work and struggle for the achievements of their goals in life. Massive portion of population from all factions of the society is always on the look out for short cuts for the achievements of their desired destinations in life. Massive fraction of students in the country like to use unfair means during the examinations for the enhancement of their grades. Masses are willing to earn more for the improvement in their life style but not through hard work and struggle so everyone is trying to get more and more through any means whether right or wrong.

It's a true saying that cheaters will not feel any hunger in the city of greed. Very similar is the situation in the so called land of pure as it always appears like the land of greedy ones. When people are over ambitious for the fulfilments of their desires, non-practical in attitude and willing to become millionaires over night fraud will definitely progress at a very rapid rate in that land and same is happening here in Pakistan.

It was the year 2006 when a school teacher from the region of central Punjab planned a multi-billion fraud scam. Teacher named as Sibtul-Husnian Shah later called as Double Shah (Due to his so called ability of doubling the money) did a massive fraud in the history of country with the help of his very sharp mind and attitude. Example of Double Shah can serve as a test case to understand the mafias involved in these type of activities with the masses, it will also make us realise that all social classes from all factions like to invite above mentioned mafias to involve in committing scams with them. It was the spring of 2006 when Double Shah left his school job and announced in his surroundings that he is going to start a business which would double the investments within very short span of time. It was very hard for anyone to believe such a proclamation at that time of recession and worst economic conditions of the country that there can be such a business which can double the principal amount within the short time span of 15 days, but even then few among his neighbours deposited their small amounts with Double Shah. First person to invest in this newly launched scheme was a driver, a neighbour of Double Shah. Astonishingly Double Shah returned their amounts within the stipulated time frame and the news spread like a fire in the premises of Gujranwala division. People from all walks of life and social classes started to hand over their life savings to him for getting their savings doubled within the promised time.

With the passage of time and with the increase in number of big fishes (some among them deposited millions of rupees with him) in his investment circle Double Shah changed his style of business. Initially he claimed to double the amount within 15 days but later the time span was increased to 30 and finally to 180 days. When initial beneficiaries of Shah's scheme started to spread Shah's repute in their surroundings a massive fraction of people from Gujranwala division and other parts of the country as well deposited heavy amounts with him. When Shah started to receive millions of rupees per day from all factions of the society he silently started transferring these amounts in foreign accounts. But he was getting too much money that was still able to fulfil few among his promised ones. With the increase of return period many among his customers or victims suspected that there was going to be a massive scam in few days but before any action could be taken, he transferred massive portion of these collected amounts in many of his foreign accounts in Dubai and Singapore. All was set and he was ready to fly from the country but was arrested on April 13, 2007 by the joint venture of National Accountability Bureau (NAB) and Police. Police officer told the media later that at the time of arrest there 2.5-3 billion PKR (25-30 million dollars) was found at his home at the time of his arrest. Shah faced a lengthy trial and was finally convicted on July 1, 2012 and sentenced to 14 years imprisonment for committing a scam of 5.6 billions that victimised thousands of Pakistanis.

Many victims of Double Shah lost the savings of their whole life time through this ponzi scheme and have still not been able to receive their principal amounts. According to a report of Daily Dawn published on May 17, 2012 some fraction of Double Shah's victims were recuperated by NAB. The report stated that NAB Punjab director Khurshid Anwar distributed cheques of total amount 32 million. As we discussed earlier that recovered amount was less than half of the total scammed amount and a very minute part of the recovered amount has been returned till now to the victims. So a vast number of Double Shah's victims are still at sixes and seven, though they are themselves to blame for their own destruction. Some media reports also stated that Police seized a major portion of wealth found at Shah's house and showed only a minute amount as recovery.

Above mentioned example of Double Shah is just a glimpse of a more larger picture, there are thousands of others in the guise of noble characters who are looting the masses of the country with every going moment with ease, comfort and liberty. One can easily find dacoits in the guise of doctors, professors, consultants, religious scholars and leaders and many more……Lets have a look at some special types of frauds going on in every corner and every field of life.

- **Frauds in Education Sector of Pakistan**

As education, health facilities and provision of instant justice are considered among basic human necessities in the civilised and modern world of the day so people from all factions of society are giving preferences to these aspects in Pakistan as well. It's a great concern for the massive population of the country that concerned government organisations associated with education, health and justice are not paying heed to the issues and challenges. The state has failed to provide the ordinary ones as per certain basic parameters of progress, prosperity and civilisations. Lower fraction of population is deprived enough and going through very miserable socioeconomic circumstances so it's not able to spend on health and education. Elite and super elite classes are not dependent on the native system for their education and health and generally prefer to go abroad for such purposes, familiar to source these services so this fraction is not much worried about the worst circumstances prevalent in public health and education departments.

Middle fraction of population (though not big in numbers as most among the population belongs to deprived classes) including upper middle and middle classes are investing on health and education in Pakistan through private sector as public sectors are not able to deliver for this educated and relatively aware fraction of the population as well.

Education is a great source of loot, fraud and corruption for the mafias involved in it, in Pakistan. Massive factions of private sector educational institutes in Pakistan are involved in great loot and fraud with the masses in the country. Substandard education is a fate of students in Pakistan in both public and private (with the exception of few organisations) sectors. Public sector is providing basic education almost free but is charging for higher education. Private sector is charging high for the both primary and higher education but is still not able to provide quality education in return. This practice is going on at a very wide level in every corner of the country and has produced severe repercussions, not only has it destroyed the education system but it is also responsible for generating a massive army of unemployable people in the society.

Private sector came in the arena of education in early 1980's in Pakistan and soon it flourished as an integral part of corporate culture of the country. Some renowned schools, colleges and universities of this sector are no doubt providing quality education (at very high cost) but massive fraction of educational institutes from private sector of the country are involved in only fraud and loot in the name of education. Majority among these privately owned schools and colleges and universities are situated in small buildings and equipped with very less and substandard furniture, laboratories, play grounds and class rooms. Many privately owned schools in Pakistan are not able to provide basic facilities like science equipments and co-curricular facilities to their students.

Teaching staff recruited in above mentioned fraction of educational institutes belong to lower income groups (lower class and lower middle class) and they are getting shameful remunerations for their services. One can't imagine that a teacher from a very deprived financial background would be able to teach well so a massive fraction of population is forced for a low quality education in Pakistan. I interviewed a girl who is attached with a familiar school system in South Punjab and getting a very minute amount for her services, her condition was very poor and confidence was shaky enough. She told me that she has done Masters in Pakistan studies from Bahudin-Zakirya University (commonly called as BZU) and is getting 8000 PKR for her services to the organisation. I asked her the reason for working for such a small amount in spite of her being so qualified; her reply to my query was quite astonishing. Let's have a look at what she said.

"When I did my Maters from BZU I had no job for a long period of time. After being unemployed for more than one year I started to work in a school and there my salary was 5000 PKR only. Later on with an experience of two years in teaching, I got a job in my current school which offered me 7000 PKR and after completing six months of service I am getting only 8000 PKR". "Sir you can't imagine the kind of exploitation they are subjecting us to", she said, "They are not running these organisations for the welfare of masses or because they possess any love for education. The owners who earn millions of rupees per month are multimillionaires but still their greed is growing more and more with the passage of time", she added.

Above mentioned example is a little glimpse of a larger picture, there are hundreds of such educational institutes in Pakistan whose earnings are not millions but in billions every year but even then they are not inclined to provide quality education to their students.

Education has become a part of corporate sector in Pakistan and considered among the highly profitable businesses, a business that requires less investment yet yields much profit. People have earned a lot from this industry but unfortunately have not improved its quality. Familiar chains of schools, colleges and universities in Pakistan are earning billions of rupees every year but not paying taxes accordingly as educational institutes are exempted from the taxes on income in Pakistan. We have discussed about various kinds of mafias involved in many sectors of life in Pakistan here we will disclose some facts about the mafia operating in the educational sector of the country. One can easily find out hundreds of privately-owned professional colleges and universities widespread in every corner of the country. These professional colleges and universities claim to provide quality education but very few among them actually do so, the remaining are making fools of the masses in the name of education and playing with the future of the youth.

Medical colleges and universities from private sector have grown at a very rapid rate during the last decade in the country. Massive fraction of above mentioned educational institutes are operating in small buildings with very few of them having equipped laboratories as per the set standards of higher education in Pakistan. I (Writer) witnessed a medical college operating in a small house with no teaching hospital; most of the private sector medical institutes in various parts of the country possess the same sort of situation.

"There is a mafia involved in running of the private medical colleges of the country", said Shahid Ali a young physician from Lahore. "When I completed my MBBS I found no job in public sector so I started working as a lecturer in a renowned medical college of private sector in Lahore. In the year 2011 when my fellow doctors were attaining the remunerations of 55,000-60,000 in government sector I was getting only 22,000 PKR. Particular medical college where I was teaching was earning 150-200 million PKR every year even then they were paying very minute salaries to faculty members. Students studying in private medical colleges in Pakistan are the children of upper fraction of the population who have not been able to attain admissions in public sector institutes, they find no solution other than getting admissions in this type of colleges. Hundreds of graduates from these colleges are occupying important portfolios in different public sector organisations with the help of their influences and by sabotaging merit."

It's a matter of fact that upper factions of the society including feudal elite, industrialists, civil-military bureaucrats and top level politicians only require a degree for their children, what is the way to attain that degree it's not their problem. According to a senior journalist from Lahore many among the senior surgeons in the country purchased degrees of MBBS for their sons from foreign fake universities during the time span of 1980 till the late 90's until private medical colleges were not established in the country. Now it's very easy for them, induction of their children in these colleges is the easiest way of attaining a medical degree without too much effort. Medical professionals of this fraction are not concerned about whether their children acquire the required skills or not, they already own medical complexes so they have secured positions in advance for their next generation where the latter will massacre the ordinary masses like their parents have been doing since so many years. A large number of young medical professionals are incompetent enough and are operating their ancestral hospitals in Pakistan. These young doctors have very low level of ethics and humanity due to very unethical atmosphere in their teaching institutes.

Private medical colleges and universities provide ease and comfort to the incompetent children of upper income groups in the country, these organisations are awarding thousands of degrees every year without any calibre testing. Politicians needed degrees to contest general elections during the time span of 2002-08 as during the regime of dictator Pervaiz Musharraff it was required that a parliamentarian should be at least a graduate. Many among the parliamentarians during that era got fake degrees from the universities of private sector in Pakistan and abroad. Several politicians in Pakistan were disqualified from their memberships during 2002-14 due to their fake degrees.

Other influential factions of the society including medical professionals also utilised these educational institutes for attaining degrees for their children as they were seeking to transfer their assets to their next generation. With the addition of income from unfair means, massive fraction of doctors in Pakistan is earning very well so this fraction of population possess lot of assets like medical complexes, agriculture and commercial lands etc. Currently business of medical colleges is very familiar among the elite community of doctors in Pakistan.

When a doctor forms an estate in Pakistan he is willing to transfer both his ancestral and professional skills to his next generation. It's a great human dilemma in Pakistan that massive factions among doctors want their children to also become doctors irrespective of abilities or interests in medical profession. This fraction of population perceives the medical profession not as a human service but as a trade under the garb of humanity. Influence of professional heredity is an integral driving force of such communities of doctors in Pakistan, so they are anyhow making their children medical professionals through private medical colleges. These children are attaining degrees at the cost of ordinary masses of the country. To recapitulate it can be said that massive fraction of private sector educational institutes in Pakistan are not only involved in loot and frauds but also producing severe type of other repercussions as well.

- **Fraud of Education and Immigration Consultants in Pakistan**

A massive fraud in the name of education and immigration consultancy is going on in Pakistan nowadays. It's a fact of the day that out of more than 192 million Pakistanis more than 40 per cent are living below the poverty line. Federal minister for Finance Mr Ishaq Dar admitted in recent days in a press briefing that more than 50 per cent of the total population in the country is earning not more than two US dollars per day. A massive fraction of the remaining 50 per cent is also a part of the very deprived class. Middle class has shrinked a lot during the last decade due to worst economic circumstances, massive fraction of previous middle class is now part of lower middle class. Similarly previous lower middle class is now fraction of lower class, lower class has gone down below the poverty line.

Poverty, unemployment, growing terrorism and non-availability of socioeconomic justice at any level are few major causes for the growing frustration and conflicts in massive fraction of population in the country. This deprived situation is leading a massive fraction of population towards absolute anger towards the state and its organs. Due to the above mentioned circumstances massive fraction of educated class from middle income group is willing to move abroad. People belonging to this massive fraction of population are seeking new destinations abroad in all directions. North American countries of USA and Canada; Oceanic countries of Australia and Newzeland; European countries of UK, Germany and France; far Eastern countries of Japan and South Korea are among the favourite destinations of the educated middle class of the country who are not willing to live any more in their home land.

Pakistan possesses a massive diaspora in middle east but this fraction is not much satisfied with their employments as compared to their counterparts in USA, Canada, Australia and Europe. All Arab countries are familiar among Pakistanis for their inhuman rules and regulations for the foreigners especially for South Asians, so they prefer Europe as a work destination. But a very deprived fraction of population is forced to work in Arab countries including Saudi Arabia, United Arab Emirates etc. on very low wages and benefits. It's a reality that Arab countries (for whom massive fraction of Pakistani population possess very emotional attitude) are treating Pakistani labour in a very inhuman manner and consider them as 'C' class residents in their countries while the Western world (massive fraction of population blames west for their misery) is taking care of the overseas Pakistanis in a very respectable and humanly way. Pakistani professionals are very less paid in the whole of Arab world as compared to Europe and Americas, so massive fraction of population in the country is willing to relocate in USA, Canada, Australia, Japan and European countries.

The September 11, 2001 terrorist attack in New York, USA by orthodox militant group who claim to be followers of Islamic religion produced severe repercussions on Pakistani educated and skilled factions of the society living abroad or desirous of settling abroad as the overall national sentiment of USA natives got prejudiced against the Islamic religion and all its followers and soon this prejudice also spread to the other North American, Oceanic and European countries. After the incident it has become much difficult for the massive fraction of above mentioned portions of the population to relocate in North America, Oceania and various parts of Europe as compared to the past. This situation has given the mafia of immigration and study consultants in Pakistan an opportunity to profiteer by exploiting the desires of the people who are willing to settle aboard at any cost in the name of foreign immigration and employment.

According to a report of Express Tribune published on August 9, 2012 Lahore high court ordered to put the name of Asim Malik in Exit Control List (ECL) for his involvement in a massive visa scam. Particular person is the chief executive officer of a visa consultancy firm named 'Future concern associates' has faced severe allegations of fraud and loot from hundreds of Pakistanis who applied for immigrations, student and business visas through them but their documents were rejected by the embassies of the destination countries. Above mentioned firm received millions of rupees in the form of consultancy fee for the arrangement of visas and immigrations but failed to deliver the desired outcomes to its clients. According to many victims, company also did not refund their fees which they were responsible to pay back in case of failure. Scam of 'Future Concern Associates' is an example of one among hundreds of other such cases that take place every year in Pakistan.

'Study and Immigration in Canada', 'Guaranteed visa of UK in one week', 'Business and family visas for Australia' and many more such type of advertisements can be found in Pakistani newspapers. Every day, magazines, billboards and even the walls try to attract and trap massive fraction of population even in these modernised and globalised times when most educated people are expected to have a keen sense of matters. Consultant mafia in Pakistan is actually playing with the dreams and emotions of a vast number of people. It's a valid question that how many among the ordinary ones will still like to live in a country where more than half of the population lives below or on the poverty line, terrorism is widespread and deep-rooted and has swallowed more than 80,000 among the ordinary masses? The situation is really desperate and most people sensing it and seeking to move abroad often get trapped by the wrong people who only seek to profiteer through exploitation.

Urbanised or even semi-urbanised middle class fraction of population including smaller industrialists, businessmen, doctors, engineers and other professionals who are earning 3-5 lakhs (0.3-05 million PKR) per month are feeling insecure in the land of pure since early 2000's. This fraction of population is very willing to relocate as compared to the feudal and industrial elite (civil-military bureaucracy also belongs to the latter fraction of elite) of the country who already possess assets abroad but are living in Pakistan as well for their political and commercial interests. Massive fraction of educated middle class is heavily dependent on these so called immigration consultants who actually are not able to connect with the embassies of foreign countries directly for visas and are cheating this fraction of population. During the last few years thousands of immigration applications, study and business visas have been pending or rejected by the embassies of North America, Oceania and countries of Europe due to incompetency or false attitude of these consultants in Pakistan.

Hundreds of thousands of Pakistani are receiving electronic mails, text messages and broachers every day about the expertise of consultants who claim to provide immigration and other visas of developed countries in the world. Hundreds of victims of these consultancy firms have lost the savings of their whole lives but were not able to achieve desired goals. Let's have a look at one such example.

"I paid 5000 US dollars (0.5 million PKR) to an immigration consultant for the citizenship of Denmark three years back in 2011 but I am still wandering near his office", said Ahmed Hassan a senior Engineer working in a semi-government organisation from Lahore. Though currently I am getting good salary but I still feel insecure in Pakistan due to heavy recession going on here since 2005, moreover many among my colleagues are more settled than me in Europe so I too have decided to settle in Scandinavia. One of my friends told me that an engineer with more than seven years work experience can easily attain the citizenship of any among the Scandinavian countries so I decided to move towards Denmark as it is among the most peaceful countries in the world. I contacted with above mentioned consultant on the suggestion of my friend, the consultant confirmed me regarding my eligibility for citizenship and demanded my documents alongside his charges of 5000 US dollars. I was reluctant to pay his fee at once but my friend told me about his expertise and I decided to pay his fee instantly, but since then I am after him and he is hiding from me now. Astonishingly one of my fellow engineers applied directly without any consultant for the citizenship of Norway and he got that within one year. Now particular consultant is neither pursuing my case in the embassy nor is he returning my money", Hassan added more.

As we discussed earlier that before the incident of 9/11 process of immigration and attaining visas of Western world was easier for the massive fraction of population. Many among the Pakistani doctors, engineers, commerce and IT professionals have settled in USA, Canada and Europe and got citizenships and resident permits during 1980-2000. After the incident of September 11 most among the countries of developed world adopted a very stringent approach towards Pakistani professionals seeking immigration in their premises leading to severe repercussions. Massive fraction of Pakistanis staying on work visas were not only denied immigrations but new lot of professionals who were waiting for opportunities in EU countries and North America during 2005-14 faced immense difficulties in getting student and work visas.

During the time span of 1980 to early 2000's Pakistani professionals were allowed to work in North America and Europe on the basis of their academic qualifications and experiences but since 9/11 it has become almost impossible for a Pakistani doctor or engineer to get a direct job in North America, Oceania and even in Europe as well. After 2005, Pakistani professionals diverted their intentions from migrations to higher studies for getting entry in above mentioned countries. As massive fraction of Pakistani professionals is willing to settle in EU countries, Oceania and North America, so they are adopting every legitimate means for it. As one such means, this fraction of population is now seeking to get admissions in still higher educational programmes of the universities of EU and North America even after having completed a professional education programme of a much high level in Pakistan.

A young Pakistani doctor or engineer having few years of work experience over here is now familiar with the fact that he/she is now no more able to get any professional position in USA, Australia or any other developed country of the world so now above fraction is trying to secure admissions in particular countries and once they enter there they find other ways like marriage, (real or paper marriage in which Pakistanis are paying fixed mounts to the residents of particular countries for resident permits) political asylums, etc. for getting citizenships.

As per records it is evident that massive fraction of Pakistani young professionals who got admissions in the Universities of North America, EU countries, Oceania and Japan never returned back home after completing higher degrees like Masters and PhD's in Engineering, FCPS, MD etc. This predicts that massive fraction among the professionals in Pakistan who is willing to get admissions in above mentioned countries is using this practice as a tool to settle there. Assessing the desires and ambitious attitude of Pakistani students for attaining citizenships, massive fraction of public universities in North America, Caribbean, EU and Oceania imposed heavy tuition fees on Pakistani students and reduced their scholarships as well. Many among the leading universities of the world are still offering scholarships to the students of Sub-Saharan Africa, Myanmar and even Afghanistan but not to Pakistanis as they feel now that Pakistani students are more interested in prolonging their stays and seek ways to settle abroad rather than focusing on their studies.

Many among the Scandinavian countries are offering free education to international students at Masters and PhD levels; countries like Sweden, Norway and Denmark were also offering free education to Pakistani students as well till late 2000, but now above mentioned countries have imposed heavy tuition fees on Pakistani students after facing the experiences of their sticking attitude. Nowadays only Germany and Finland among the EU countries are providing free higher education to Pakistani students but these two countries have reduced their quotas for Pakistanis as compared to the near past.

Mafias operating in the name of immigration and education abroad in Pakistan are still making fool of students by claiming to arrange their free studies abroad. 'Free study in Sweden', '100% free education in Norway', 'Scholarships available for Denmark and Finland' and many such more advertisements in newspapers, magazines, billboards and everywhere in the country are trying to entice the educated fraction of youth since a long span of time. But majority among propagated consultants are frauds involved in exploiting the wealth and emotions of the youth with ease and comfort and feel no accountability for it.

Above mentioned so called immigration and study consultants demand heavy amounts for the arrangement of admissions and scholarships in the universities of Europe. Most among these consultants claim that they possess links with the officials of Public universities in North America, Oceania and Europe and they can secure admissions for their clients on the payment of 2-10 lacs (0.2-1 million) but most among these so called experts fail to do so. Massive fraction of foreign education consultants trap students in the name of scholarships, this fraction takes heavy fees from their clients on the promise of providing them scholarships in top universities of the world. Massive fraction of students remain unfamiliar with the intricate details of the admission process as many among them feel so excited at the prospect of studying in Europe or America that they neglect the proper investigations about universities and other formalities and put all such matters on the shoulders of consultants. These consultants cheat them by providing admissions in ordinary private sector universities as they possess links with the officials of these universities so not only they take heavy charges from students but also get commissions from the administration of those universities. When students reach there they feel shocked to find that the promises made by the consultants have not been delivered, they are not given any scholarships and also they do not find the aura of prestige typical of top level European and American public universities.

As we discussed earlier that most among the top level public universities in Europe are not offering any more scholarships to Pakistani students. With the exception of few universities in Finland and Germany all other public universities situated in EU countries are now charging heavy tuition fees from Pakistani students so studying in Europe has gone out of reach from the upper middle class of the country as well. Finland and Germany though still award free education to Pakistani students but their criteria are strict enough and massive fraction of Pakistani students is not able to attain that. Free education Universities in Finland provide admissions on the basis of very strict merit, these universities not only demand high academic grades but also require high proficiencies in both English (At least seven bands out of nine are required in International language testing, IELTS) and finish languages which is a very difficult task for massive fraction of students in Pakistan. Similarly, German Universities demand at least two year deposit of expenditures (upto 15000 Euros) in a German bank alongside with deposition of a nominal fee. Public sector German universities also demands high proficiency in German and English languages. Education consultants in Pakistan dealing in foreign study programmes mostly hide these facts from their clients as they are greedy, they extract their own charges surreptitiously and students who apply through them either get rejected by the universities or embassies when they apply for visas.

Students in most parts of the world are not allowed to take up job at all or only get permission to work for specified limited working hours in a week during undergoing study programmes, even the highest level programmes like PhD. Nowadays pursuing studies while working is a common trend all over the world. In higher level programmes students are free to choose the days and timings of their classes, for the remaining days or time they are free to work. Generally working students prefer to attend classes for three to four days in a week so as also be able to work, but as per rules of most European and American institutes they cannot take up work requiring more than eighteen or at the most twenty hours. Many consultants in Pakistan fool candidates who approach them for getting admissions in foreign universities by telling them that they can study and work together and earn a lot of money, many among their clients belong to lower middle class so they put their own or their parent's entire life savings at stake and get admissions abroad as per the suggestions of consultants but when they reach their destinations they are accosted by severe situations.

Ali Qasim, a twenty three years old graduate from Lahore told me (writer) that once he visited an education consultant in Lahore who claimed that he was a graduate from Oxford University, London. During his meeting with me he tried to convince me for taking admission in a private university of UK. He propagated that there are enough opportunities of earning in United Kingdom even while studying, and that he too was earning 1600-2000 pounds during his education tenure. Qasim further added that as he had a keen interest in international affairs and was familiar that UK was still facing the aftershocks of Euro zone debt crises so he found it astonishing for a student to earn such a big amount from a job of limited working hour schedule. Yet, the consultant went on convincing him but Qasim was in search of a scholarship instead of studying abroad on his parents expenditures as his parents were bearing his responsibility from a long span of time, so he decided to reject the consultant's offer. Qasim expressed to me (writer) that if the consultant was earning 2000 pounds during his studies as was claimed by him, then after completing his studies he could have earned at least 3000 pounds per month, yet instead of being abroad the consultant's presence in Pakistan seemed strange.

A massive fraction of immigration and education consultants operating in Pakistan claim to have relationships with both public sector universities and embassies of above mentioned countries so they propagate this a lot in their advertisements. Many youngsters of rural upper middle class fraction of the society who are not familiar with globalisation of world through modern techniques including proper utilisation of internet become victims of this mafia very easily. Let's have a look as to the kind of people involved in education consultancy business in Pakistan.

"One of my class fellows who dropped out from university due to low grades in 2005 did different ordinary jobs for a long span of time", said Salman Massod a twenty eight years old guy from Lahore. "He went to Spain in 2008 where he worked as a labourer for almost five years, luckily he got a chance to enter into a paper marriage with a Spanish girl due to which he got resident permit over there yet he is still not able to get citizenship of that county. But nowadays he is running an education and immigration consultancy firm to counsel about scope of education in Europe and Australia. It looks very astonishing that a person who is not qualified more than intermediate level is guiding people (or destructing them) about the highest level of study and immigration programmes of Europe, this can only happen in Pakistan", Masood added more.

- **Quackery in Pakistan**

After discussing too much about fraud in the name of education and immigration let's have a look on another type of fraud which is much prevalent in Pakistan. Quackery is no doubt among very serious issues of modern day Pakistan and it's producing very severe repercussions on massive deprived factions of the population. As we discussed earlier that more than 90 per cent of total population in the country is deprived even of the basic necessities of life in this land of pure. Basic education, pure drinking water, instant justice and provision of hygienic living standards are the basic responsibilities of any civilised government in the world but governments here in the so called land of pure have always failed to fulfil their duties.

It's a matter of fact when states are not able to deliver for their citizens the result always appears in the form of frustrations, conflicts and disorders and same is going on here in Pakistan. State owned health, education and other departments in Pakistan are not working for the benefits of masses so deprived social classes are forced to connect with quacks in every field of life.

Generally a person who pretends professionally or publically to have skills, knowledge or qualification which he or she does not possess is called as quack. It's a great dilemma of modern day Pakistan that people of genuine talent have become like an endangered species with only a very minute fraction of them still remaining in the country, talent either is not in proper utilisation or is forced for migration. Quacks are free to play with the health and future of ordinary ones in Pakistan; they utilise massive fraction of population as a tool for committing frauds in the name of health and education in Pakistan. In previous part of the chapter we had some discussion about frauds in education sector, now we will discuss its presence in some other fields of life as well.

Quacks in Pakistan are looting commoners with their smart tools in every field of life but this mafia has produced worst repercussions in the medical field. According to Random house dictionary, quackery is the promotion of unproven or fraudulent medical practices and this is widely spread in Pakistan. Massive factions among medical practitioners in the country hold no licenses or in other words are not qualified for the job of a physician or surgeon but are still practicing with ease and comfort. This fraction of frauds feels no accountability for killing people or causing damage to their prime organs due to incompetent attitude. With more than 50 per cent population of the country living below poverty line or at its edge, basic healthcare facilities are non-familiar to a vast majority of population. Moreover, mafia operating in private sector hospitals is making sure (with the help of public health officials) that services of public sector health institutes always remains out of reach from ordinary ones so massive fraction of lower income group (even lower middle and middle classes as well) is heavily dependent on quacks in modern day Pakistan as its almost impossible for them to bear the expenditures of quality private sector Hospitals like Agha Khan hospital in Karachi and Shukat Khanum Memorial Hospital in Lahore.

Quackery in the fields of medicine and surgery is among the major causes of deaths in Pakistan every year. Massive fraction of government hospitals (almost 99.99 per cent) possesses miserable circumstances due to many reasons like corruption, incompetency and non-professional attitude of doctors etc. When quality hospitals from the corporate sector are only accessible by the super elite and elite factions of the population and government hospitals are in very miserable circumstances then what will the masses do? They possess no options with the exception of getting treatments from quacks which they have been doing since a long span of time.

When commoners who are economically deprived enough are treated by quacks they face a huge risk of being inflicted by medical complications and disorders (fortunate enough among them loose their lives instantly due to the reactions of medication or surgery but less fortune ones have to suffer for their entire lives due to incompetency and ignorance of these quacks operating in every corner of the country) for their whole life spans. According to a report of Daily the News published on November 18, 2013, Dr Anil Arora chairman of Sri Ganga Ram Hospital (New Delhi, India) said during his visit to Ganga Ram Hospital Lahore that majority of deaths in Pakistan belongs to quackery. According to Dr Arora patients of hepatitis in Pakistan are getting severe complications due to lack of qualified staff and getting treatments through quacks. He also stated that liver patients are more carefully handled in India as compared to Pakistan so he offered a free training programme for Pakistani doctors to deal with such patients.

Immense poverty no doubt has played a vital role for the proliferation of a widespread network of quacks but massive corruption of health officials in Pakistan is also playing its part for the enhancement of quackery in the country. Massive fraction of drug Inspectors or other officials appointed by the government for the cure of quackery receive heavy bribes from this fraction or mafia. This type of bribe is commonly called as monthly (a monthly stipend is presented by the mafias operating in the country to corrupt government officials for ensuring the continuity of their businesses) which is a very influential and traditional way for making these health officials keep mum against the issue of quackery prevalent in each street and town of the country. Doctors in public hospitals have been found to humiliate the ordinary masses and treat their patients in a very inhuman way so that the patients instead of coming to public hospitals where they are entitled to get treatment at low costs have no other option than approaching the private hospitals for treatment which is much expensive, the miserable circumstances in public hospitals are purposely created so as to avoid work and responsibilities but due to being government organisations. This conduct in no way affects their inflow of funds and monthly salaries.

As quacks are not qualified so in order to make money they show more humble and friendly attitude towards patients which attracts a large fraction of population towards them including a massive rural population of the country. Let's have a look as to the kind of attitude doctors possess with the ordinary masses of the country especially those from rural and backward areas of the country.

"Once I went to a district head-quarter hospital in Khanewal (a very backward district of South Punjab) due to headache and flu", said Ghulam Abbas a thirty nine year old labourer. "There was a huge crowd of patients but doctor was busy in gossiping with a lady fellow. He used to divert his attentions towards patients once in fifteen minutes or so for a moment or two and then again tilted his face towards the lady sitting with him. He was not giving more than 20 seconds to a patient for check up. It was 11:30 am when he announced that he was going for tea and thereafter he came back after almost one hour. After twenty minutes of his return my turn came, is seemed obvious that he was in a great hurry to save his precious time, he instantly almost snapped at me and asked my problem to which I could reply insufficiently and briefly and without bothering to examine me properly he instantly scribbled a medicine on a paper", Abbas added more.

Quacks are dealing with all types of severe diseases without any fear in Pakistan, they are doing surgeries of complicated diseases as well which is leading to great repercussions. One can easily find matriculate or sometimes almost illiterate orthopaedists, gynaecologists, dentists and general physicians in every street of the country. If someone from the deprived fraction of the population has gone through any accident and broken his bone he will directly contact with a quack orthopaedist (Pehalwan Jee) instead of going to a government hospital. Similarly, women of lower income group are familiar to approach dais (so called skilled women who utilise their skills for the birth of children) during pregnancies and for child birth. It's a great dilemma of modern day Pakistan that its death rate of pregnant women during and after the child birth is very high as compared to its neighbours Iran and India. According to a report of Daily the Nation more than 20,000 women die every year in Pakistan during pregnancy and child birth. Report also stated that UNICEF declared Pakistan among the most alarming countries possessing worst circumstances for women in the world.

Pakistan has a high rate of maternal mortality of 276 maternal deaths per 10,000 births which is very high in comparison to the developed world. "Pakistan has the highest rate of mother mortality in Asia after Afghanistan", said Dr Ali Muhammad Mir on the occasion of International Mother's Day on May 14, 2014. "Both infant and mother mortality is prevalent due to uneducated and non-skilled ladies who are involved during the child birth."

It's a great dilemma of modern day Pakistan that illiterate and poorly skilled dentists widespread in the country are spreading HIV/AIDS and Hepatitis to a great extent through their unhygienic instruments used during dental treatments and surgeries. Dental healthcare is not only too expensive (out of reach of massive fraction of population) in private hospitals but it also costs much in public sector hospitals as well. Treatment of teeth can go up to millions in quality hospitals of private sector in Pakistan so even middle class fraction of population is not able to get cure of teeth in private hospitals of the country. More than 99 per cent public hospitals in the country possess none or rare facilities of dental surgeries. Dentists working in these government hospitals always suggest their patients to visit them in their private clinics in the evenings for even ordinary treatments. Having to face such severe circumstances commoners are forced to approach quack dentists widespread in every corner of the country and expose themselves to the risk of contracting AIDS and other severe transmittable diseases as a result of faulty treatments.

- **Quacks and Sexual Health**

Sex has always been a great matter of concern for most of the Pakistanis and they like to spend on it as well. Conflicts, frustrations and many types of depressions have caused various impacts on their sexual abilities. Most among the Pakistani men are always willing to enhance their sexual abilities due to many reasons. Polygamy is familiar among rural men even in lower income groups and to meet the challenges of polygamy they need immense sexual power. Unfortunately massive fraction of population is not able to consult with professional sexologists as they too are expensive enough like dentists. Government hospitals again are not able to provide guidance or treatment to the commoners who contact them for that particular purpose.

Massive fraction of population in the country especially the males like to contact quacks for the cure of their sexual diseases. Quacks are familiar with the reality that sexual health is among the core issues of massive fraction of male population in the country so they are utilising smart techniques for the enhancements of their revenues. Quacks dealing in sexology are much rich as compared to their counterparts in the fields of general medicine, surgery and dentistry. This fraction of population is involved in exploiting the emotions of massive fraction of population through very attractive advertisements.

'Men never grow old', 'Amazing magical medicine for making your nights perfect', 'One doze of our medicine will make you fit like a horse', and many more such advertisements can be easily found in print, electronic and social media of the country with references of quacks. A fraction of quacks likes to advice everyone in the country for the improvements in their sexual health through their services.

- **Some Other Facts about Quackery in Pakistan**

It's very difficult to produce real numbers about the quacks in Pakistan as they are widespread and deep rooted among both urban and rural areas of the country. Rural areas in the country including villages, small towns and adjacent areas alongside cities are worst effected by quackery due to lack of public sector hospitals and doctors.

Quacks operating in metropolitan cities including Karachi, Lahore, Rawalpindi, Multan, etc. are also working with the same daring attitude and comfort like their counterparts in smaller cities and towns. The few public sector hospitals in these cities which also possess severe circumstances are not able to provide even basic healthcare facilities to massive fraction of resident population. According to standards of World Health Organisation (WHO) at least one physician is required per 1000 population but in Pakistan hardly one doctor is available per 10,000 population.

General physicians working in public sector hospitals are also not much qualified, they mostly are qualified till the level of Bachelor degree in medicine and surgery and when called for a more in depth diagnosis they fail to do so due to lack of knowledge and expertise. Physicians working in public and even private hospitals of the country are not working accordingly, mostly are operating like pharmacists as massive fraction among them prefer to ask patients about their diseases and then suggest them medicines instead of tracing the causes and consequences of diseases and then treating them accordingly. Most among the doctors working in public hospitals of the country are not only incompetent but they possess very inhuman attitude towards the deprived fraction of population which is forced to approach them due to worst economic circumstances. Due to incompetency of these doctors, educated lower middle class fraction of the population also prefers quacks alongside the very deprived fraction of the population as they feel that experienced quacks are much better than incompetent doctors working in public hospitals of the country.

Relatively less educated middle class fraction of population also feels that quacks are far better than graduate doctors working in public hospitals and there are many reasons for this belief as well. We have discussed earlier that the attitude of physicians and particularly of the specialised ones is very inhuman towards their patients in public and sometimes in private hospitals as well. This fraction of doctors possesses a strong materialistic attitude which is causing thousands of deaths every year in Pakistan; these doctors ignore patients in public hospitals for their own commercial interests. Even if a patient is critical enough this greedy fraction of doctors will not entertain them in the public hospital but instead will suggest them to visit their private clinics so as to extract money.

There is another cruel practice going on in public sector hospitals of the country which is not to entertain serious patients so as to hide the incompetency of doctors. Thousands among seriously injured ones (due to road accidents or violence, terrorism etc) are dying every year in Pakistan because of the cruel and non-cooperative attitude of doctors. When an injured one is rushed to a public hospital large number of doctors refuse to treat him for avoiding consequences in future and this has produced severe repercussions on the society. This practice is not only going on in public sector hospitals but also in private sector hospitals, although the latter kinds of medical complexes are earning millions of rupees every month but in case of emergencies they also adopt a cruel attitude.

"I was a regular visitor of a private clinic as the owner (doctor) was my friend", said Imran Abbas a young guy from Khanewal. One day one among my friends got injured in a road accident, I rushed him to the clinic of my friend (though public hospital was not too far away from the place of incident but I decided to go to a private clinic to avoid formalities which sometimes could be longer than one's life). After examining the critical condition of the patient, the doctor on duty refused to treat him. I requested him to call the owner of clinic-cum-hospital, it was an astonishing moment for me when the owner (my so called friend) came out and he too took the same stance like his serving doctor. I requested both of them to give some treatment to the injured one but they constantly told me to take him to Multan. Their reluctant attitude continued, they did not even provide first aid to the injured person and my friend died in front of them. The doctors said that I have to register a statement of death for my friend stating in it a time that was before the arrival in that particular hospital. At that moment I thought that large number of the doctor community of Pakistan has lost all moral values", Abbas added more.

Above mentioned kind of attitude has produced severe repercussions on the minds of the masses and major part of population possess a very hate ridden attitude towards doctors and they prefer to contact quacks. A Shah (name disguised due to specific reasons) is a very familiar quack working in a town of South Punjab. He possesses no degree (formally literate) but he is running a big hospital in the countryside of a district in rural Punjab. As large number of population in the town admires the abilities and humble attitude of the quack so his earning is more than a qualified surgeon. A doctor working in district hospital of the particular district (from where quack belongs) was quite envious of the above mentioned quack so he decided to start his own hospital opposite to the hospital of the quack. It may look apparently astonishing but it is a reality that after a span of one year the doctor decided to close his hospital in that town as lot of population preferred consulting a quack over a qualified doctor. I enquired into the matter and got very surprising result, let's have a look.

"A Shah (Quack) is a very kind and down to earth person", said Ali Khan a twenty seven years old guy from the town where the quack is running his hospital. "The doctor who came from city was a proud man who had enough belief on his abilities but massive fraction of population rejected him as they love Shah a lot. We all know that Shah is not a qualified doctor but his dealing with patients is very good. He is not too demanding as well and charges only fifty rupees from a person, moreover he is experienced enough and lot of population in town feels that his recommended medicines are more effective than those of the qualified doctors practicing in Multan so why should we pay five hundred rupees to a doctor from the city for the same sort of treatment?", Khan added more.

Another big reason for the widespread network of quackery is the massive brain drain in the fields of medicine and surgery in Pakistan. Currently, total number of qualified physicians serving in Pakistan are 120,000, a large number of experts in the above mentioned fields have migrated from the country during the last two decades. At least 10,000 trained Pakistani doctors are serving in United States only. According to some other statistics more than 30,000 Pakistani doctors (2012 statistics) are working all around the world other than USA. Some elite medical institutes of the country are familiar for arranging the migration of their graduates, for example in the year 2004, 900 out of 1100 graduates of Agha Khan medical university (the top private sector medical university in the country) left Pakistan for the purpose of post graduation. Only 40 from the above mentioned doctors came back to Pakistan.

Massive brain drain in the fields of medicine and surgery has left only average and ordinary minds in Pakistan which is producing severe repercussions. So these ordinary minds are killing population or have got full liberty for this purpose. To recapitulate all regarding medical quackery in Pakistan, it can be said that the number of quacks in Pakistan is more than four times than that of the qualified doctors in the country so at least there are 0.8-1 million quacks which suggests that the masses are at a great risk of medical complications through them. The State as of now has been inept in undertaking any worthwhile measures regarding this looming hazard to human health and life. In future if requisite steps are not taken to reduce medical quackery in the country circumstances will become more severe.

- **Religious Quackery in Pakistan**

We discussed in previous chapter that religion is widely utilised for socioeconomic and political injustices and discriminations, here we shall discuss the manner in which these fraudulent factions of the society utilise religion for their commercial interests as well. Islam is the widely practiced and most dominating religion in Pakistan and Muslims of Pakistan are the second highest population of the Islam community after Indonesia. Among 192 million Pakistanis 95.2 per cent follow the Islamic faith. Religious quacks like their other counterparts in the society are familiar for looting the ordinary citizens of the country by utilising their smart techniques. Like too many means used for exploitation, religion too is widely used for corruption, frauds, and commercial interests in this part of the world without any fear and accountability.

Like political dynasties there are specific religious dynasties as well in Pakistan that are utilising the beliefs of their followers as a tool for income generations. If political dynasties are the centres of corruptions, nepotisms and socioeconomic injustices for the massive sections of population religious dynasties too are involved in spreading frauds and discriminations through the religious quacks associated with them.

Like many other profitable businesses, religion is also a pure business here in the land of pure. Religious leaders of all types are getting benefits in the name of their self-created estates of religious norms, values and traditions. We will not discuss religion as a tool of politics (we will discuss that in next chapter), here in this chapter we will only discuss familiar types of religious quackeries in Pakistan.

Making a fool of people in the name of religion or spiritualism is the easiest way of fraud in Pakistan. No qualification, no professional experiences and no repute is required for attaining the guise of a spiritual or religious leader commonly called as Peer Sahib in Pakistan. Anyone who does not possess any employment and following can work as a peer baba and these babas (so called spiritualists) feel full liberties for committing different types of frauds as accountability of mafias is almost impossible in the land of pure. This mafia is widely utilising religion as an emotional weapon for the achievements of their satanic desires and heinous goals.

Every day one can easily find dozens of stories related to these fake spiritual leaders involved in various kinds of crimes. A large number of fraudulent religious leaders in Pakistan are involved in heinous activities like rape of women and children, scams of money, violence and extremism etc. According to a recent reported incident a peer raped a girl and her mother in their home in the southern district of Punjab. Peer Javed Shah entered in the house of her follower lady at mid night and told that lady (house lady) that her house was occupied by evil djinns and he (Peer) will ostracize this evil. Thereafter, Javeed Shah repeatedly raped Shahzadi (the follower lady) and her daughter and ran away.

Amils or magicians (black magic is very familiar in Sub-continent for the achievement of one's desired goals) are considered as super human beings in most parts of the sub-continent. Many among the spiritual leaders in Pakistan also claim that they are familiar with black or spiritual magic which they can utilise for the solutions of human problems. As massive fraction of population in this part of the world is going through immense social, economical and spiritual problems so they like to contact with these peers, babas and amils in the hope of finding some sort of relief in their lives. These religious quacks are committing severe socioeconomic frauds and heinous crimes with their followers. Thousands of people are victimised by these peers every year and loose assets of their lives and respect.

Fact of the day in modern day Pakistan is very severe enough for massive fraction of population. Unemployment is touching the skies, currently more than 15 per cent of total population is without any job, terror, conflicts and discriminations are widespread and deep-rooted. Moreover, nepotism has destroyed the system of merit and calibre, large section of population in the country is following the path of materialism. Due to these types of circumstances commoners and even the upper factions of the society are willing to resort to some magic for the solutions of their problems.

Almost every religion in the world has always been utilised as a source of satisfaction, spiritual purifications and relief from psychological problems since the ancient times. A great number of religious people in the world like to adopt spiritualism for the solutions of their problems. Islam is among the widely practiced religions in the world, Muslims are second in population after the Christians in the world and their count is between 1.35-1.5 billions. A significant number of Pakistani Muslims are among those who are greatly inspired by spiritualism as was propagated during yester years by the sufis and saints of the Sub-continent. Bahudin-Zakriya of Multan, Usman Ali Marwandi - commonly called as Data Sahib of Lahore, Lal Shabaz of Sehwan, Moin – U-din of Ajmer (Rajasthan, India) and many others have inspired the Muslims of this part of the world. Above mentioned sufis and saints played a vital role for the spread of Islam in the Sub-continent. True followers of these sufis and saints who are carrying their legacies are fully involved in spreading old traditions of Islamic spiritualism all over the world. Hundreds of thousands of people are getting benefits (Spiritual purifications and relief from depressions and conflicts) from the methods and guidelines described by ancient saints even in this modern world.

Tombs and shrines of pious saints are visited by millions of people every year. Hundreds of thousands in Pakistan possess strong faiths in saints and pray to them for the solutions of their problems. Massive fraction of population in the country believes that saints and Sufis who worshipped the Almighty for their whole lives (sacrificed their pleasures for the will of God) have attained such positions in God's realm that their voice is now much more influential as compared to that of the ordinary ones in the court of God so who so ever will try to attain the blessings of these saints (by visiting their shrines regularly) will get the goodwill of God.

Emotional attachments of large section of population with spiritualism and with saints and Sufis are widely utilised by fake peers for the achievements of their commercial goals. Massive fraction of population in the country likes to regard some people as their spiritual leader as they believe that some spiritually gifted or inclined persons are capable of purifying sinful souls and can show them the right path. Majority among the population looks willing to utilise the spiritual knowledge of their leaders for the predication of future, massive fraction among the commoners possess strong faith on the divine connections of their spiritual leaders. This section of population feels that spiritual leaders are super human beings and possess great connections with the almighty, but many gullible people among them are not able to distinguish between the real and false spiritualists and often get swayed by imposters who claim to have divine connections. Now let's have a look as to how this approach is leading the masses towards the path of destruction.

"Everyone in this world is keen to know about their future and the right decisions for them for the coming time", said Ali Hussein a religious scholar. Curiosity of weak believers has always been greatly utilised by fake peers for their own commercial interests. No one knows about the future except the almighty but when people come to know that any amil or peer predicts about the future they get attracted by him and try to utilise his powers (so called) for the betterment of their life in future. These kinds of followers are not only spending enough on this fraction of peers but they are also helping in the massive advertisements of above mentioned fraction of peers and so called magicians. But reality is totally different; these peers possess no knowledge of future and are not even familiar with the basic principles of Islam. Prayers, observing fasts during the holy month of Ramadan and other basic Muslim principles, norms and values are unimportant for this fraction of so called religious leaders", Hessian added more.

Islam describes human beings as the combination of both body structure and soul; both physical and spiritual elements of human beings have their own requirements of satisfaction. Muslims likes to offer prayer (being the order of Almighty) for the purifications of their souls and inner satisfactions. Similarly other actions and norms are followed to abide orders of the Almighty and to preserve the Islamic traditions. Religious leaders (Ulema's), saints and Sufi's play the role of a spiritual guide (path defining anchors) for the benefit of the masses, but as genuineness is no more a trait of the massive fraction of population so they become a target of false religious leaders who utilise religion as a tool of fraud and corruption.

Massive fraction of religious quacks in Pakistan widespread in every corner of the country claim themselves as stakeholders of spiritual and traditional Islamic values. This section is making money through various ways such as by providing explanation of dreams as massive fraction of population here feels that dreams can predict the future and help in planning their life in a better way. These quacks are also involved in providing consultations to a fraction of population for future planning and decision-making in the light of their so called spiritual knowledge. Like many other professions there is no certain limitation or qualification for the adoption of the profession of a peer or spiritual leader. One can easily find hundreds of these so called spiritual experts widespread in cities, towns and villages of the country.

Another great dilemma of spiritual families in Pakistan is the influence of heredity. Like political dynasties there exist certain religious and spiritual dynasties as well. Let's have a look on some very familiar spiritual dynasties of the country following the influence of heredity. Famous religious dynasties like Shah Rukan–e-Alam in Multan, Shah Jeewana in Jhang and many others are following the influence of heredity and kinship for transferring the post of Sajdah Nasheen (Successors) of a spiritual leader. People other than the family of spiritual leader (even if pious enough) are not eligible for the above mentioned titles. Most spiritual leaders in Pakistan are enjoying important portfolios only on the basis of heredity and kinship, moral altitude stands nowhere in this race.

Demonology is another very important tool of these fake peers and amils utilised for making money at higher level. Demonology basically is a study of demons or beliefs about demons and also deals with super natural beings which are not Gods. These super natural beings are commonly called as moakils or djins described as creatures of Almighty by Holy Quran. This short of spiritual experts of amils which claims to have connections with supernatural beings is very widespread in the country. Lot of commoners like to visit these amils or peers very frequently for the solution of their complicated problems, diseases and conflicts but more than 99 per cent among these amils possess no connections and knowledge about super naturals. They even do not possess the factual information about dijins and demons. Above mentioned fraction of so called peers are only spreading crime, fraud and loot in the society. Media reports in the recent past has revealed their bitter faces several times but they still feel liberty in carrying on with their practice as massive fraction of population still have faith on their abilities.

- **Quackery in Astrology in Pakistan**

Astrology is a study of several systems of divination based on the premise that there is a relationship between astronomical phenomena and events in the human world. Astrology is an ancient knowledge and its roots are associated with Second millennium BCE (before Christ era). Hellenistic, Babylon and Decanic astrological studies are old branches of this field-familiar for dealing in horoscopes. Horoscope is an astrological chart or diagrammatic representing of the positions of suns, moons, planets and sensitive angles at the limit of an event. Medieval Muslim Arab astrologers including Ali Bin Rizwan, Ibrahim Al-Fazri, Ali Kindi, Iben-e-Younis and Abu Ishaq Al-Zarqawi presented many new ideas and theories and solved several complications in above mentioned field.

Famous book of Alkindi (also known as Alkindus), 'Book of judgment of stars' comprises of forty chapters of innovative matter including rays, eclipse and spirituality of planets. Greek, Egyptians, and American astrologers of ancient and modern times also served the humanity with their efforts and innovations utilised especially for weather predictions, predictions of hurricanes, floods and other natural phenomenon affecting human life.

Astrology in Pakistan is a great source of money-making by looting the masses through various means by the mafias involved in it. Like their other counterparts quacks in the field of astrology are also involved in corruption and frauds. Quacks belonging to this fraction like to utilise the title of professor for themselves, doing so provides them lot of liberty in committing massive frauds with the masses. Similar to medical and religious fields, quacks in the field of astrology are also widespread and deep-rooted in every corner of the country. Quacks dealing with horoscope astrology and its allied fields like palmistry are 99.99 per cent frauds. This fraction of so called experts possesses absolutely no knowledge about astrology in any sense.

Palmistry is an allied field of astrology and possesses importance all over the world. Massive fraction of population in Pakistan as well likes to contact palmists for the predictions of their futures. One can easily find thousands of palmists doing their businesses in every large and small city of the country. Like many other fraudulent factions of the society thousands of fraud palmists and other kinds of astrologers are also running their operations without any kind of accountability with ease, comfort and liberty. Very few among these hundreds of thousands of astrologers in Pakistan would be familiar with the positions of sun, moon, planets and eclipses and only rare ones can calculate the horoscopes accordingly.

'Speed of stars and your future', 'I can change your fate with my powerful knowledge', 'Super naturals are my slave, can do anything on my order', 'After getting massive power from the demons Bengali baba in Pakistan now' and many such more captions can be easily found in the advertisements of newspapers, magazines, electronic and social media everywhere in the country. This fraction of so called professionals are equally distributed in both larger and smaller (even in towns and villages) cities of the country but very rare among them are the real professionals.

Abdullah Shokat Ch. commonly called as Mamo is considered as a top astrologer of the country. Mamo now eighty is familiar for his some true predictions about the future incidents and personalities. According to Wikipedia (the free encyclopaedia) he has predicted correctly about the political events of 1971 in Pakistan and formation of Bangladesh. He has also predicted correctly about the hurricanes of 2005 (Rita and Katrina) in United States and assassination of former prime minister of Pakistan Benazir Bhutto (2007). His much critically analysed prediction about Pak-India cricket match in ICC world cup 2011 went wrong. Mamo was born in India (Delhi) before the partition of Sub-continent and got the knowledge of astrology from Pundit Ragonath Sharma and he is serving in this field since last fifty years. With the exception of Mamo and few others, massive fraction of astrologers and palmists in Pakistan are not educated and trained enough about their fields so they just spreading rumours and crime in the name of astrology.

It would be an astonishing matter for any other country (with the exception of Pakistan) that it is possible for some people to practice in a field with ease and liberty without possessing any basic knowledge about it. While visiting across the country many among the foreigners have noticed the hundreds of thousands of wall writings and badly managed bill boards which looks like an astonishing manner of advertisement to them but most astonishing fact to which they are unfamiliar is that that the massive fraction of these street wall writings belongs to fake peers, astrologers and so called magicians.

Widespread and very vocal electronic media in Pakistan has produced vast opportunities for every type of professionals to propagate their skills to the masses. Bulk of astrologers/palmists is also utilising this tool to enhance their businesses. This section of astrologers hold key importance during cricket matches of Pakistan and other countries (even during FIFA world cup), General elections and during some other events of national level. This fraction of astrologers are frequently asked about the results of the matches during live transmissions of international sports events but truly speaking 99.99 per cent among them have failed to deliver true predictions.

Astrologers invited during sports events in recent past appeared very non-professional with almost no expertise of their fields. Almost none among them was ready to give straight forward predictions. During Asia Cup cricket tournament of April 2014 held in Sri Lanka a match between arch rivals India and Pakistan got too much hype (as it usually does) so massive fraction of news channels started their live transmissions about the match analysis, they also invited many astrologers for the predictions about the match but it looked very astonishing when none among this fraction was able to produce a true prediction. Many among them were very conscious of having to deliver their views, this suggests that either they possessed no knowledge about astrology or they forgot everything in front of the television cameras. Let's have a look at one example of a famous astrologer who had put forth his predictions about the particular match on a famous television channel.

"Stars are in favour of India but if Pakistan's batting performance (as bowling is always been a hall mark of Pakistani cricket team) improves that day the match can turn in favour of Pakistan. If Pakistan has to win then Capitan Misbah and middle order has to perform well otherwise circumstances will be difficult for Pakistan". I was astonished at his so called expert opinion and thought that was this the opinion of an astrologer or a street cricket viewer? Interestingly Pakistan won by one wicket at the end, Misbah and Umar Akmal from middle order failed to give any performance. If I was there to face the media then I could have given a better opinion than him, I thought.

Above mentioned example was only a little glimpse of a much larger picture, there are thousands other examples which one can easily find in every corner of the country. According to a senior reporter from Lahore a lady astrologer who is now part of a famous TV show was a professional prostitute for a long span of time. It was shocking news for me so I asked how she became an astrologer then. The reply was even more shocking, "One among her beneficiaries was the producer of that particular show so he introduced her as an astrologer reporter", said the reporter.

- **Frauds of Non Governmental Organisations in Pakistan**

A non-government organisation (commonly called as NGO) is generally described as an organisation which utilises its revenues for the benefits of masses without depending on conventional government agencies. Some NGOs however are funded by different governments but most NGOs in the world are generating their funds with the help of corporate sector and through charities from all income groups. Big giants of corporate sector in the world are utilising NGOs as a tool for building a benevolent image.

Different kinds of NGOs operating across the developed world are playing their parts in the progress, prosperity and socioeconomic betterment of the masses. NGOs in most parts of Europe, America, Oceania and Far East are involved for the provision of quality education, better health facilities, community development, elimination of crimes and evils and for developing awareness among the masses for their rights. Non-government organisations are divided into four categories in most of the developed world and are accordingly playing their roles for the betterments of their relevant societies and whole world. Let's have a look at some specifications of NGOs.

Community-based NGOs are working within small towns; communities in most of Europe, North America and Oceania are enjoying the services of above mentioned NGOs. Another type of NGO that is working in cities of massive fraction of developed world for providing services within the premises of districts is called as city-based NGOs. Nationwide NGOs possess networks in the whole country. International organisations (NGOs) possess world wide networks which are serving in different countries and regions on the basis of their specialties. Most among the international NGOs are working for the elimination of poverty and injustice from the world. Many among them are working for the provision of human rights to the deprived factions of third world countries. Some NGOs are specialised in matters of children and women rights and these are also focusing on most deprived parts of the world.

Oxfam, Ducere foundation and Save the Children are some very famous NGOs possessing the world wide networks that are operating for the elimination of poverty and protection of children.

Oxfam is an international organisation which possesses networks in more than ninety four countries in the world and is familiar for providing solutions for the alleviation of poverty. **Oxfam** was founded in 1942 in United Kingdom; it is based on the agenda of rights which is commonly called as rights-based approach. This approach stated that every human being is entitled to the following rights: (1) Right to a sustainable livelihood (2) Right to basic social service (3) Right to life and security (4) Right to hearing and speaking or freedom of expression or listening (5) Right to have an identity. **Oxfam** is considered as the world's largest social welfare providing network with funds of more than 300 pounds (estimated, 2008), more than 6000 employees and operations in ninety four countries and eight regions of the world.

If we make comparison among different countries and regions of the world with respect to the operations of the NGOs we will find USA on top as per this ranking criterion. United States has the largest number of NGOs, more than 1.5 million NGOs are providing their services for the citizens of United States. Russia possesses 277,000 active NGOs working for the betterment of masses. Though India apparently possesses the largest number of Non-government organisations in the world of 2 millions but more than half among these organisations are not properly active or ghost ones, they get funds from local and international donors but are not doing anything for the welfare of the deprived masses.

Fact of the day is very severe about the NGOs in Pakistan as it's very difficult to estimate about the real numbers of Non-government organisations in the country. According to **Transparency Watch** total numbers of NGOs working in Pakistan are 25,000-35,000 though, the NGOs though functional but are very minute in numbers as compared to other countries. Role of an NGO is relatively different in Pakistan as compared to NGOs working in Europe, United States and some other parts of the world. Massive fraction of NGOs working in Pakistan is involved in corruptions and frauds and is looting both public money as well as grants from international donors. More than 90 per cent of above mentioned NGOs are fake/ghosts but yet–receive heavy grants and charities from the western world in the name helping deprived factions of the society but actually they spend all the funds on their own personal interests.

Different media reports in the recent past have unveiled the faces of this fraction of population (NGO owners in Pakistan) that are only involved in corruptions and frauds in the guise of social welfare. This fraction is earning billions of rupees every year due to local and international funding by making a fool of local donors since a long span of time but their real victims are foreigners. Representatives of these NGOs visit EU countries alongside with North America and Oceania every year and collects massive funds in the name of economically deprived Pakistanis.

As more than 50 per cent of total population in the country is below or on the edge of poverty line so Pakistan stands in last numbers in the world with respect to education and health facilities to its citizens, massive fraction of NGOs operating in the country utilise these worst circumstances for their own commercial interests in a very smart way. It's a great dilemma of modern day Pakistan that most among the Non-government organisations belong to elite and super elite classes of the country. Wives of industrialists and Senior civil and military bureaucrats are greatly involved in the business of NGOs in Pakistan. Nowadays some other factions from elite like property tycoons etc., are also running NGOs in Pakistan. Some factions of educated upper middle class of population including professors, journalistic elite (including anchors and editors) and doctors are also part of this mafia.

As we discussed earlier Pakistan very few facilities for the commoners in the fields of education, health, instant justice, and community services so these shortcomings are widely propagated in western world by this mafia, they convince the western countries that they are the best ones to serve these deprived factions. They are also familiar with the fact that country possesses high rate of crime against women. Women are sexually abused very frequently in this part of the world, used as bonded labour and exploited in many other ways as well. Women issues are also a great source of income for massive fraction of NGO's in Pakistan, this fraction of non-government organisations portray miserable circumstances of Pakistani women to the world and collect funds in the name of women upliftment. Lot of NGOs working for the cause of human rights and justice in Pakistan collect massive funds from the western world every year but circumstances are becoming worst for women in Pakistan with every passing year.

With very few exceptions majority among 35,000 NGOs in Pakistan possess very loose structures. System of governance is weakly designed to avoid transparency and accountability. Some NGOs in the country are government-funded and are operating in both urban and rural areas of the country in different projects but these government-funded organisations are also facing severe criticism from different factions of the society due to their alleged scams in various projects. Government of Pakistan also has no solid structure for the accountability and monitoring of these NGOs.

Most among the NGOs working in Pakistan are foreign-funded and possess hidden agendas and interests. This fraction of NGOs has also been in the shadows of severe criticisms since a long span of time. Massive fraction among these Non-government organisations have to face the challenge of proving their national integrity and patriotism to the institutes of national security. If we categorize the NGOs in Pakistan we will find various types of agendas of different organisations. Massive factions of NGOs in Pakistan claims to provide facilities in social sector. This fraction of organisations gets enough local and foreign aids and grants from various sources. Local funds are generated through charities, donations of upper income groups and some times by Zakat, (provision of 2.5 per cent of total income every year for the elimination of poverty, its among the most basic Islamic principles applied on every Muslim) NGOs that utilise religion (Islam) as a tool are getting enough revenues in the form of Zakat every year. A fraction of Islamic NGOs in Pakistan is involved in militant activities and promotion of their self-created models of Islam.

Another type of NGOs in the country is involved in policy issues and debates such as foreign and economic policies, global problems etc. This fraction of non-governmental organisation is very active among the educated upper middle class. This fraction of organisation is operating through seminars, walks and different other activities which inspires the educated middle class of the country. Most among these organisations also possess global agendas and interests, massive fraction of population in the country believes that these NGOs are following the dictations of their exterior masters.

Another among the types of NGOs in Pakistan is operating for the provision of emergency services such as rehabilitations after the natural disasters like earthquakes, floods etc. Being a third world country Pakistan possesses almost no infrastructure to face natural disasters (country is not even equipped to face the necessities of population in normal circumstances). Pakistan has been facing different types of natural disasters since a long span of time (since its creation) but has still not been able to prepare itself to meet this challenge. Floods, earthquakes and hurricanes have remained an integral part of the country's life span but any government has still not been able to establish any organisation to meet the challenges of natural disasters. Few NGOs no doubt have made good contributions in the past for the rehabilitations and relief after the natural disasters.

Mir Khaili-U-Rehman foundation (MKRF), an NGO working under the umbrella of Jang media group (largest media house in the country) has played a vital role for the rehabilitations of flood victims in 2010 and 2012. MKRF has also played its part in education sector, above mentioned organisations has launched a massive movement for the elimination of illiteracy through its allied institutes including Daily Jang (largest circulated newspaper in the country) and Geo news (highest rated news channel of the country). Above mentioned media group is running largest media campaign in the country for the right of education to every child of Pakistan, but organisations like MKRF are very few in Pakistan and massive fraction of NGOs is involved only in loot and fraud.

NGOs working for education, health and community services have been known to be involved in great loot and corruption with public funds during the recent past in the country. As business of NGOs in Pakistan is possessing lot of money so it has attracted upper middle class and section of celebrities like showbiz and sports personalities as well alongside fraction of the conventional elite. It's almost become a fashion in Pakistan among the privileged classes of the country to make money in the name of deprived factions of the society and every one among them is attaining their profits through above mentioned mechanism. Educated upper section of the society has adopted such smart ways of making money through this tool that many among them are now multi-billionaires.

Many celebrities in Pakistan including former and serving cricket stars, actors, singers and other public figures are utilising their NGOs not only for soft image building but also for generating massive funds. Imran Khan the cricketer-cum-politician (Chairperson of Pakistan Tehrek-e-Insaf, the third largest political party of the country) also faced severe criticism by his opponents for utilising his social work for political and commercial interests. Khan founded Shokat Khanum memorial cancer hospital on December 29, 1994 named after his mother (Shokat Khanum). Land for above mentioned project was given by government of Pakistan and construction of that mega project was completed with the help of charities and donations of masses. According to political opponents of Imran Khan, the hospital is now widely utilised as a tool of political and commercial interests of Khan. Imran Khan is not only the lone example there are dozens of other celebrities as well-involved in social work but are facing severe criticisms from different factions of society for utilising their projects for self-projections and attaining commercial interests.

Ibrar-Ul-Huq, a singer turned politician also faced same sort of criticism for utilising his NGO for political and commercial interests. According to his opponents he appointed his brother as an executive director of his organisation which was running on public charities and donations. Opponents of Ibrar claim that he has collected billions of rupees in form of donations and charities from abroad but has spent only a very minute fraction of it for the welfare of masses. As NGOs are exempted from the taxes in Pakistan so massive fraction of both educated elite and public figures are involved in this business as they feel that this is the easiest way of making and saving money.

"More than 95 per cent among the raised funds of NGO's operating in Pakistan are going in the kitties of owners or are misused", said Dr Ahtashm Mubashir, staff member of a health NGO. "They (owners) collect funds from both Pakistan and abroad in the names of education, health and community services for the poor and socially deprived factions of the society but these funds are utilised for purchasing vehicles and luxurious life style and much among it is spend on wine and women by this fraction of population. These beasts (indicating the NGO owners) humiliate their country fellows by projecting their poverty and injustice to the western world but the collected funds from the west are rarely spent on the deprived factions of the society. This heinous practice is going here with absolute liberty and no one is here to make above mentioned fraction accountable", Mubashir added more.

Advocacy and lobbying NGOs are also receiving heavy funds from abroad. This fraction of NGOs are usually operating in the field of women rights and are propagating their character as a guardian of human rights in Pakistan. Like their sister organisations working in the fields of health and education this fraction of NGOs are also humiliating their fellow countrymen abroad. Representatives of these NGOs also visit Europe, Oceania and American continent every year and collect heavy funds through Pakistanis living in that part of the world. This fraction of NGOs is continuously propagating about the miserable circumstances of human rights in Pakistan to the western world and also projecting themselves as the well wishers of these deprived factions of the society. This is a fact of the day that conditions of human rights in Pakistan are severe enough but the way in which above mentioned organisations are describing it are not acceptable by majority among the masses.

Many among the Non-government organisations in Pakistan have been criticised by massive fraction of population for their hidden agendas. One school of thought (centre right) in Pakistan blames NGOs working for human rights for working against national ideology and Islamic culture and traditions. This fraction of society claims that the above mentioned organisations are promoting western culture and agendas in the guise of women welfare and human rights.

Utilisation of public money through various projects has always been a great matter of concern for most of the Pakistanis. Massive portion of government officials and politicians are involved in loot and corruptions in different kinds of public projects. Reports of Transparency international, Pew research centre Washington and some other reputed organisations of the world have described the country among the most corrupt ones in the world during the recent past. This practice of ongoing and massive corruption in different government departments has produced great repercussions on private sector organisations working in social sector. This fraction of society too now is trying its level best to get massive share with the utilisation of smart techniques.

Fourth Military ruler of the country Pervaiz Musharraff was favoured enough by western world during his regime (1999-2008) due to some of his policies including an active participation of Pakistan against ongoing war against terrorism. After 9/11 Pakistan became an important ally of United States and NATO (North Atlantic Treaty Organisation) against Taliban and Al-Qaeda and got the aid of more than 20 billion dollars in return from United States and allies but no goodness from this massive aid has been effected as is evident from the faces of deprived Pakistanis, large portion of this aid has been squandered by the corrupt bureaucrats and politicians involved in various public projects. Currently, Pakistan is the largest aid receiving country in the world from United Kingdom which has been providing financial and technical aid to Pakistanis for the enhancement of their socioeconomic conditions. UK has given more than 665 million pounds to Pakistanis during the fiscal year 2012-13. Now the question arises that when such massive foreign aid which is provided to different governments in such an organised way has failed to deliver for the masses then what to expect from those aids that the NGOs receive individually for deprived Pakistanis?

Massive fraction of Non-government organisations have also adopted the culture of loot and corruption like the different public sector organisations, some of these public sector organisations are playing the role of donor agencies of NGOs operating in the country. When NGOs working in social sector have to pay bribes to the officials of public sector organisations for various purposes like registrations, release of funds etc., then how could they themselves be untouched by corruptions? Another issue is that of accountability, different types of NGOs are involved in the collection of massive funds from Pakistan and abroad for investment in various projects, yet information as to the number of such projects in the pipeline is not furnished and government is unaware of such details and is also inept of conducting an external audit of these organisations.

According to a report of Daily Dawn published on August 21, 2010 massive fraction of fake NGOs collected funds for the victims of flood (a severe flood struck Pakistan in the summer of 2010) from Pakistan and abroad and flew away. Flood of 2010 produced severe repercussions on a massive fraction of population. More than 1800 lost their lives according to official records while independent sources claim that casualties were near about 5000. Economic losses were also not too minute, already deprived economy got the shock of at least 44 billion dollars. At least 25 million population of the country was directly affected by this severe flood and at least 10 million were displaced from their homes during the months of July and August when one-fifth portion of the country was drowned under water. Perceiving this massive flood as an opportunity hundreds of fake NGOs started fund raising in the name of helping victims in various parts of the country and abroad as well. Names of many NGOs who established their camps in Karachi, Lahore, Rawalpindi and many other cities of the country for collecting funds for poor floods victims were very unfamiliar for massive fraction of masses. This fraction of NGOs was able to collect heavy funds from the masses as massive fraction of population in the country was feeling sympathetic towards the flood victims at that time. Since then nobody knows where these NGOs have gone, flood victims who were already deprived enough are still living in miserable circumstances.

According to a senior journalist from Karachi, "Most small and medium sized NGOs-are dependent on foreign aids and are doing absolutely nothing for the welfare of masses in the society. Some relatively bigger organisations possessing widespread networks in the country are running a few projects for the deprived classes of the country so as to sustain their reputations, but this work is too minute for bringing any significant positive change in this deprived fraction of society", he added more.

Another reality about the NGOs working in Pakistan is very severe and that is that the expenditures on their propagations is much higher than their actual work. To attain maximum funds from local and international donors massive fraction of large scale NGOs are resorting to media management in a smart way. With the utilisation of media (as there is no free lunch so media houses are also getting benefits from these sort of organisations) this fraction of NGOs propagate about their fake projects of social welfare and attract international donors particularly and attain massive funds which are utilised for their own welfare only. Let's have a look at one such example so as to understand the relation between this fraction and media.

"A feudal-cum-politician lady from South Punjab (considered as most backward area in the country) is running an NGO in the field of education. She visits UK every year (for spending summer) where she has introduced herself as a social worker and human rights activist (can there be any other joke apart from this?). Sources say that she collects massive funds for the poor and deprived population of her area from there but the amount she distributes among that particular fraction of population looks very shameful. According to a senior school teacher of her constituency once she distributed school uniforms in a government girls school during a ceremony in which she arrived with a massive crowd of journalists and photographers and hardly distributed uniforms among 100 girls, according to teacher the expenditure was not more than 70,000-80,000 of all this exercise but she described it as a great mile stone in her speech. The photographers captured the snap of every single girl who got uniform and many among them were posted in the newspapers of the next day alongside a news article of three columns.

Above mentioned example is a little glimpse of a larger picture, there are thousands of such NGOs widespread in every corner of the country which are collecting funds of millions of pounds and dollars every year from abroad and are doing nothing other than fraud and corruption in the name of the welfare of the ordinary masses of the country. Let's have a look at another side of the picture.

Pakistan would be probably the only country in the world where criminal gangs and mafias are attaining their desired goals in the guise of NGOs. Businesses of prostitution, drugs and human smugglings are widely going on here in guise of these organisations. According to a report of Al-Jazeera (famous News channel and online newspaper operated from Qatar, widely considered as the only independent media house in the whole Arab world) published and broadcasted on September 8, 2012 Pakistan has become an off limit country for the NGOs. The report stated that dozens of NGOs operating in Pakistan are involved in heinous crimes and are facing no accountability from concerned provincial governments and the federal government has also shown a criminal silence in this regard as well. According to a senior journalist from Islamabad some NGOs in Karachi, Lahore and Islamabad are running brothels in the posh colonies for the pleasures of the ruling elite of the country and helping this fraction for the attainment of their desired goals. An investigative reporter of SAMA T.V., in his programme 'May Hon Kon' (Who am I?) exposed an NGO that was involved in the heinous businesses of drug supply and prostitution in Surgani town Karachi. The reporter was very much threatened by the staff (who claimed to have the support of the local police station) of particular NGO during the reporting again and again. According to another crime reporter a very renowned social worker lady from Multan is also running the same sort of business in the guise of a beauty salon. Above mentioned lady is also very influential in the region of South Punjab and possesses relationships with political and bureaucratic elite.

To recapitulate all it can be said that the role of an NGO is very important for the alleviation of socioeconomic injustice in any society but massive fraction of NGOs in Pakistan are not playing their parts accordingly. Above mentioned fraction is either involved in massive corruption and fraud or fulfilling their exterior agendas, hence conflicts and frustrations are growing at a rapid rate in the society through this faction.

Acronyms

ANP : Awami National Party, a progressive political fraction that has roots in the Northern part of the country
BBC : British Broadcasting Corporation
BZU : Bhaudin Zakriya University, Multan
BJP : Bhartiya Janata Party (India)
CPI : Corruption Precipitation Index
CJP : Chief Justice of Pakistan
CSP : Civil Servant of Pakistan, utilised for describing bureaucracy
CNG : Compressed Natural Gas
COAS : Chief of Army Staff
CM : Chief Minister
DMG : District Management Group, primer fraction of bureaucracy
DCO : District Coordination Officer
DPO : District Police Officer
DSP : Deputy Superintendent of Police
DHA : Defence Housing Authority, posh residential areas restricted for the military elite of the country
EU : European Union
FATA : Federally Administrated Tribal Areas
GDP : Gross Domestic Product
ICT : Islamabad Capital Territory
ICS : Indian Civil Servant
INC : Indian National Congress (India)
IMF : International Monetary Fund
IJT : Islami Jamet-e-Talba, student wing of orthodox political group Jamat-e-Islami
JIP : Jamat-e-Islami, Pakistan political group representing Islamic clerics
ISPR : Inter Services Public Relation, an allied institute of Pakistan Army

JUI (F) : Jameat-Ulmay Islam Fazal, a political group representing Islamic orthodoxy
KPK : Khyber Pukhtunkhwa, province in North West of the country
LJ : Laskir-E-Jhangvi, a banned orthodox militant group
LESCO : Lahore Electric Supply Corporation
MW : Mega Watt, unit representing production of Electricity
NICL : National Insurance Corporation Limited
NTM : Network Television Marketing
NESPAK : National Engineering Services Pakistan
NGO : Non Governmental Organisation
NAB : National Accountability Bureau
PSP : Police Services of Pakistan, representing the bureaucratic cadre of Police in Pakistan
PEMRA : Pakistan Electronic Media Regularity Authority
PAS : Pakistan Administrative Services
PTV : Pakistan Television, state owned news and entertainment outlet
PIA : Pakistan International Airlines
PKR : Pakistani Rupee, representing the basic unit of currency
PML (N) : Pakistan Muslim League Nawaz Group
PTI : Pakistan Tehrek –e-Insaf party
PPP : Pakistan People's Party
PCO : Provisional Constitutional Order
RBC : Red Blood Cells
RPO : Regional Police Officer
SP : Superintendent of Police
SCP : Supreme Court of Pakistan
SSP : Sipah-e-Sahba Pakistan, a banned militant organisation
SDPI : Sustainable Development Policy Institute
SHO : Station House Officer, in charge of a Police Station
TTP : Tehrek-e-Taliban Pakistan, a militant movement for the provision of orthodox Islamic norms and laws in the country
UNESCO : United Nations Scientific Educational and Cultural Organisation
WBC : White Blood Cells
WAPDA : Water and Power Development Authority

References and Statistics

- Al-Jazeera TV
- BBC
- Daily Dawn
- Daily The News
- Daily Express Tribune
- Daily Pakistan Today
- Daily Times (Pakistan)
- Daily The Nation
- The Guardian London
- Los Angeles Times (USA)
- Federal Bureau of Statistics, government of Pakistan
- ARY News Pakistan
- Dawn News
- Geo News
- SAMMA TV
- Pakistan A HARD COUNTRY by Peter Paul Anatol Leven
- Pew Research Centre, Washington
- Human Rights Commission of Pakistan
- National Commission for Justice and Peace
- Transparency International
- Sustainable Development Policy Institute

Index